FO
FROM

FAMOUS **OD** KITCHENS

THE BRAND NAMES COOK BOOK

Edited by Marguerite English/Sponsored by Saran Wrap

Designed, produced, and © 1961
by Western Printing and Lithographing Company

Printed in U.S.A.

Library of Congress Catalog Card Number 61-10871

Sponsored by Saran Wrap, -
a trademark product of The Dow Chemical Company

SPECIAL OFFER TO READERS OF THIS BOOK:

If you have enjoyed this cook book and would like to have
additional copies, send $1.00 per book (check, money order, or
cash) to Cook Book, P.O. Box 447, The Dow Chemical Company,
Midland, Michigan.

TABLE OF CONTENTS

INTRODUCTION

Cookery means . . . the knowledge of all herbs, and fruits, and balms, and spices; and of all that is healing and sweet in fields and groves, and savory in meats; it means carefulness, and inventiveness, and watchfulness, and willingness, and readiness of appliance; it means the economy of your great-grandmothers, and the science of modern chemists; it means good tasting, and no wasting; it means English thoroughness, and French art, and Arabian hospitality; and it means, in fine, that you are to be perfectly, and always, "ladies"—"loaf-givers."

JOHN RUSKIN
The Ethics of the Dust

Delicious, eye-appealing food is the result of a three-way partnership: quality products, tested recipes, and an *interested* cook.

Food From Famous Kitchens is a collection of recipes that represent the most carefully tested foods in the world, supported by millions of dollars in research, development, and marketing. Quality is implicit in the Brand Names products included here. Together they form a roll call of excellence, providing you with a very special guarantee.

These recipes are neither expensive nor difficult to prepare. Their ingredients are to be found in supermarkets and grocery stores across the country. The recipes are as traditional as Thanksgiving, and as modern as tomorrow.

The art of cooking is incomplete without *you*. Recipes are the manufacturers' guides, but the style is yours. Style, as defined by Webster, is "a distinctive or characteristic mode of presentation, construction, or execution in any art." A style of your own is an attainable goal; it is the most desirable of all the culinary arts.

I have not attempted to tell you how to cook; there are

hundreds of books on the market which handle that problem more than adequately. Instead, *Food From Famous Kitchens* makes suggestions, offers ideas, and provides the basis for success. The rest is up to you. Be conscious of your kitchen art, and practice it. The answer to the question, "How do I learn to cook?" always has been, still is, and always will be "Cook!"

This book would not have been possible without the assistance of many people—so many that I cannot possibly express my gratitude to all of them here. But I would like to mention the following whose recipes and advice fill the pages of *Food From Famous Kitchens*.

Helen C. Hamilton of Best Foods, Division of Corn Products Company; Rachael Reed of The Borden Company; Mrs. Giovanni Buitoni of Buitoni Foods Corp.; Patricia Collier of Dole Corporation; Dolores Elliott of The Dow Chemical Company; Alice Hutchinson of The R. T. French Company; the General Foods Kitchens; Mabel Stegner of Grocery Store Products Company; Regina Frisbie of Kellogg Company; Don Poirier of Kretschmer Wheat Germ Corp.; Mary Collins of McCormick & Co., Inc.; Janet Taylor of Ocean Spray Cranberries, Inc.; the Home Economics Department of Pet Milk Company; Lois Ross of The Quaker Oats Co.; Bernadine Landsberg of Red Star Yeast & Products Co.; J. M. Thul of The Seven-Up Company; Ann Williams-Heller of American Skultuna Inc.; Virginia Schroeder of Standard Brands, Inc.; Marjorie Zimmerman of Stokely-Van Camp, Inc.; Gertrude Austin of Sunkist Growers, Inc.; Betty Lee Bennet of Uncle Ben's, Inc.; Deborah A. Hale of United Fruit Company; and Virginia Skelton of The American Institute of Food Distribution, Inc.

Marguerite Engberg

ACKNOWLEDGMENTS

The following major companies have contributed a selection of their finest recipes to make *Food From Famous Kitchens* possible. Their co-operation and good will are gratefully acknowledged.

THE EDITOR

Ac'cent International
American Dehydrated Onion & Garlic Association
American Lamb Council
American Skultuna Inc.
The Angostura-Wuppermann Corp.
Best Foods, Division of Corn Products Company
The Borden Company
Brazil Nut Association
Buitoni Foods Corp.
Burnham & Morrill Co.
Calavo Growers of California
California Almond Growers Exchange
California Packing Corporation
The Campbell Soup Company
The Chun King Corp.
Diamond Walnut Growers, Inc.
Dole Corporation

The Dow Chemical Company
The R. T. French Company
General Foods Corporation
Green Giant Company
Grocery Store Products Co.
George A. Hormel Co.
Hueblein, Inc.
Hunt Foods, Inc.
Kellogg Company
Knox Gelatine, Inc.
Kretschmer Wheat Germ Corp.
Thomas J. Lipton, Inc.
Louisiana Yam Commission
Paul Masson Vineyards
McCall's Magazine
McCormick & Co., Inc.
McIlhenny Company
National Biscuit Company
National Red Cherry Institute
The Nestlé Company
Ocean Spray Cranberries, Inc.

Pan American Coffee Bureau

Penick & Ford, Ltd.

Pet Milk Company

Poultry and Egg National Board

The Procter & Gamble Company

The Quaker Oats Co.

Red Star Yeast & Products Co.

The Seven-Up Company

Spanish Green Olive Commission

Standard Brands, Inc.

Star-Kist Foods, Inc.

Stokely-Van Camp, Inc.

Sunkist Growers, Inc.

Uncle Ben's, Inc.

United Fruit Company

The Welch Grape Juice Company, Inc.

MENUS

In this section, you will find recipes selected from this book, assembled in logical and tasteful menus. Some menus are heartier, others lighter, to suit your need or fancy. The page numbers next to recipes are for your convenience.

BREAKFAST
Scrambled Eggs
Sausage-Stuffed Apples (p. 94)
Beverage

Melon Slices
Orange Pancakes and Sauce (p. 208)
Fried Pork Tenderloin
Beverage

Orange Juice
Creamed Eggs (p. 117)
Breakfast Ham
Toast   Preserves
Beverage

Iced Bouillon
Puffy Wheat Germ Omelet (p. 120)
Cranberry Muffins (p. 212)
Beverage

Fruit Juice
Toast Cups A La Eggs (p. 119)
Bacon or Sausage
Beverage

Melon
Gingerbread Waffles (p. 209)
Bacon and Sausage
Beverage

Sliced Fresh Pears
Continental Pancakes (p. 207)
Beverage

Baked Grapefruit (p. 274)
Poached Eggs and Canadian Bacon on Toast
Beverage

LUNCH
Curried Chicken 'N' Rice (p. 103)
Broiled Tomatoes (p. 161)
Batterway Rye Bread (p. 216)
Cantaloupe with Raspberry Sherbet
Beverage

Vichyssoise Supreme (p. 42)
Veal-and-Vegetable Ring (p. 192)
Biscuit Fingers (p. 205)
Assorted Cheese and Fruit
Beverage

Melon and Berry Cocktail
Chateau-Rice Broil (p. 138)
Bowl of Iced Vegetables
Black Bottom Pie (p. 232)
Beverage

Cool Avocado Soup (p. 42)
Spaghetti with Cheese Balls (p. 128)
Pineapple
Beverage

BRUNCH
Beer Omelet Royale (p. 120)
Country Sausage and Bacon
Oatmeal Refrigerator Rolls (p. 221)
Beverage

Cranberry Juice
Corned Beef Ring with Cheese Yams (p. 67)
Cucumber-Asparagus Salad (p. 186)
Golden Corn Bread (p. 206)
Beverage

Tomato Juice
Salmon Loaf with Whipped Potato Topping (p. 47)
Savory Broiled Eggplant (p. 153)
Jam Muffins (p. 203)
Beverage

DINNER
Guacamole Dip with Crackers (p. 18)
Shrimp Creole (p. 55)
Artichoke Hearts
Assorted Breads
French Concord Tarts (p. 236)
Beverage

Cheese Soup (p. 31)
Baked Pork Chops (p. 86)
Baked Idaho Potato
Italian Salad Bowl (p. 185)
Fresh Fruit
Beverage

Royal Chicken Consommé (p. 35)
Veal Chops with Walnut Sauce (p. 73)
Whipped Potato-Stuffed Tomato (p. 162)
Green Beans Rosemary (p. 152)
Quick Cherry Muffins (p. 203)
Rum Custard (p. 263)
Beverage

Golden Velvet Soup (p. 33)
Orange Duck en Casserole (p. 111)
Whipped Potato Soufflé (p. 132)
Spinach Salad with California Dip (p. 18)
Frozen Fruit Sherbet (p. 271)
Beverage

Cherry Soup (p. 40)
Polynesian Beef (p. 66)
Chinese Vegetables (p. 154)
Assorted Breads or Chow Mein Noodles
Almond Cookies (p. 345)
Beverage

Italian Tri-Color (p. 129)
Salade Nicoise (p. 190)
Garlic Bread
Black Walnut Ice Cream (p. 267)
Beverage

SUPPER
Crabmeat Jambalaya (p. 37)
Saffron Rice
Coffee Coconut Meringues (p. 349)
Fruit
Beverage

Spareribs with Sauerkraut (p. 89)
Parsley Dumplings
Bavarian Mint Pie (p. 228)
Beverage

APPeTIZeRS

The selection of appetizers for any occasion—even the most casual—speaks volumes about your home, your hospitality, your approach to entertaining. As you will see from the recipes that follow, preparing appetizers is easy and fun to do; but prepare them carefully and serve them artfully.

Keep cold things cold and hot things hot. Check frequently to see that trays are kept filled and attractively arranged. Remember that appetizers should maintain the spirit of the occasion. If your guests are coming from a football game, give them something hearty; if they have come for dinner, give them appetizers that will complement the meal.

It is best to center your creative efforts around one or two choice dishes, supplementing these with dips and simple canapés. Pastry filled with tiny sausages, stuffed mushroom crowns, delicately-spiced kebabs, bite-size meat balls, guacamole and cheese dips are always popular. For a change of pace, try marinating chicken thighs in barbecue sauce, then broiling and serving them. Fondues are especially well-liked; you will find several in the pages that follow.

Many metropolitan hostesses, faced with the necessity of entertaining hungry guests who are dropping in between work and the theatre or a late dinner, are providing what amounts to a cocktail buffet. Patés, sliced ham and turkey, and assorted trays of thinly-cut bread, help to allay hunger pangs far into the evening.

DEVILED HAM DIP
Pet Milk Company

1 2- to 3-ounce package softened white cream cheese
⅓ cup Pet Evaporated Milk
1 1- to 2¼-ounce can deviled ham
1 tablespoon sweet pickle relish, drained
1 tablespoon horseradish, drained
¼ teaspoon salt

Blend cream cheese and evaporated milk. Add deviled ham, pickle relish, horseradish, and salt, and mix well. Chill thoroughly. Use as a dip for crackers or potato chips. Makes about 1⅓ cups.

Note: If mixture seems too stiff for easy dipping, add a little more evaporated milk until of the desired consistency.

OLIVE CHEESE DIP
Spanish Green Olive Commission

1 cup creamed cottage cheese
½ cup mayonnaise
2½ teaspoons prepared horseradish
Dash Tabasco
Dash cayenne
Dash salt
1 teaspoon grated onion
½ cup finely chopped pimiento-stuffed green olives
Potato chips or cooked shrimp

Combine cheese, mayonnaise, horseradish, Tabasco, cayenne, salt, and onion; blend well. Fold in olives. Serve as a dip for potato chips or shrimp. Garnish as desired. Makes about 1¾ cups. (See illustration 4.)

CALIFORNIA DIP
Thomas J. Lipton, Inc.

1 package Lipton Dehydrated Onion Soup

1 pint commercial sour cream

Stir onion soup as it comes from package into sour cream and blend thoroughly. Use as dip with potato chips.

GUACAMOLE
McIlhenny Company

1 large ripe avocado, peeled and cubed

2 3-ounce packages cream cheese

2 teaspoons lemon or lime juice

¼ teaspoon Tabasco

¼ teaspoon salt

½ teaspoon Worcestershire Sauce

Mash avocado; add softened cream cheese and remaining ingredients. Blend until smooth. Use as dip for cheese wafers, potato chips, crisp crackers. Makes about 1½ cups.

Note: Quantities of sour cream in above recipe may be varied to suit individual taste. This dip should be covered with Saran Wrap, and stored in the refrigerator until served. Leftovers should be kept under refrigeration.

BEER-CHEESE FONDUE
National Biscuit Company

3 pounds Cheddar cheese
1 12-ounce can beer

1 clove garlic, sliced
Chippers and Triscuit Wafers

Melt 3 pounds cheese with beer over low heat or in chafing dish. Add garlic. Keep hot and serve with the crackers.

CONTINENTAL FONDUE
National Biscuit Company

1 pound Swiss cheese, grated
⅔ cup dry white wine

1 clove garlic, crushed
Pepper
Ritz Crackers

Combine cheese, wine, garlic, and pepper. Stir over low heat until cheese melts and ingredients are well blended. Serve immediately in chafing dish. Delicious dipped up with crackers.

CURRY EGG BALLS
Best Foods, Division of
Corn Products Company

6 hard-cooked eggs
¼ cup Hellmann's or Best Foods Real Mayonnaise
¼ teaspoon curry powder
¼ teaspoon salt

Pepper
¼ cup finely chopped walnuts
¼ cup dry bread crumbs
2 tablespoons margarine

Chop the eggs very fine; mix in mayonnaise, curry powder, salt, and a dash of pepper. Shape into 24 balls. Sauté the walnuts and bread crumbs in the margarine; roll egg balls in crumbs. Makes 24 balls.

CROUSTADES AND SHRIMP
Best Foods, Division of
Corn Products Company

Croustades:

1 1-pound loaf of unsliced bread	Margarine

Remove crusts from half of the loaf. Cut into 16 ¼-inch or 32 ⅝-inch squares. With a sharp paring knife or scissors, scoop out center of each square. Leave ⅛- to ¼-inch on sides and bottom. Dip in melted margarine with top side down. Place on baking sheet and bake in 450° oven 3 to 5 minutes, or until golden brown.

Shrimp Filling:

1 4½-ounce can shrimp	3 tablespoons Hellmann's or
¼ cup finely chopped celery	Best Foods Real Mayon-
2 scallions, finely chopped	naise
Salt and pepper	1 teaspoon lemon juice

Combine the ingredients and fill the croustades with the mixture. Or spread on crisp crackers, slightly toasted.

STUFFED SHRIMP HORS D'OEUVRES
Best Foods, Division of
Corn Products Company

30 shrimp, cooked and cleaned	¼ teaspoon thyme
¼ cup Roquefort cheese	¼ cup Hellmann's or Best Foods Real Mayonnaise
¼ cup cream cheese	1 teaspoon lemon juice

Slit the shrimp. Cream the cheese and thyme together to form a paste; add mayonnaise and lemon juice, and blend well. Spread a generous layer of filling over half of shrimp and top with other half. Chill. Serve with food picks.

TUNA IN A CUCUMBER
National Biscuit Company

1 7-ounce can tuna fish
¼ pound cream cheese
1 tablespoon mayonnaise
1 tablespoon lemon juice
½ teaspoon salt
¼ teaspoon pepper
1 tablespoon pickle relish
3 small cucumbers
Ritz Crackers

Mix first 7 ingredients together; chill. Core centers of cucumbers. Stuff tuna mixture into the cucumbers. Chill and slice. Serve on the crackers.

STUFFED MUSHROOM CROWNS
Grocery Store Products Co.

2 6-ounce cans Broiled-in-Butter Mushroom Crowns
1 3-ounce package cream cheese
½ teaspoon onion juice
2 teaspoons lemon juice
2 tablespoons diced toasted almonds
⅔ cup chopped leftover turkey
⅛ teaspoon salt
Paprika

Drain mushrooms and remove stem ends with top of knife or small melon-baller. Finely chop the stems. Soften cream cheese at room temperature. Add the chopped mushroom stems, onion and lemon juice, almonds, turkey, and salt. Heap mixture in hollow of each mushroom crown. Dust lightly with paprika. Serve cold. Makes about 50 stuffed crowns.

BLEU CHEESE IN A MELON
National Biscuit Company

½ pound bleu cheese   1 cantaloupe
½ pound cream cheese   Waverly Wafers
¼ cup heavy cream

Thoroughly blend together 2 cheeses and thin mixture with the heavy cream. Scoop melon balls from cantaloupe. Spoon cheese dip into the cantaloupe shell. Serve with crackers and melon balls on cocktail picks.

HEAVENLY SWISS-ROQUEFORT TRIANGLES
The Borden Company

½ cup (¼ pound) butter   1 teaspoon Worcestershire
1 3-ounce portion Borden's   Sauce
   Napoleon Roquefort   4 Borden's Natural Swiss
   Cheese   Cheese Slices
                              18 pimiento stuffed olives

Let butter and Roquefort cheese stand at room temperature until softened. Combine butter, Roquefort cheese, and Worcestershire Sauce; blend well. Spread each cheese slice with Roquefort-butter mixture. Cut into small triangles, ½ inch at base. Cut each olive into about 4 slices. For each hors d'oeuvre, alternate on toothpick: 1 olive slice, cheese triangle, and olive slice. Makes about 3 dozen.

CHEESE-NUT BALL
The Dow Chemical Company

Soften equal parts of sharp Cheddar, cream, and blue cheese. Season well. Mix in chopped walnuts and minced parsley. Form in ball. Roll in minced parsley and finely chopped walnuts. Wrap in Saran Wrap until ready to serve. Serve with a variety of crisp crackers.

CARAWAY LOAF
National Biscuit Company

1½ pounds cream cheese
1½ pounds Cheddar cheese, grated
¼ cup milk
4 tablespoons caraway seeds
1 tablespoon Worcestershire Sauce
Corn Thins

Mix all ingredients except Corn Thins. Shape into a loaf by forming into a long roll. Chill in Saran Wrap until firm, about 4 hours. Slice and serve on Corn Thins.

Variations

ANCHOVY LOAF. Blend the first 3 ingredients with 1 2-ounce tube of anchovy paste. After chilling, slice and serve on Triangle Thins.

COFFEE LOAF. Combine first 3 ingredients with 1 tablespoon instant coffee and 2 tablespoons sugar. Chill. Slice and serve on Wheat Thins.

SNAPPY HAM-AND-CHEESE PINWHEELS
The Borden Company

2 3-ounce packages Borden's Cream Cheese
1 5-ounce jar Borden's Blue Cheese Spread
½ teaspoon onion juice
5 slices boiled ham, 4¾ x 6¾ x ⅛-inch

Soften cream cheese and blue cheese spread at room temperature. Beat cream cheese until smooth and fluffy. Gradually beat in blue cheese spread. Stir in onion juice. Divide into 5 portions. Spread each portion on a slice of ham; roll each tightly, jelly-roll fashion. Wrap in Saran Wrap. Chill in refrigerator until firm enough to slice smoothly, about 4 to 6 hours. Rolls may be prepared the night before and stored in the refrigerator until ready to use. Just before serving, slice rolls into ¾-inch thick pinwheels. Makes 30 ¾-inch wheels.

OLIVE PINWHEEL SANDWICHES
Spanish Green Olive Commission

1 8-ounce package cream cheese, soft
1 tablespoon milk
1 teaspoon grated onion
½ teaspoon prepared horse-radish

Food coloring
1 loaf unsliced white or whole wheat bread
Small pimiento-stuffed green olives

Combine cheese, milk, onion, and horseradish; beat until well blended. Tint cheese mixture as desired with food coloring; blend well.

Trim crusts from bread. Cut bread into lengthwise slices about ¼-inch thick. Run rolling pin lightly over each slice, starting at narrow end. Spread bread with cheese mixture. Place 3 to 4 olives across short end. Starting at end with olives, roll up bread tightly. Wrap rolls in Saran Wrap and chill several hours. Cut into slices ¼-inch thick. Makes about 2½ dozen sandwiches. (See illustration 4.)

HOT PARMESAN-AND-ROMANO CHEESE PUFFS
The Borden Company

3 egg whites
Pinch of cayenne

1 3-ounce canister Borden's Grated Parmesan and Romano Cheese

In heavy saucepan, melt fat to depth of 3 inches. Heat fat to 350° on deep fat thermometer, or until a cube of day-old bread browns in 1 minute. Beat egg whites until stiff but not dry; fold in cayenne and cheese (mixture will decrease in volume when cheese is added). Drop by teaspoonfuls into fat. Cook until delicately browned on all sides, about 3 to 4 minutes. Remove from fat with a slotted spoon; drain on absorbent paper. Dust with paprika. Serve hot. Makes about 30 puffs.

CHEESE CURL-A-WAYS
The Borden Company

1 3-ounce Borden's Pippin Roll	1 9½-ounce jar large stuffed olives, drained
	26 carrot curls

Let cheese stand at room temperature until softened. Cut slice from base of each olive; reserve. Remove pimiento stuffing; fill each olive with cheese. Insert toothpick through carrot curl; place olive slice on toothpick and insert through center top of cheese-stuffed olive. Makes about 26.

LIVER PATE MOLD
Best Foods, Division of
Corn Products Company

1 8-ounce roll of liver paste	1 package cream cheese
2 tablespoons lemon juice	¼ cup mayonnaise
1½ teaspoons grated onion	1 tablespoon capers
3 tablespoons Hellmann's or Best Foods Real Mayonnaise	

Blend the liver paste, lemon juice, onions, and mayonnaise until a smooth paste is formed. Pack into a small mold or shape into small cake. Chill. Blend the cream cheese with ¼ cup mayonnaise. Spread on paté as icing and decorate with capers. Wrap in Saran Wrap. Set in coldest part of refrigerator several hours. Makes 8 to 10 servings.

MUSHROOM-NUT CANAPE SPREAD
Grocery Store Products Co.

3 ounces shelled Brazil nuts
1 3-ounce can chopped Broiled-in-Butter Mushrooms

1 3-ounce package cream cheese
¼ teaspoon celery salt
¼ teaspoon salt
Toast rounds

Put Brazil nuts through food chopper, using finest knife. Drain mushrooms and chop very fine. Combine nuts, mushrooms, and cream cheese with seasonings. Spread on tiny toast rounds. Place under moderately hot broiler a few minutes before serving. Makes 48 small canapés.

CHICKEN LIVER 'N' SHRIMP SPREAD
Best Foods, Division of
Corn Products Company

Combine ½ cup chopped, cooked chicken livers; ½ cup finely chopped shrimp; 2 tablespoons finely minced green pepper; ¼ cup Hellmann's or Best Foods Real Mayonnaise; and ¼ teaspoon grated onion. Chill. Makes 1 cup.

OLIVE BOLOGNA FINGERS
Spanish Green Olive Commission

6 slices bread
Prepared mustard
12 slices bologna

Mayonnaise
18 pimiento-stuffed green
olives, sliced

Trim crusts from bread and cut into 2½-inch fingers. Spread bread fingers with mustard. Cut each slice bologna over mustard. Top with mayonnaise and garnish with olive slices. Makes 2 dozen fingers. (See illustration 4.)

CHEESE-CAVIAR SPREAD
National Biscuit Company

1 tablespoon red caviar
Lemon juice
1 8-ounce package cream
cheese

1 large tomato
Waverly Wafers

Mix the caviar with a dash of lemon juice and the cream cheese. Serve in a scooped-out tomato, with additional caviar topping the spread. Mixture should be at room temperature when served for easy spreading on the crackers.

CREAMY CARROT AND OLIVE SPREAD
Spanish Green Olive Commission

1 8-ounce package cream
cheese, softened
1 tablespoon milk
½ cup shredded carrot

½ teaspoon grated onion
½ cup chopped pimiento-
stuffed olives
Melba toast rounds

Combine cheese and milk; beat until blended. Add carrot, onion, and olives; mix well. Spread on toast rounds. Garnish with carrot flowers, if desired. Makes about 1½ cups. (See illustration 4.)

OLIVE EGG SALAD CANAPE SPREAD
Spanish Green Olive Commission

4 hard-cooked eggs, finely chopped

3 tablespoons finely chopped celery

3 tablespoons finely chopped onion

⅓ cup chopped pimiento-stuffed green olives

¼ cup mayonnaise

Salt and pepper to taste

Melba toast rounds

Combine eggs, celery, onion, olives, and mayonnaise; mix well. Season with salt and pepper. Spread on toast rounds. Garnish with olive slices, if desired. Makes about 1⅔ cups. (See illustration 4.)

SOUPS

Soup has made a comeback all over America. It has reappeared at breakfast, and as a bracer for the departing guest. At midnight it is a tranquilizer.

If you are short of time rely on a reserve shelf of canned and frozen seafood and vegetables. Chowder in any disguise is suitable in an emergency or for a carefully planned supper.

Breakfasts often tend to become stereotyped. Try serving soup to your family early in the morning; it will surprise and delight them. Serve breakfast soups from a pottery breakfast jug, a heat-resistant carafe, a heated casserole, a colorful mixing bowl, or a silver pitcher. Garnish soups with crisp bacon bits, croutons, pretzel pieces, bite-size cereal or cereal flakes, chopped or sliced egg, oyster crackers, toast squares or triangles, grated cheese, shredded chipped beef, poached egg, frankfurter pennies, toasted rye curls, shredded apple (in bouillon), lemon slices, grated lemon rind, or slivers of dried apricots.

RICE-AND-TOMATO BOWL
The Campbell Soup Company

1 10½-ounce can Campbell's Condensed Tomato Soup

1 soup can water
¼ cup cooked rice

Combine ingredients in saucepan. Heat thoroughly. For variation, use ½ cup cooked noodles instead of rice. Makes 2 to 3 servings.

PUREE MONGOLE
The Campbell Soup Company

1 10½-ounce can Campbell's Condensed Green Pea Soup
1 10½-ounce can Campbell's Condensed Tomato Soup

1 cup milk
1 cup water
Curry powder (optional)

Blend soups, milk, and water in saucepan. Heat, but do not boil. Add a dash of curry powder, if desired. Makes 4 servings.

CREAM OF BROCCOLI SOUP
General Foods Corporation

1 10-ounce package Birds Eye Chopped Broccoli
4½ cups vegetable liquid and milk
3 tablespoons butter
2 to 3 teaspoons grated onion

3 tablespoons flour
1 teaspoon salt
Dash of pepper
½ cup light cream or top milk
1 chicken bouillon cube

Cook broccoli as directed on package. Drain, reserving liquid. Add milk to make 4½ cups. Melt butter in heavy saucepan. Add onion and sauté 1 minute. Then add flour, salt, and pepper, and stir until blended. Add milk mixture and the cream gradually, stirring constantly. Add bouillon cube. Cook over low heat until thickened, stirring constantly. Add broccoli and heat thoroughly. Serve in bowls or cups. Garnish each serving with a dash of paprika. Makes 6½ cups, or 6 to 8 servings.

CHEESE SOUP
Thomas J. Lipton, Inc.

2 tablespoons Lipton De-
  hydrated Onion Soup
1 cup boiling water
2 tablespoons butter or margarine
2 tablespoons finely grated
  carrot
2 tablespoons flour
3 cups milk
1 cup grated cheese
½ teaspoon salt
Pepper
⅛ teaspoon dry mustard

Stir dehydrated onion soup into boiling water and simmer 10 minutes. In saucepan, melt butter or margarine and sauté carrot until tender, about 3 to 5 minutes. Blend in flour, then soup mixture. Stir until thickened. Add milk, cheese, and seasonings. Heat, stirring constantly, but do not boil. Makes 4 servings.

1 Prime rib of beef in a regal pose. Select well-aged beef—and remember that fat is important to flavor. Photo courtesy of Ac'cent International.

2 Fruits of the sea, deep-fried to a golden crispness, are a perfect finger-food, and explain the popularity of assorted seafoods for informal parties. Photo courtesy of The Procter & Gamble Company

3 Stuffed Pork Chops (p. 88) appropriately follow bean-with-bacon soup. Buy double-thick chops, and have your butcher cut a pocket along the side of each. Fill with stuffing before simmering; serve with yams and zucchini. Photo courtesy of The Campbell Soup Company.

4 A tray of hors d'oeuvres as pretty as this is well worth the time and effort it requires. On the tray: Olive-Egg Salad Canape Spread (p. 28); Olive Pinwheel Sandwiches (p. 24); Creamy Carrot and Olive Spread (p. 27); Olive-Bologna Fingers (p. 27). In the bowl: Olive Cheese Dip (p. 17). Photo courtesy of Spanish Green Olive Commission.

5 Apples are as natural with pork as mint is with lamb for a side dish or garnish. A newer way to include both is to bake them with a. stuffing of sausage, onion, and crackers. See Sausage-Stuffed Apples (p. 94). Photo courtesy of National Biscuit Company.

6 For soup with a difference, float Frozen Raviolettes in a bowl of beef bouillon. Sprinkle with grated Parmesan cheese and follow with assorted fruit for dessert. Photo courtesy of Buitoni Foods Corp.

7 Shrimp Creole (p. 55) is synonymous with New Orleans, and its popularity is widely established. Serve over rice, and accompany with a salad and fruit or sherbet to complete the menu. Photo courtesy of The Seven-Up Company.

8 Ham is a holiday favorite, especially when prepared with any one of a variety of fruit glazes. This one, made with whipped currant jelly, pineapple rings, and maraschino cherries, is unusual, a dramatic dish to feature. See Ruby Red Glazed Pineapple-Ham (p. 91). Photo courtesy of Dole Corporation.

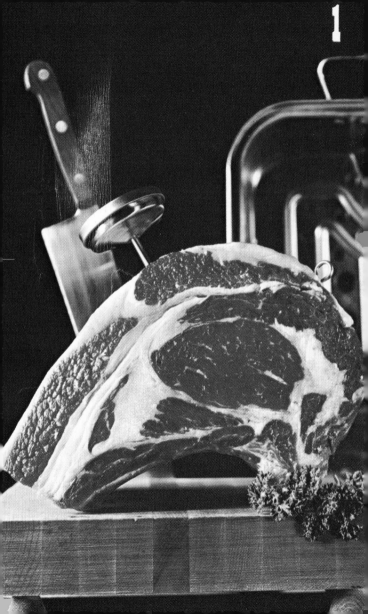

GOLDEN VELVET SOUP
General Foods Corporation

1 12-ounce package Birds
  Eye Cooked Squash
2 cups milk
1 teaspoon grated onion

1 teaspoon salt
Dash of pepper
Dash of celery salt
1 tablespoon butter

Place frozen block of squash in saucepan. Add milk, onion, salt, pepper, and celery salt. Heat slowly, stirring often, until squash is thawed and milk comes to a boil, about 12 minutes. Remove from heat, add butter, and stir until melted. Serve in cups or bowls. Garnish each serving with a sprig of parsley. Makes about 3 cups, or 4 servings.

CREAM-POTATO-MUSHROOM SOUP
The Borden Company

¼ cup butter
½ pound fresh mushrooms,
  chopped
½ cup chopped onion
1½ cups boiling water
1 envelope Borden's Instant
  Whipped Potatoes
½ teaspoon salt

¼ teaspoon pepper
¼ teaspoon thyme
Dash nutmeg or mace
2 cups milk
¼ cup sherry (optional)
1 egg yolk
2 cups Borden's Sour Cream

Melt butter in large, heavy saucepan; add mushrooms and onion; sauté until onion is tender. Stir in water, potato flakes, seasonings, and milk. Bring to boiling point, but do not boil. Beat sherry with egg yolk; blend in sour cream; stir into soup. Cook until heated throughout. Serve with croutons and chopped parsley. Makes 1½ quarts.

Note: If desired, 1 to 2 cups cooked lobster, shrimp or crabmeat may be added with sour cream mixture.

ELEGANT MUSHROOM SOUP
American Dehydrated Onion
& Garlic Association

1 4-ounce can mushrooms
1 tablespoon butter
1 10½-ounce can condensed
    cream of mushroom soup
Drained mushroom liquor

¼ cup dry sherry
1 cup cream
1/16 teaspoon nutmeg
1½ teaspoons instant
    minced onion

Drain mushrooms, saving liquor. Sauté mushrooms lightly in butter. Blend in all remaining ingredients, and heat slowly just to boiling point. Serve in small heated soup bowls. Makes 4 to 5 servings.

MINESTRONE
Hunt Foods, Inc.

½ cup olive or vegetable oil
1 clove garlic, minced
2 cups chopped onion
1 cup chopped celery
4 tablespoons chopped pars-
    ley
1 6-ounce can Hunt's To-
    mato Paste
1 10½-ounce can beef or
    vegetable broth, undiluted
9 cups water
1 cup coarsely chopped
    cabbage

2 carrots, thinly sliced
2 teaspoons salt
¼ teaspoon pepper
⅛ teaspoon sage
1 1-pound can kidney beans
1 zucchini squash, thinly
    sliced (optional)
1 cup green beans or peas,
    frozen or canned
1 cup elbow macaroni
Grated Parmesan cheese

Heat oil in large pot. Add garlic, onion, celery, and parsley; cook until soft. Stir in Hunt's Tomato Paste and next 7 ingredients. Mix well, bring to boil. Lower heat, cover, and simmer slowly 1 hour. Add remaining ingredients except cheese. Cook 10 to 15 minutes more, or until macaroni is tender. Serve piping hot with plenty of Parmesan cheese. When covered with Saran Wrap, it keeps well in refrigerator; reheats nicely. Makes 8 servings.

FALL GARDEN BORSCHT
Thomas J. Lipton, Inc.

6 cups water
1 pound beef chuck, cut into 1-inch cubes
2 packages Lipton Dehydrated Onion Soup
¾ cup celery, cut into 1-inch pieces
2 cups sliced raw beets
1½ cups sliced carrots
1 small head cabbage, cut into wedges
1 bay leaf
1 cup coarsely grated raw beets
1 6-ounce can tomato paste
2 tablespoons vinegar
1 teaspoon salt
Commercial sour cream

In large kettle, place water, beef, onion soup, celery, sliced beets, carrots, cabbage, and bay leaf. Cover and simmer 2 hours. Stir in grated beets, tomato paste, sugar, vinegar, and salt. Cover and simmer 15 to 20 minutes. Serve topped with sour cream. Makes 8 to 10 servings.

ROYAL CHICKEN CONSOMME
Calavo Growers of California

1 3-inch stick cinnamon
4 whole cloves
1 quart chicken broth (fresh, canned, or bouillon cubes)
1 Calavo Avocado

Add spices to broth and simmer 10 minutes; strain and discard spices. Cut avocado in half lengthwise; remove seed and skin. Cut into slices and place 3 or 4 slices in each soup bowl. Pour in the hot, spiced chicken broth and serve at once. Makes 4 servings.

CREAM OF CHICKEN BISQUE
Paul Masson Vineyards

4 tablespoons butter	Dash powdered garlic
4 tablespoons flour	(optional)
1¼ cup chicken broth	¾ cup minced cooked
½ teaspoon salt	chicken
1 onion, cut in half	1 egg yolk
1 stalk celery, cut in pieces	⅓ cup Paul Masson Dry
3 cups milk	Sherry
	Whipped cream (optional)

Mix butter and flour over low heat to bubbling paste. Add broth, salt, onion, and celery. Stir until creamy; cover and cook over low heat for 15 minutes, stirring as necessary to prevent lumping. Strain liquid into pot; add milk, minced chicken, and garlic powder. Cook until creamy. In a separate bowl, thin an egg yolk with a little of the hot soup; then stir into the soup pot. Add sherry. (Do not boil after addition of egg yolk and wine.) Crest servings with whipped cream, if desired. Makes 4 to 6 servings.

SHRIMP GUMBO DELUXE
Grocery Store Products Co.

2 tablespoons butter	1½ teaspoons salt
½ cup chopped onion	½ teaspoon pepper
1 6-ounce can sliced Broiled-in-Butter Mushrooms	1 package frozen white fish fillets
2 1-pound cans or 4 cups tomatoes	2 4½-ounce cans shrimp, deveined
2 6-ounce cans tomato paste	1 cup okra, cooked or canned
⅛ teaspoon thyme	2 cups precooked rice
1 bay leaf	
1 sprig parsley, chopped	

Melt butter and sauté onion until just tender, about 5 minutes. Drain mushrooms and add mushroom broth, tomatoes, tomato paste, thyme, bay leaf, parsley, salt, and pepper to onion in skillet. Bring to quick boil, lower heat, and simmer 1 hour. Meanwhile thaw and flake white fish fillets. When sauce has simmered to a good consistency, add white fish, shrimp, okra, and mushrooms. Heat thoroughly, about 10 minutes. Prepare precooked rice according to package directions. Serve Gumbo over steaming hot rice in soup plates. Makes 6 to 8 servings.

CRABMEAT JAMBALAYA
National Biscuit Company

2 6¼-ounce cans crabmeat
2 tablespoons butter or margarine
¾ cup chopped onion
1 pound cooked ham, diced
1 clove garlic, crushed
1 beef bouillon cube
1 cup boiling water
2 6-ounce cans tomato paste

2 tablespoons parsley, chopped
1 teaspoon salt
¼ teaspoon thyme
⅛ teaspoon pepper
⅛ teaspoon cayenne
⅛ teaspoon chili powder
1 bay leaf
Triscuit Wafers

Flake crabmeat. Heat butter or margarine in saucepan over low heat. Add onion, ham, and garlic, cooking over medium heat until onion is transparent. Dissolve bouillon cube in boiling water. Add to mixture along with the next 8 ingredients. Cover, bring to boiling. Add crabmeat pieces, simmer about 5 minutes. Serve hot on crackers. Makes 8 servings.

AVOCADO BISQUE
Calavo Growers of California

1 10½-ounce can condensed cream of chicken soup
1½ soup cans of rich milk
1 tablespoon instant minced onion
¼ teaspoon chili powder
1 teaspoon water
1 tablespoon lemon juice
2 medium Calavo Avocados
Salt

Combine soup, milk, and instant minced onion; heat slowly. Stir chili powder into water and lemon juice. Cut avocados in half; remove seed and skin. Purée avocados with chili mixture. Blend into hot soup; heat a few minutes longer but be careful not to overheat or boil. Add salt to taste. Makes about 1 quart.

BOSTON FISH CHOWDER
The Angostura-Wuppermann Corp.

2 pounds fresh cod or haddock
¼ pound salt pork, chopped
2 medium onions
2 medium cooked potatoes, sliced
2 cups rich milk, scalded
1 tablespoon butter
2 teaspoons Angostura Aromatic Bitters
Salt and pepper to taste

Wash fish, remove bones and skin. Cut into 1-inch pieces. Cook skin, bones, and trimming in 2 cups water for 20 minutes to make stock. Strain. Fry salt pork, add onions and cook until soft but not brown. Add potatoes and the strained fish stock. Cook all together for 5 minutes. Add cut-up fish and simmer about 10 minutes longer. Add the scalded milk. Add butter and bitters. Season well with salt and pepper. Serve with crackers.

SEA SHELL CHOWDER
Buitoni Foods Corp.

1 8-ounce package Buitoni Shell Macaroni
½ pound bacon
2 or 3 tablespoons butter
1 onion, chopped
1 quart milk

1 quart heavy cream
2 to 3 bouillon cubes
1 to 2 cups cooked lobster chunks
Salt and pepper
1 tablespoon minced parsley

Cook macaroni. Fry bacon evenly and set aside. Using a large kettle, sauté onion in butter. Add milk and cream; heat to scalding. Dissolve bouillon cubes in ½ cup of the hot milk and return to kettle. Crumble bacon and add it together with remaining ingredients. Serve piping hot. Makes 8 servings.

QUICK VEGETABLE CHOWDER
American Dehydrated Onion
& Garlic Association

1 tablespoon instant minced onion
1 10½-ounce can tomato soup
1 10½-ounce can consommé or broth
1 7½-ounce can tomatoes

1 No. 303 can whole kernel corn
2 tablespoons butter or margarine
2 tablespoons chopped parsley

Combine all ingredients except parsley, and heat just to boiling. Add parsley and serve. Makes 4 to 6 servings.

CORN CHOWDER
American Dehydrated Onion
& Garlic Association

1 15-ounce can cream style
   corn
1 10½-ounce can cream of
   mushroom soup
1½ teaspoons instant
   minced onion

⅛ teaspoon nutmeg
½ teaspoon salt
Pepper
1½ cups light cream
½ cup Chablis or sauterne

Blend all ingredients in a saucepan. Heat slowly until piping hot, stirring now and then. Makes about 1 quart.

CHERRY SOUP
National Red Cherry Institute

1 can (1 pound) red sour
   pitted cherries (water
   pack)
⅓ cup sugar
2 teaspoons corn starch

¼ teaspoon salt
¼ teaspoon cinnamon
½ cup orange juice
½ cup red wine
Sour cream (optional)

Drain cherries; reserve liquid. Chop drained cherries very fine or put in electric blender. Mix together sugar, corn starch, salt, and cinnamon in saucepan. Stir in reserved cherry liquid, chopped cherries, and orange juice. Place over medium heat and cook, stirring constantly, until mixture comes to a boil; boil ½ minute. Remove from heat; stir in wine. Serve hot or cold. Top each serving with a spoonful of sour cream; sprinkle with slivered orange rind. Makes 6 servings.

BEAN SOUP

Bean Soup has appeared consistently in a place of honor on the menu of the House of Representatives Restaurant in Washington since a day in 1904 when Speaker Joseph G. Cannon discovered that it had been omitted. Bitterly disappointed, Speaker Cannon demanded its permanent re-instatement, and the generations of law-makers which have followed him to Congress have sustained its popularity. Here is the famous recipe, quoted as it appears on the House Restaurant menu:

---

2 pounds No. 1 white Michigan beans
Cover with water and soak overnight.
Drain and re-cover with water.
Add a smoked ham hock and *simmer slowly* for about 4 hours until beans are cooked tender. Then add salt and pepper to suit taste. Just before serving, bruise beans with large spoon or ladle, enough to cloud.

(Serves about 6 persons.)

COLD SOUPS

CURRIED CHICKEN BISQUE
Best Foods, Division of
Corn Products Company

1 chicken bouillon cube
2 cups water
1 10-ounce can cream of chicken soup

½ cup Hellmann's or Best Foods Real Mayonnaise
½ teaspoon curry powder

Dissolve bouillon cube in 1 cup boiling water. Blend chicken soup, mayonnaise, and curry powder. Add remaining water and bouillon slowly. (Beat with rotary beater if lumps are present.) Heat just to boiling point and then chill thoroughly. Garnish with whipped cream, if desired. Makes 4 servings.

VICHYSSOISE SUPREME
The Borden Company

3 cups water
1 medium onion, chopped
¼ cup chopped fresh parsley
4 chicken bouillon cubes
2 tablespoons butter
1 teaspoon salt

⅛ teaspoon pepper
3 cups (1½ pints) Borden's Light Cream or Half-and-Half
1 envelope Borden's Instant Whipped Potatoes

Place water, onion, parsley, bouillon cubes, butter, and seasonings in large saucepan; bring to boil. Stir; cover. Simmer over low heat until onions are tender, about 12 minutes. Add cream and bring to boiling point. Remove from heat; stir in potato flakes. Let stand 3 minutes. Chill well. Garnish with chopped chives. Makes about 6 cups.

COOL AVOCADO SOUP
National Biscuit Company

4 tablespoons flour
¼ teaspoon onion salt
⅛ teaspoon chili powder
2⅔ cups chicken bouillon

2 ripe avocados
⅔ cup light cream
2 teaspoons lemon juice
Shredded Wheat Juniors

Mix flour, onion salt, and chili powder together. Add a little chicken bouillon to form a thin paste. Stir flour mixture into rest of bouillon. Stir over heat until mixture comes to a boil. Remove from heat. Peel avocados. Cut off 4 slices for garnish. Mash rest of avocado through a sieve. Stir into chicken bouillon and lemon juice. Stir mixture over ice until very cold. Stir in cream. Pour into chilled cups and garnish with slice of avocado. Serve with the cereal.

COLD CONCORD SOUP
The Welch Grape Juice Company, Inc.

1 quart Welch's Grape Juice
2 cups cold water
Juice and grated rind of 1
    lemon
1 clove

1 tablespoon corn starch
1 pint commercial sour
    cream
6 mint sprigs (optional)

Combine grape juice, water, lemon juice, and clove. Heat to simmer stage. Thoroughly combine sugar and corn starch. Stir gently into first mixture. Cook over low heat, stirring constantly, until mixture comes to a boil. Cook over very low heat for 15 minutes. Cool. Chill. At serving time pour into soup bowls; garnish each serving with pinch of grated lemon rind and generous dollop of sour cream. Add mint sprig if desired.

PEACH-AND-ORANGE SOUP
Standard Brands, Inc.

1 package Royal Orange
    Gelatin
1 cup thawed frozen sliced
    peaches, drained and
    diced

2 cups boiling water
½ cup cold water
½ cup peach syrup

Mix gelatin and peaches in a large bowl. Add boiling water and stir until dissolved. Add cold water and peach syrup and stir in. Pour into bouillon cups and chill. Or pour into shallow pan, chill, and spoon into glass bouillon cups. Garnish with pieces of lime or lemon, or sprigs of fresh mint. Makes about 1 quart.

FISH and SEaFOOD

High in protein and low in fat, with generous supplies of Vitamins A and D, fish and seafood are vitally important in well rounded diets. Shellfish contain natural supplies of minerals as well; oysters and clams are particularly high in iron.

Almost all fish—and many shellfish—are attractively priced, easily within the reach of every pocketbook. Canned tuna deserves special mention for this reason, and for its versatility in casseroles, chowders, and salads.

Here you will find a host of exciting innovations, as well as new applications of familiar fish and seafood dishes. Make a thorough sampling, not just on meatless Fridays, but on any day of the week. Do not overcook fish. It is moist, cooks quickly, and is one of the most subtly flavored foods.

FISH

MEDITERRANEAN FISH ROLLS
Hunt Foods, Inc.

2 pounds fillets of flounder,
   sole, or perch
Juice of ½ lemon
Salt and pepper
2 tablespoons vegetable or
   olive oil
¼ cup chopped onion
1 clove garlic, minced
1 6-ounce can Hunt's To-
   mato Paste

1½ cups water
½ teaspoon salt
¼ teaspoon pepper
¼ teaspoon oregano
¼ cup dry white wine
   (optional)
Lemon wedges
Parsley

Cut fillets in half lengthwise. Sprinkle with lemon juice, salt, and pepper. Roll up with Tasty Mushroom Stuffing and fasten with toothpicks. Place in greased 10 x 6 x 2-inch baking dish. In a skillet, cook onion and garlic in oil until soft. Add tomato paste mixed with water, salt, pepper, and oregano. Simmer, uncovered, 20 minutes. Add wine, if you wish, and pour over fish. Bake in 375° oven for 35 minutes, or until fish flakes easily. Baste occasionally. Garnish with lemon wedges and parsley. Makes 6 servings.

Tasty Mushroom Stuffing:

1 2-ounce can finely
   chopped mushrooms
2 tablespoons fine dry bread
   crumbs

3 tablespoons grated Parmesan cheese
1 tablespoon parsley,
   chopped

Combine these ingredients and spread over fillets.

FISHERMEN'S CODCAKES
The Borden Company

1 4-ounce package dehy-
  drated shredded salt codfish
2½ cups water

1 egg, slightly beaten
1 envelope Borden's Instant
  Whipped Potatoes
4 tablespoons butter

Soak codfish in 1½ cups of the water for 2 minutes; drain and press to remove moisture. Discard liquid. Combine egg, remaining water, potatoes, and codfish; blend well. Let stand 1 minute. Shape into 6 cakes. Melt butter in skillet; sauté cakes until golden brown on both sides. Serve with tomato sauce and lemon wedges. Makes 6 cakes.

EPICURE'S BAKED HALIBUT
The Seven-Up Company

Baked Halibut:

2 pounds halibut steak
1 7-ounce bottle 7-Up

½ cup fine bread crumbs

Pour 7-Up in a shallow bowl. Spread bread crumbs on waxed paper. Dip halibut in 7-Up, then in crumbs, and place in a greased shallow baking pan. Reserve 7-Up. Bake in 450° oven for 10 to 15 minutes, or until tender. Serve with Epicure's Sauce. Makes 4 servings.

Epicure's Sauce:

2 tablespoons margarine
½ small green pepper,
  minced
1 small onion, minced
1 branch celery, chopped

1½ tablespoons flour
1 teaspoon curry powder
Tabasco
Reserved 7-Up

While the halibut is baking, melt margarine in a pan and add green pepper, onion, and celery. Cook over low heat until vegetables are softened, about 5 minutes. Mix in flour, curry powder, and a dash of Tabasco. Stir in remaining 7-Up and cook over low heat, stirring constantly, until mixture begins to boil. Pour over baked fish.

SALMON LOAF WITH WHIPPED POTATO TOPPING
The Borden Company

Salmon Loaf:

2 tablespoons butter	½ cup finely chopped sweet
¼ cup finely chopped onion	gherkins
1 1-pound can salmon, well	½ cup milk
drained	1 egg
½ cup dry bread crumbs	1 teaspoon butter

Melt 2 tablespoons butter in small skillet; add onion and sauté until tender. In a bowl, combine salmon, bread crumbs, sweet gherkins, ½ cup milk, egg, and 1 teaspoon butter. Add onion mixture. Butter 8½ x 4½ x 2½-inch loaf pan. Lightly pack salmon mixture in pan; cover top with aluminum foil. Bake in 350° oven for 1 hour, or until lightly browned and firm. (Remove aluminum foil during last 20 minutes of baking.) Remove from oven. Loosen loaf from sides of pan with spatula. Turn out onto warm platter.

Potato Topping:

3 cups water	2 tablespoons butter
1 teaspoon salt	2 envelopes Borden's In-
1 cup milk	stant Whipped Potatoes

Combine water and 1 teaspoon salt in large saucepan. Bring to boil. Remove from heat. Add milk immediately. Add butter and potato flakes. Stir with fork until liquid is absorbed. Whip briskly. With fork, swirl potatoes over top and sides of loaf. If desired, garnish with parsley and sliced olives. Makes 6 servings.

SAVORY SALMON RING
Kretschmer Wheat Germ Corp.

1 can salmon
1 cup Kretchmer Wheat Germ
½ cup coarse dry bread crumbs

2 tablespoons minced onion
2 eggs, slightly beaten
1 can condensed cream of celery soup

Combine ingredients and mix well. Pack into a buttered 9-inch ring mold. Bake in a 350° oven 50 minutes, or until the center is firm. Remove from oven. Let stand about 5 minutes. Turn out onto heated serving platter. Accompany with heated tomato sauce. Makes 4 to 6 servings.

SOLE AMANDINE
Best Foods, Division of
Corn Products Company

1 pound fillets of sole or flounder
Flour
Salt and pepper
¼ cup Mazola Margarine
4 cups peeled chopped fresh tomatoes
½ clove garlic, minced

1 tablespoon Mazola Margarine
½ teaspoon tarragon
½ teaspoon salt
⅛ teaspoon pepper
¼ cup blanched almonds, slivered and toasted

Dip fillets lightly in flour seasoned with salt and pepper. Melt margarine in a skillet over low heat. Add fillets and fry 2 to 3 minutes, or until golden brown. Turn carefully and brown other side. Meanwhile, combine tomatoes and remaining ingredients in a large skillet. Cook about 2 minutes, or until tomatoes are heated. Arrange tomatoes on shallow platter and place fillets on top. Garnish with slivered almonds. Makes 4 servings.

TUNA-AND-CORN PIE
Star-Kist Foods, Inc.

1 family-size can Star-Kist
   Tuna
1 12-ounce can creamed
   corn

Mashed potatoes
Tomatoes, sliced in sections

Place tuna and corn in greased 1½-quart casserole, alternating tuna with corn and ending with tuna. Top with mashed potatoes. Decorate with tomato sections. Bake at 375° for 15 minutes. Makes 4 to 6 servings.

TUNA TIMBALES
Star-Kist Foods, Inc.

1 7-ounce can Star-Kist Tuna
2 tablespoons chopped
   onion
3 eggs, separated
2 tablespoons salad oil
½ cup milk

1½ cups soft bread crumbs
1 teaspoon finely minced
   parsley
½ teaspoon salt
⅛ teaspoon pepper
2 teaspoons lemon juice

Lightly brown undrained tuna and onion in oil. Add beaten egg yolks and remaining ingredients, folding in stiffly beaten egg whites last. Turn into greased cups and bake in pan of hot water in 350° oven 30 minutes, or until firm in center. Unmold and serve hot with your favorite sauce. Makes 6 servings.

TUNA-CHICKEN CURRY
Star-Kist Foods, Inc.

1 cup uncooked rice
1 can cream of chicken soup
½ cup milk
1 teaspoon curry powder

1 6- to 7-ounce can Star-Kist
   Tuna
1 cup crushed pineapple,
   drained (optional)

Cook rice. Put chicken soup in saucepan with milk and curry powder; stir until well blended. Heat. When mixture is hot, add tuna and pineapple; mix well. Garnish with toasted coconut or salted peanuts. Makes 4 servings. (See illustration 38.)

TUNA CAPRI
The Borden Company

8 slices fresh bread	⅛ teaspoon pepper
Butter, soft	½ cup Borden's Grated Parmesan and Romano Cheese
3 tablespoons butter	
3 tablespoons flour	
1¾ cups milk	2 tablespoons chopped pimiento
½ teaspoon Worcestershire Sauce	
¼ teaspoon salt	1 7-ounce can tuna fish, drained

Cut crusts from bread. Spread both sides with the softened butter. Press into cups of 2-inch muffin pans. Bake in 375° oven 10 to 12 minutes. While toast cups are baking, melt 3 tablespoons butter in saucepan. Stir in flour. Gradually stir in milk, keeping mixture smooth. Add seasonings. Cook over medium heat, stirring constantly, until mixture is thickened. Stir in cheese. Cook over low heat until cheese is melted. Add pimiento and tuna fish. Spoon into toast cups and sprinkle with additional cheese. Makes 4 servings.

CRAB

CRABMEAT CAKES
Thomas J. Lipton, Inc.

1 cup soft bread crumbs	1 teaspoon Worcestershire Sauce
2 tablespoons salad oil	
1 pound crabmeat	¼ cup California Dip (see page 18)
2 eggs, separated	
1 teaspoon salt	¼ cup butter
½ teaspoon dry mustard	

Toss bread crumbs with salad oil until oil is absorbed, then add to the crabmeat. Beat egg yolks; add salt, dry mustard, and Worcestershire Sauce, and combine with crab-bread crumb mixture. Beat egg whites until stiff and fold into mixture. Then fold in California Dip. Melt butter in skillet. Drop crabmeat cake mix by spoonsful into hot melted butter and cook until golden brown on each side. Makes 6 servings. Cover with Saran Wrap and refrigerate if prepared in advance.

DEVILED CRAB GOURMET
Diamond Walnut Growers, Inc.

2 cups cooked crabmeat, or
2 6½-ounce cans
½ cup toasted coarsely
chopped Diamond Walnuts
2 hard-cooked eggs, diced
½ cup mayonnaise
2 teaspoons lemon juice
1 teaspoon Worcestershire
Sauce
¼ teaspoon dry mustard
¼ teaspoon salt
Dash of cayenne pepper or
Tabasco
1 cup buttered crumbs

Heat oven to 400°. Flake crabmeat; toss with walnuts and eggs. Mix mayonnaise with seasonings and add. Spoon into baking shells or small, shallow baking dish. Cover with buttered crumbs. Bake about 20 minutes, or until golden brown. Top each serving with a sprig of parsley. Makes 4 servings.

Note: Flaked, cooked, or canned shrimp can replace crab in this recipe. Or canned tuna or salmon may be used.

RICE-STUFFED CRABS
Uncle Ben's, Inc.

1 cup Uncle Ben's Converted Rice
2 tablespoons minced onion
3 tablespoons butter
2 tablespoons flour
½ cup light cream

1 teaspoon salt
1 cup flaked crabmeat
1 tablespoon lemon juice
1 tablespoon chopped parsley
3 egg whites, stiffly beaten

Cook rice according to the directions on the package. Sauté onions in butter for 5 minutes, stir in flour; add salt and cream, and cook 5 minutes, stirring until thickened. Add crabmeat, rice, and seasonings; cook over moderate heat 5 minutes longer. Fold gently into egg whites. Turn into crab shells or small ramekins. Bake in 350° oven 20 minutes, or until done. Makes 8 servings.

LOBSTER

ROCK LOBSTER A LA CAPETOWN
The Angostura-Wuppermann Corp.

5 tablespoons butter or margarine
1 tablespoon minced onion
4 tablespoons flour
2½ cups milk
½ teaspoon salt
⅛ teaspoon pepper

½ teaspoon Angostura Aromatic Bitters
½ cup diced celery
2 6- to 8-ounce South African rock lobster tails, cooked

Melt butter or margarine. Add onion and cook 2 minutes over very low heat until slightly tender, but not brown. Stir in flour until well blended. Add milk gradually, while stirring over low heat. Add salt, pepper, bitters, and celery. Remove lobster meat from shells, break into small pieces and add. Mix well and place in individual shallow baking dishes. Brown lightly in 425° oven. Makes 5 to 6 servings.

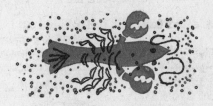

SEAFOOD CASSEROLE
Hueblein, Inc.

3 cups homemade or canned cheese sauce
2 tablespoons A-1 Steak Sauce
2 cups cooked elbow macaroni

1 cup lobster meat
1 cup shrimp or crabmeat
1 cup sautéed mushrooms
Bread crumbs

Mix all ingredients together and pour into buttered casserole. Top with bread crumbs and bake 30 minutes at 350°. Makes 6 servings.

MEXICAN LOBSTER STEW
Green Giant Company

1 12-ounce can Mexicorn Brand Corn
1 6½-ounce can lobster meat or ½-pound cooked lobster in pieces

2 tablespoons butter
1 cup cream
Salt and pepper

Combine corn, lobster, and butter; heat over low heat. Add cream; salt and pepper to taste. Heat thoroughly. Makes 4 servings.

SCALLOPS

SAUTEED SCALLOPS
McIlhenny Company

1½ pounds scallops
¼ teaspoon salt
¾ cup fine dry bread crumbs

⅓ cup butter or margarine
⅛ teaspoon Tabasco

Sprinkle scallops with salt; roll in bread crumbs. Melt butter in skillet; add Tabasco. Add scallops and cook over high heat, turning until scallops are browned on all sides. Serve with tartar sauce. Makes 4 servings.

SCALLOPS AND MUSHROOMS EN BROCHETTE
Grocery Store Products Co.

1 pound sea scallops
½ teaspoon Kitchen Bouquet
¼ teaspoon salt
¼ teaspoon celery salt
¼ teaspoon paprika

¼ teaspoon dry mustard
2 teaspoons salad oil
1 teaspoon lemon juice
¼ pound sliced bacon
1 6-ounce can Broiled-in-Butter Mushrooms

Place scallops in mixing bowl. Sprinkle with Kitchen Bouquet and the seasonings. Toss lightly with fork to coat evenly, then add salad oil and lemon juice; mix gently again. Cut bacon in 2-inch strips and cook just until transparent, not crisp. Drain on absorbent paper. Drain mushrooms, reserving broth for other use. Arrange them with scallops and bacon alternately on individual skewers. Place skewers on rack of preheated broiling compartment. Broil 4 inches from moderate heat for 6 minutes. Turn and broil for another 6 minutes. Serve immediately, garnished with tomato wedges and parsley or water cress. Makes 4 servings.

SHRIMP

SHRIMP CREOLE
The Seven-Up Company

½ cup chopped green onions
3 garlic cloves, minced
⅓ cup vegetable oil
¼ cup flour
1 8-ounce can tomato sauce
1 7-ounce bottle 7-Up

1 pound shelled shrimp, cooked
2 bay leaves
1 teaspoon salt
½ teaspoon thyme
Cooked rice

Brown green onions and garlic in heated oil 5 minutes, stirring occasionally. Stir in flour, then add tomato sauce and 7-Up. Cook over low heat, stirring, until mixture boils. Add shrimp, bay leaves, salt and thyme. Cook over low heat 15 minutes, stirring occasionally. Remove bay leaves and serve mixture over rice. Makes 4 servings. (See illustration 7.)

WILD RICE-SHRIMP CASSEROLE
The Chun King Corp.

1 can cream of mushroom soup
2 tablespoons chopped green pepper
2 tablespoons chopped onions
2 tablespoons melted butter
1 tablespoon lemon juice

2 cups Nokomis Wild Rice, cooked
½ teaspoon Worcestershire Sauce
½ teaspoon dry mustard
¼ teaspoon pepper
½ cup cheese, cubed
½ pound cleaned shrimp, uncooked

Mix all ingredients together thoroughly. Pour into greased 1½-quart casserole and bake in 375° oven for 30 to 35 minutes. Makes 4 servings.

SEAFOOD SUPREME
Pet Milk Company

½ cup finely cut onion
1 4-ounce can mushroom stems and pieces, undrained
2 tablespoons butter or margarine
1 10½-ounce can cream of mushroom soup
⅛ teaspoon pepper
1 teaspoon Worcestershire Sauce
2 drops Tabasco
1 cup Pet Evaporated Milk
⅔ cup sliced stuffed olives
1 4½-ounce can shrimp, well drained
1 7-ounce can tuna, well drained

In a 10-inch skillet, brown onion in butter or margarine. Add mushroom stems and pieces, cream of mushroom soup, pepper, Worcestershire Sauce, and Tabasco and stir until smooth. Cover and cook over medium heat 1 minute. Remove from heat and stir evaporated milk in gradually. Add olives, shrimp, and tuna. Stir just until combined and heat to steaming hot (do not boil). Serve over toast points, chow mein noodles, or hot rice. Makes 6 servings.

SHRIMP SAUCE IN GRITS RING
The Quaker Oats Co.

Grits Ring:
5 cups boiling water
1¼ cups Quaker or Aunt Jemima Enriched Hominy Grits
1¼ teaspoons salt
½ cup chopped green pepper
2 tablespoons chopped pimiento

Slowly stir grits into boiling salted water; cover and cook for 25 minutes, stirring frequently. Stir in green pepper and pimiento. Pour into greased 8-inch ring mold and let stand 20 to 25 minutes. (If desired, you may prepare this ahead of time and reheat. Cool it slightly; cover with Saran Wrap and refrigerate. To heat, place over pan of boiling water for 15 to 20 minutes.) Unmold onto plate and fill center with Shrimp Sauce.

Shrimp Sauce:

½ pound sliced mushrooms
2 tablespoons butter or margarine
1 10½-ounce can cream of chicken soup
¼ teaspoon pepper
¼ teaspoon salt
¾ cup milk
3 cups chopped shrimp, cooked

Sauté mushrooms in butter until tender. Stir in soup, pepper, salt, and milk. Add shrimp and simmer about 10 minutes. Makes 4 to 6 servings.

SHRIMP TEMPURA
Best Foods, Division of
Corn Products Company

1½ pounds raw medium shrimp
Squash
Egg plant
Whole green beans
1 recipe Tempura Batter
Mazola Corn Oil for frying

Shell and clean shrimp. Cut squash, egg plant, and beans into pencil-thin slices. Dip pieces of shrimp and vegetables into Tempura Batter; drain. Meanwhile, heat corn oil in heavy skillet or kettle to 375°. Corn oil should be at least 1-inch deep, but should not fill skillet or kettle more than ⅓ full. Fry food, turning to cook both sides; it will brown only very slightly during cooking. Drain on absorbent paper. Serve immediately with soy sauce on bed of fluffy rice. Makes 4 servings.

Tempura Batter:

¼ cup Argo Corn Starch	1 cup water
¾ cup flour	1 egg

Sift corn starch and flour together. Stir in water, then egg. Beat with rotary beater until well blended.

M°ATS

Americans eat about 160 pounds of meat per person a year, as compared to the Russians who get along on 65 pounds, and the Australians who consume a thumping 234 pounds. Although we are largely a beef-eating nation, tastes vary widely in different regions. New England and the Far West lead in beef consumption, with California alone accounting for one-quarter of the national total. More than half the lamb produced in this country is eaten in New York City. The Southerner traditionally favors pork; so much so that it may appear on his table as often as three times a day.

The cooking of meat has figured in more controversies than any other food subject, and is a topic to be approached with the utmost tact among knowledgeable hostesses. The following chart, however, is one on which there should be a minimum of disagreement.

The Cuts to Roast

BEEF. Standing ribs, rolled ribs, rump (high quality), loaf.
VEAL. Leg, loin, rack, shoulder (bone in), cushion-style shoulder, boned and rolled shoulder, loaf.
PORK. Center cut loin, blade loin, sirloin (bone in) or boneless sirloin, Boston butt, fresh or smoked picnic, fresh or smoked ham, smoked shoulder butt, spareribs, ham loaf.

LAMB. Leg, shoulder (bone in), cushion-style shoulder, boned and rolled shoulder, loaf.

The Cuts to Broil

BEEF. Rib, club, tenderloin (filet mignon), T-bone, porterhouse, tip, sirloin, and top round steaks; patties.

SMOKED PORK. Bacon, Canadian-style bacon, ham slices, sliced smoked shoulder butt.

LAMB. Shoulder, rib, loin and sirloin chops; English lamb chops; steaks; patties.

VARIETY MEATS. Sweetbreads, brains, veal or lamb liver, kidneys.

The Cuts to Panbroil

BEEF. Rib, club, tenderloin (filet mignon), T-bone, porterhouse, tip, sirloin and top round steaks; patties.

SMOKED PORK. Bacon, Canadian-style bacon, ham slices, sliced smoked shoulder butt.

LAMB. Shoulder, rib, loin and sirloin chops; English lamb chops; steaks; patties.

VARIETY MEATS. Sweetbreads, brains, veal or lamb liver, kidneys.

The Cuts to Braise

BEEF. Pot roasts; arm, blade, round and flank steaks; short ribs; plate; brisket; cross cut shanks.

VEAL. Breast; steaks; rib, loin and kidney chops; cubes.

PORK. Shoulder steaks, chops, spareribs, tenderloin, hocks.

LAMB. Shoulder chops, breast, neck slices, shanks.

VARIETY MEATS. Sweetbreads, brains, liver, veal or lamb kidneys.

The Cuts to Panfry

BEEF. Thin rib, club, tenderloin (filet mignon), T-bone, porterhouse, sirloin and top round steaks; patties.

VEAL. Arm, shoulder, sirloin, round steaks; rib, loin, kidney chops.

SMOKED PORK. Ham slice, bacon, Canadian-style bacon.

FRESH PORK. Thin shoulder steaks; rib, loin chops; tenderloin.

LAMB. Shoulder, rib and loin chops; patties.
VARIETY MEATS. Sweetbreads, brains, liver, veal or lamb kidneys.

The Cuts to Cook in Liquid

BEEF. Neck, shank, flank, heel of round, plate, brisket, short ribs, corned beef, stew meat.
VEAL. Neck, breast, riblets, flank, shoulder, shank, heel of round, stew meat.
SMOKED PORK. Ham, picnic, shoulder butt, shank.
LAMB. Neck, breast, riblets, flank, shank, stew meat.
VARIETY MEATS. Heart, kidney, tongue, brains, sweetbreads.

Allow a minimum cooling-off period of 10 minutes for roasts. (The same advice applies to fowl.) Even the sharpest knife will make an irregular cut when the meat is too hot. Leftovers will look better and handle more easily if the original servings are carved with care.

BEEF

BEEF BOURGUIGNON DIJONNAIS
Paul Masson Vineyards

5 medium onions, peeled and sliced
2 tablespoons bacon drippings
2 pounds lean bottom round of beef, cut into ¾-inch cubes
1½ tablespoons flour
Pinch of salt
Pinch of pepper
Pinch of dried marjoram
Pinch of dried thyme
½ cup condensed beef bouillon
1 cup Paul Masson Burgundy, Pinot Noir, or Cabernet Sauvignon
1 pound sliced fresh mushrooms

Fry the onions in bacon drippings until brown, and set aside. Sauté beef (free of all fat or gristle) in the same bacon drippings (adding a little more if necessary) until cubes are browned on all sides. Then sprinkle over them flour, salt, pepper, marjoram, and thyme. Add beef bouillon and wine. Stir mixture well to blend, then let simmer as slowly as possible for 3¼ hours. The mixture during this cooking should barely bubble occasionally. (If necessary, put an asbestos mat under the skillet.) If the liquid cooks away, add bouillon and wine in the proportion of 1 part of stock to 2 parts of wine to keep the beef barely covered.

After the mixture has cooked for 3¼ hours, return the browned onions to the skillet and add sliced fresh mushrooms. Stir together well, and let cook for ¾ to 1 hour longer. Again, it may be necessary to add a little more stock and wine. The sauce should be thick and dark brown.

ITALIAN MEAT ROLLS
Hunt Foods, Inc.

1½ pounds round steak, ¼-inch thick	3 tablespoons olive or vegetable oil
Salt and pepper	1 6-ounce can Hunt's Tomato Paste
3 strips bacon	
1 cup fresh bread crumbs	2 cups hot water
¼ cup chopped onion	1 clove garlic, minced
¼ cup chopped parsley	1½ teaspoons salt
¼ cup grated Parmesan cheese	¼ teaspoon pepper
	Pinch of basil or marjoram
	Cooked spaghetti

Cut steak into 6 oblong pieces. Sprinkle with salt and pepper. Pound thin with edge of plate. Top each with ½ strip of bacon. Mix crumbs, onion, parsley, and cheese. Spread over bacon. Roll up and secure with toothpicks or string. Brown gently on all sides in hot oil. Mix tomato paste and remaining ingredients, except spaghetti. Pour over rolls. Cover tightly and simmer 1½ hours, or until tender. Remove toothpicks and, if you like, slice rolls into pinwheels. Serve with spaghetti. Makes 4 servings. Can be frozen wrapped in Saran Wrap.

OLD-COUNTRY SPAGHETTI AND POT ROAST
Hunt Foods, Inc.

1 2-pound chuck pot roast, 2-inches thick
1 clove garlic, quartered
2 tablespoons olive oil
2 tablespoons butter
1 clove garlic, minced
1 small onion, chopped
2 teaspoons oregano
1 teaspoon thyme
½ teaspoon basil
⅛ teaspoon cinnamon
1 teaspoon salt
¼ teaspoon pepper
2 6-ounce cans Hunt's Tomato Paste
3½ cups water
1 pound spaghetti, uncooked
Grated Parmesan or Romano cheese

Make 4 slits in roast and insert quarters of garlic. Tie meat if necessary to hold shape. Heat oil and butter in large kettle. Brown meat slowly on all sides. Remove meat and lower heat. Add minced garlic and next 7 seasonings. Cook gently about 5 minutes, being careful not to burn. Return meat. Mix tomato paste with water, and pour over meat. Bring to full boil. Lower heat and cover loosely. Simmer slowly about 2 hours, turning meat occasionally. When meat is tender and sauce thickened, cook spaghetti. Drain and put in shallow dish. Cover with most of the sauce. Sprinkle with cheese, and mix lightly. Serve with remaining sauce and sliced meat. Makes about 6 servings.

SKILLET BEEF STEW
Thomas J. Lipton, Inc.

3 tablespoons butter
1 clove garlic, minced
2 pounds beef chuck, cut in 1½-inch cubes
1 cup California Dip (see page 18)
3 tomatoes, peeled and chopped
½ teaspoon salt
⅛ teaspoon pepper
1 teaspoon fresh chopped dill or ¼ teaspoon dried dill
2 tablespoons flour
½ cup Marsala

Melt butter in skillet; add garlic and meat. Brown meat well on all sides. Whip the California Dip with rotary beater, and to it add tomatoes, salt, pepper, and dill. Pour sauce over the meat. Cover and simmer for about 1½ hours, or until the meat is tender. Blend flour and wine together, stir into the meat mixture, and cook 5 minutes longer. Makes 6 servings.

MEAT LOAF
Thomas J. Lipton, Inc.

2 eggs	¾ cup warm water
1 package Lipton Dehydrated Onion Soup	1½ cups soft bread crumbs
⅓ cup catsup	2 pounds ground beef

Beat eggs slightly. Stir in soup mix, catsup, and water; blend in crumbs and meat. Shape into loaf or pack in loaf pan and bake in 350° oven for 1 hour. Makes 6 servings. Refrigerates well when wrapped in Saran Wrap.

ROLLED MEAT LOAF WITH BLEU CHEESE DRESSING
National Biscuit Company

1 pound lean ground beef	1 4-ounce can mushrooms, drained and chopped
½ teaspoon salt	2 tablespoons crumbled bleu cheese
⅛ teaspoon pepper	
¼ cup finely chopped onion	1 6¼-ounce package Nabisco Bleu Cheese Crackers, finely rolled (about 2 cups crumbs)
1 egg, lightly beaten	
2 tablespoons butter or margarine, melted	

Mix together first 5 ingredients. Shape on waxed paper into a rectangle about 9 x 7-inches and about 1-inch thick. Blend together remaining ingredients for stuffing. Heap stuffing in center of meat and spread to edges. Using the waxed paper, roll meat over stuffing and seal by patting meat together at top and ends. Remove paper and bake in shallow pan in 350° oven 40 minutes. Makes 4 servings. Excellent for freezing wrapped in Saran Wrap.

WIGWAM PIE

The Chun King Corp.

Crust:

3/4 pound ground beef
1 egg
1/2 cup Chun King Chow Mein Noodles, coarsely crushed

3 tablespoons chopped onions
1/2 teaspoon salt
1/4 teaspoon pepper

Mix together all ingredients and press into 9-inch pie pan to form crust.

Filling:

1 can condensed tomato soup
1 can Nokomis Pre-Cooked Casserole of Wild Rice
3 tablespoons chopped green pepper

1/2 cup cheese, shredded
1 1/2 cups Chun King Chow Mein Noodles (balance of can)

Mix soup, wild rice casserole, green pepper, and cheese. Pour into meat crust. Sprinkle with chow mein noodles. Bake in 375° oven 35 to 40 minutes. Makes 6 wedge servings.

POLYNESIAN BEEF
The Chun King Corp.

1 pound ground beef
2 tablespoons shortening
½ cup Chun King Water
  Chestnuts, sliced
1 4-ounce can mushrooms,
  undrained
½ cup raisins

1 package frozen peas
½ cup bouillon
1 teaspoon curry powder
1 tablespoon Chun King
  Soya Sauce
6 slices unpeeled oranges
½ cup salted cashews

Brown beef in shortening. Add water chestnuts, mushrooms, raisins, peas, bouillon, curry powder, and soya sauce. Break block of peas apart with fork and gently toss mixture to blend. Top with slices of unpeeled orange. Cover closely and cook over low heat 15 minutes. Add nuts and serve with Fried Rice (see page 135). Makes 4 servings.

FRIKADELLER
Hunt Foods, Inc.

1 pound ground beef
1 pound ground veal
¼ cup minced onion
½ cup dry bread crumbs
1 teaspoon salt
¼ teaspoon pepper
½ teaspoon Worcestershire
  Sauce

2 eggs, beaten
3 tablespoons vegetable oil
2 8-ounce cans Hunt's To-
  mato Sauce
½ cup water
1 tablespoon chopped parsley
½ cup dry white wine

Combine beef, veal, onion, crumbs, seasonings, and eggs; toss lightly. Shape into rolls about 3-inches long and 1-inch thick. Brown on all sides in oil in skillet. Add tomato sauce, water, and parsley. Cover. Simmer 30 minutes. Place meat rolls on cooked noodles. Add wine to sauce. Pour over noodles and meat. Makes 6 to 7 servings. Wrap leftovers in Saran Wrap and place in refrigerator.

COUNTRY PIE
Hunt Foods, Inc.

The Crust:

½ 8-ounce can Hunt's To-
  mato Sauce
½ cup bread crumbs
1 pound ground beef
¼ cup chopped onion

¼ cup chopped green pep-
  per
1½ teaspoons salt
⅛ teaspoon oregano
⅛ teaspoon pepper

Combine these ingredients and mix well. Pat meat mixture into bottom of a greased 9-inch pie plate, and pinch
1-inch flutings around the edges. Set aside.

The Filling:

1⅓ cups precooked rice
1½ 8-ounce cans Hunt's Tomato Sauce
1 cup water

½ teaspoon salt
1 cup grated Cheddar
  cheese

Combine rice, tomato sauce, water, salt, and ¼ cup of
the cheese. Spoon rice mixture into meat shell. Cover. Bake
in a 350° oven 25 minutes. Uncover and sprinkle top with
remaining cheese. Return to oven and bake, uncovered, 10
to 15 minutes longer. Makes 5 or 6 servings.

CORNED BEEF RING WITH CHEESE YAMS
Louisiana Yam Commission

4 cups corned beef, cooked
2 cups soft bread crumbs
¼ cup chopped onion
2 eggs, slightly beaten
1 cup milk
2 teaspoons prepared
  horseradish

½ cup milk
2 cups grated American
  cheese
6 medium Louisiana Yams,
  cooked, peeled, and cut
  in half lengthwise
Paprika

Chop corned beef, very fine. Mix corned beef, bread crumbs, onion, eggs, milk, horseradish, and mustard. Turn into greased 8-inch ring mold. Bake in 375° oven 45 minutes to 1 hour, or until firm.

Combine ½ cup milk and cheese; cook over low heat to melt cheese, stirring constantly. Add yams to cheese sauce. Heat. Unmold corned beef ring, fill center with yam mixture. Sprinkle with paprika.

GLAZED CORNED BEEF WITH PRUNES
California Packing Corporation

5 pounds lean corned beef	⅓ cup vinegar
1 onion	⅓ cup brown sugar, packed
2 stalks celery	⅓ cup water
4 sprigs parsley	2 teaspoons prepared mustard
2 bay leaves	
Whole cloves	1 cup uncooked Del Monte Prunes
⅓ cup Del Monte Catsup	

Cover corned beef with water in large kettle and simmer with onion, celery, parsley, and bay leaves until meat is tender, about 3 to 4 hours. Remove meat to shallow baking pan and score fat. Stud with cloves. Blend catsup, vinegar, brown sugar, water, and mustard. Pour over meat. Add prunes to meat. Bake in a 350° oven about 1 hour, basting frequently with the sauce. Makes about 8 servings.

OLD-FASHIONED LIVER PATTIES
The Angostura-Wuppermann Corp.

1⅓ pounds beef liver,
    ground
1 cup cooked rice
1 teaspoon salt

¼ teaspoon pepper
1 tablespoon Angostura Aromatic Bitters

Combine all ingredients. Form into patties; sauté or broil until golden brown and done. Arrange as a garnish around a big platter of French fried onions. Makes 4 servings.

SCALLOPED LIVER AND CABBAGE
Grocery Store Products Co.

1 pound beef liver, sliced
1 teaspoon Kitchen Bouquet
1 teaspoon salt
⅛ teaspoon pepper
3 tablespoons fat
2 quarts finely shredded cabbage, 1½ pounds

¼ cup butter or margarine
2 tablespoons minced onion
¼ cup flour
½ teaspoon salt
⅛ teaspoon mace
1 teaspoon mustard
⅛ teaspoon pepper
2 cups milk

Cover liver with boiling water and soak for 5 minutes. Drain well and blot dry with paper toweling. Remove any tubing or skin. Cut in thin, finger-length strips. Place in bowl, sprinkle with Kitchen Bouquet, salt, and pepper, and toss lightly until evenly coated. In 9-inch frying pan melt fat. Add dredged liver and brown lightly. Meanwhile, shred cabbage and place in saucepan in 1 inch of boiling, salted water. Steam for 5 minutes. Drain. Melt butter in saucepan. Add onion and sauté 1 minute. Combine and stir in flour and dry seasonings. Add milk and cook, stirring constantly, until sauce thickens. Combine cabbage and sauce and place in 11 x 7 x 2-inch baking dish. Place liver on top and bake, uncovered, in a preheated 350° oven until thoroughly heated, about 20 minutes. Makes 4 to 6 servings.

VEAL

CHERRY VEAL POT ROAST
Grocery Store Products Co.

3½- to 4-pound veal rump roast
1 tablespoon Kitchen Bouquet
1 teaspoon salt
½ teaspoon pepper
½ teaspoon ground ginger
2 tablespoons fat
1-pound can sour cherries
2 tablespoons corn starch
2 tablespoons sugar

Brush entire surface of meat generously with a mixture of Kitchen Bouquet, salt, pepper, and ginger. Melt fat in Dutch oven over moderate heat and brown roast on all sides. Place rack under roast. Drain cherries. Add ½-cup cherry juice to roast; cover and cook over low heat 1¾ hours. When roast is done, remove and place on warm platter. Skim fat from drippings. Blend together corn starch, sugar, and remaining cherry juice. Stir into drippings, bring to a boil, and stir constantly until thick and smooth. Add cherries; heat. Serve with veal roast. Makes 6 to 8 servings. Will freeze well, protected with Saran Wrap.

STUFFED VEAL SHOULDER
National Biscuit Company

4-pound boned veal shoulder
8 slices bacon
½ cup medium chopped onion
2 packets Premium Saltine Crackers, coarsely crumbled
¼ teaspoon pepper
3 tablespoons finely chopped dill
¼ teaspoon garlic powder
1 chicken bouillon cube
1 cup boiling water

Have butcher cut pocket in meat. Fry bacon until well done. Drain on paper towels. Crumble. In same skillet, sauté onion until golden brown. Add bacon and onion to cracker crumbs; then add pepper, dill, and garlic powder; blend well. Dissolve bouillon cube in water, add to crumb mixture. Fill cavity with stuffing. Bake uncovered in 300° oven at least 2 hours, 30 minutes to the pound. Serve with Sour Cream Sauce (see page 171).

VEAL CASSEROLE

Grocery Store Products Co.

1 pound boneless shoulder veal
1½ teaspoons Kitchen Bouquet
2 tablespoons fat
½ cup finely diced onion
1 clove garlic, finely minced
½ cup finely diced celery
½ cup finely diced green pepper
1 19-ounce can tomatoes
¾ cup water
1½ teaspoons salt
½ teaspoon chili powder
¼ teaspoon curry powder
1 cup converted rice

Cut veal in ½-inch cubes, then place in bowl and sprinkle with Kitchen Bouquet. Mix well to coat meat evenly. Melt fat in frying pan. Add meat and brown lightly over moderate heat. Add onion and garlic and continue cooking for about 5 minutes, stirring frequently. Add celery, green pepper, contents of can of tomatoes, water, salt, chili powder, and curry powder. Bring to boil. Add rice. Pour mixture into greased 1½-quart baking dish. Cover tightly and bake in 350° oven until rice is fluffy and done, about 45 minutes. Serve immediately. Makes 4 to 6 servings. Saran Wrap will protect this casserole nicely for refrigerating or freezing.

OSSO BUCO (BRAISED VEAL SHANKS) WITH GREEN BEANS AND CARROTS

American Skultuna Inc.

½ cup salad oil
1 clove garlic, puréed or finely chopped
3 veal shanks, cut up
Flour
1 tablespoon minced onion
2 small carrots, finely chopped
1 stalk celery, finely chopped
2 bay leaves

1 28-ounce can whole tomatoes
1 cup sauterne or bouillon
2 tablespoons minced parsley
1 tablespoon finely grated lemon
Salt and pepper to taste
½ pound whole green beans
½ pound whole carrots

Heat oil and garlic in base pot of Skultuna Steamer for Split-Level Cookery®. Dust meat lightly with flour; add to oil and brown on all sides, about 10 minutes. Add onion, carrots, celery, bay leaves, tomatoes, and sauterne or bouillon. Blend well. Simmer for 1½ hours. Cover meat with a few clean lettuce leaves to cover liquid entirely and float on top. Cook over medium heat for about 30 minutes with ½ pound whole green beans and ½ pound whole carrots in inset pot of steamer. Remove covered inset pot and set aside.

Remove lettuce leaves from base pot. Blend minced parsley and lemon rind into meat dish; season with salt and pepper. To serve, place meat in warm serving dish and surround with vegetables. Season the beans with marjoram and the carrots with celery salt. Makes about 4 servings.

Note: For dessert serve Steamed Apricot Pudding (see page 339) which may be cooked at the same time as meat in the inset pot of steamer. If pudding is not done at the end of the first 1½ hours, return it to inset pot and continue cooking along with vegetables.

ORIENTAL VEAL CHOPS
California Packing Corporation

1 cup uncooked rice
1 teaspoon salt
1 10½-ounce can condensed onion soup
1 teaspoon thyme
Salt and pepper
4 thick veal chops, about 2 pounds

2 tablespoons shortening
½ cup water
2 tablespoons lemon juice
¾ cup pitted cooked Del Monte Prunes
1 11-ounce can mandarin oranges

Combine rice, salt, onion soup, and thyme in shallow baking dish. Salt and pepper the chops; brown in shortening. Add water to pan drippings and pour over rice. Arrange chops over rice; sprinkle with lemon juice. Cover and bake in a 350° oven for 30 minutes. Uncover and place the cooked prunes and mandarin oranges on chops, pouring syrup from oranges over all. Cover; bake 20 minutes longer. Garnish each chop with a green pepper ring at serving time, if desired. Makes 4 servings.

VEAL CHOPS WITH WALNUT SAUCE
Diamond Walnut Growers, Inc.

8 large veal chops
2 tablespoons butter or margarine
Salt and pepper to taste
¼ teaspoon crumbled dried marjoram
½ cup dry white table wine
½ pint commercial sour cream

1 2¼-ounce can liver paté
¾ cup coarsely chopped Diamond Walnuts, ground in blender
Salt to taste
Hot buttered green noodles
Seedless grapes or hot crab apples for garnish
Walnut halves

Brown chops well on both sides in melted butter or margarine. Sprinkle with salt, pepper, and marjoram. Pour in ¼ cup of the wine; cover and simmer slowly 15 minutes, or until chops are tender. Meanwhile, in top of double boiler, mix together sour cream, paté, ground walnuts, and the other ¼ cup wine. Place over hot water and heat through. Season with salt to taste. At serving time, turn noodles out on a hot platter; arrange chops over them. Pour wine drippings from cooking chops into the walnut sauce and stir to blend. Spoon sauce over chops and noodles. Garnish with grapes and walnut halves. Makes 8 servings.

VEAL CHOPS PARMESAN IN WHITE WINE
Paul Masson Vineyards

4 ¾-inch thick veal loin chops, with kidneys attached	Flour
	Grated Parmesan cheese
Fresh lime juice	2 tablespoons butter
Salt and pepper	¾ cup Paul Masson Dry
Melted butter	Sauterne

Sprinkle the chops on both sides with lime juice, then with salt and pepper. Brush with melted butter; sprinkle with flour and Parmesan cheese, patting the cheese into the chops so that they are well coated. Let stand for a few minutes, then turn the chops and repeat on other side. When completed, let the chops stand for about 1 hour. When ready to cook, sauté the chops in a heavy skillet quickly in 2 tablespoons butter until they are browned on both sides. When chops are browned on second side, pour the wine into the skillet. Cover and simmer slowly for 30 to 40 minutes.

VEAL ROLL WITH WALNUTS
Grocery Store Products Co.

1 pound boneless veal cutlet, 1½-inches thick	2 tablespoons fat
1 teaspoon Kitchen Bouquet	2 tablespoons flour
2 tablespoons minced parsley	⅔ cup water
½ cup chopped walnuts	1 3-ounce can sliced Broiled-in-Butter Mushrooms
1 teaspoon salt	½ cup finely diced celery
⅛ teaspoon pepper	1 cup sliced carrots
	1 bay leaf

Brush both sides of veal with Kitchen Bouquet. Sprinkle with parsley, nut meats, salt, and pepper. Roll up as for jelly roll. Tie in place. Melt fat over moderate heat in Dutch oven. Brown veal on all sides. Blend together and add flour, water, and contents of can of mushrooms. Cook, stirring frequently, until sauce thickens. Add carrots, celery, and bay leaf around veal roll. Cover and cook over low heat until meat is tender, about 45 minutes. Remove bay leaf. Arrange meat on serving platter with sauce from pan. Garnish with water cress or parsley. Makes 4 servings.

VEAL SCALLOPINE
Hunt Foods, Inc.

2 pounds veal cutlet, cut wafer-thin	2 teaspoons sugar
½ cup flour	1 teaspoon salt
Salt and pepper	Pepper to taste
½ cup olive or vegetable oil	1 bay leaf
1 6-ounce can Hunt's Tomato Paste	Few cloves
1¾ cups hot water	½ cup dry white wine or sherry (optional)

Roll veal in flour seasoned with salt and pepper. Brown gently in oil. Combine tomato paste with all ingredients except wine. Pour over veal. Cover, and cook over low heat 30 minutes, or until tender. Add wine, if you wish. Bring quickly to a boil. Serve immediately. Makes 5 to 6 servings.

STEAK-AND-VEAL KIDNEY PIE
Paul Masson Vineyards

1 pound lean tenderloin of beef, minced fine	½ teaspoon salt
	A little pepper
1 pound lean veal kidney, minced fine	1 glass Paul Masson Pale Dry Sherry
8 fresh sliced mushrooms	1 teaspoon Worcestershire Sauce
1 onion, chopped fine	
2 hard-cooked eggs, chopped	1 cup brown sauce or a good beef or veal gravy with 1 teaspoon beef extract
½ teaspoon chopped parsley	

Mix all the ingredients together. Place in a deep casserole and cover with pie crust. Bake in 375° oven 50 minutes to 1 hour. Makes 4 to 6 servings.

LAMB

BAKED KEBABS
Hunt Foods, Inc.

2 pounds boned lamb shoulder	4 slices bacon, quartered
	Salt and pepper
4 small potatoes, peeled and halved	2 8-ounce cans Hunt's Tomato Sauce
2 onions, quartered	1 cup water
1 green pepper, cut into squares	1 tablespoon Worcestershire Sauce
3 small carrots, cut into 2-inch pieces	4 whole cloves

Cut meat into 2-inch cubes. Arrange alternate pieces of meat and vegetables on metal skewers, spacing bacon between vegetables. Sprinkle with salt and pepper. Place in shallow 12 x 9 x 2-inch pan. Mix tomato sauce with remaining ingredients. Pour over kebabs. Bake in 350° oven, basting frequently, about 2 hours, or until tender. Makes 4 servings.

SWEDISH BOILED LAMB
American Skultuna Inc.

2 to 2½ pounds lamb shoulder or breast	Salt
4 peppercorns	Ground black pepper to taste
1 bay leaf	1 pound wax beans
12 sprigs fresh dill	6 to 8 new potatoes

Have butcher cut meat into 4 to 6 pieces according to servings desired. Place meat in base pot of Skultuna Steamer for Split-Level Cookery®; cover with boiling water. Bring to boil; skim. Add peppercorns, bay leaf, dill sprigs, about 1 tablespoon salt for each quart water, and ground pepper. Cover and simmer for 1 hour.

Cover meat with a few clean lettuce leaves to cover liquid entirely and float on top. Place inset pot over base pot containing 1 pound of wax beans and 6 to 8 new potatoes to be cooked for the meal. Cover and continue cooking over medium heat for about 35 minutes, or until vegetables are tender.

Serve in warm serving dish, garnished with dill. Sprinkle

beans with melted butter or lemon butter; dust potatoes with salt. Dill Sauce (see page 173) goes well with this dinner.

LAMB STEW WITH CROUTONS
American Lamb Council

1½ pounds lamb shoulder, cubed
½ cup sliced onions
2 cups stock or bouillon
1 medium head cauliflower, broken in cauliflowerets
2 cups canned tomatoes
1½ cups cooked lima beans
1½ teaspoons salt
¼ teaspoon pepper

3 tablespoons all-purpose flour
¼ cup chopped canned pimientos
¼ cup butter or margarine, melted
½ cup grated Parmesan cheese
2 cups ½-inch bread cubes

Combine lamb and onions. Cook over low heat until lamb is browned on all sides. Add stock or bouillon. Cover and cook over low heat 30 minutes. Add cauliflowerets, tomatoes, lima beans, salt, and pepper. Cook until cauliflowerets are tender, stirring occasionally. Add a little of lamb liquid to flour; blend. Add to lamb mixture with pimientos. Cook until slightly thickened, stirring constantly.

Meanwhile, combine melted butter or margarine, grated cheese, and bread cubes; mix well. Broil 3 to 4 inches from source of heat 2 to 3 minutes, or until lightly browned. Serve stew topped with croutons. Makes 6 servings.

LAMB CHOPS WITH FRUIT STUFFING
California Packing Corporation

2 cups cooked Del Monte Prunes
½ cup chopped onion
1 cup chopped celery
½ cup butter or margarine

2 quarts soft stale bread crumbs
½ teaspoon powdered thyme
Salt
6 shoulder lamb chops

Cut cooked prunes from pits into small pieces. Cook onion and celery slowly in butter until transparent. Pour over bread crumbs, tossing to blend. Sprinkle with thyme and ½ teaspoon salt and mix. Blend in prunes. Turn into a shallow greased baking dish. Brown chops on both sides in hot, lightly greased skillet. Salt the chops. Arrange chops on stuffing and cover. Bake in a 325° oven for 1 hour. Makes 6 servings.

PROVINCIAL HOT POT
The Borden Company

¼ cup butter
6 loin lamb chops
6 large onions, chopped
3 cloves garlic, minced, or ⅜ teaspoon garlic powder
2 cups Borden's Homogenized Milk
2 bouillon cubes
¼ cup finely chopped parsley or parsley flakes
2 bay leaves

1½ teaspoons salt
2 teaspoons ginger
½ teaspoon pepper
1 9-ounce package frozen green beans
1 10-ounce package frozen corn
1 2¼-ounce envelope Borden's Instant Whipped Potatoes

Melt butter in large deep skillet. Sauté lamb chops until brown on both sides. Reduce heat; add onions and garlic; sauté until onions are tender. Stir in milk, bouillon cubes, and seasonings; cover skillet. Simmer mixture for 15 minutes. Cook frozen vegetables according to package directions. Drain well. Place in bottom of 2-quart casserole. Arrange chops over vegetables. Strain liquid in which chops were simmered. Pour ¾ cup of this liquid over the chops. To remaining liquid, add enough water to make 1½ cups. Use this liquid for potato topping.

To prepare potato topping: Follow package directions for preparing instant whipped potatoes using the 1½ cups of above liquid in place of the water and milk. Omit butter and salt. Arrange these flavored potatoes between the chops. Bake in 350° oven about 15 minutes, or until the potatoes are slightly browned. Makes 6 servings.

LAMB RIBLETS WITH SPAGHETTI
American Lamb Council

2 4- to 5-pound breast of lamb rib sections, cut in 2-rib portions	4 medium onions
	1 lemon
	Cooked spaghetti
Salt and pepper	Parmesan cheese
Smoked salt (optional)	

Brown lamb ribs on both sides over moderate surface heat or in a 400° oven. Drain off the fat. Arrange the lamb in a roaster with a tight-fitting cover. Sprinkle lightly with salt, pepper, and with bit of smoked salt, if desired.

Tuck in between lamb pieces 4 onions and lemon, very thinly sliced. Combine ingredients for Barbecue Sauce for Lamb (see page 172) and pour over the lamb and onions. Cover tightly. Bake in a 325° oven for 1½ hours, or until fork tender. Spoon the sauce over the ribs 2 or 3 times during this period, adding a bit of water if necessary to keep sauce from sticking to pan. Uncover and bake 15 to 20 minutes more. Serve piping hot with butter-tossed spaghetti, and Parmesan cheese, and a mixed vegetable salad. Makes 8 servings.

CHA CHA CHILI
American Lamb Council

1 pound ground lamb	1 8-ounce can tomato sauce
¼ cup grated Parmesan cheese	2 1-pound cans red kidney beans
½ teaspoon garlic salt	2 teaspoons chili powder
1 medium onion, chopped	½ teaspoon salt
1 medium green pepper, chopped	Cooked rice

Combine lamb, cheese, and garlic salt; mix well. Shape into 1-inch balls. Cook over low heat until browned on all sides. Add onion and green pepper; cook 5 minutes. Add tomato sauce, beans, chili powder, and salt; mix well. Cover and cook 45 minutes, stirring occasionally. Serve over rice. Makes 4 servings.

SHEPHERD'S PIE
American Lamb Council

2 packages instant whipped potatoes
¾ cup grated Cheddar cheese
1 10-ounce package frozen Brussels sprouts
2 cups diced cooked lamb
1 tablespoon all-purpose flour

2 tablespoons salad oil
2 cups well-seasoned gravy
¾ cup drained cooked small onions
1 cup sliced cooked carrots
¼ cup canned pimiento strips
Salt and pepper to taste

Prepare potatoes following package directions. Add cheese, mix well. Cook Brussels sprouts, drain. Coat lamb with flour; heat fat or oil and add lamb. Cook over medium heat until lamb is browned; add gravy, sprouts, onions, carrots, pimientos, seasoning. Stir. Heat to serving temperature, stirring frequently. Turn into greased 2½-quart casserole and top with potatoes. Bake in 425° oven for 15 minutes. (See illustration 12.)

LAMB CURRY WITH RICE
Uncle Ben's, Inc.

½ cup sliced onion
½ cup diced celery
1 clove garlic, minced
2 tablespoons fat
1½ cups lamb gravy or stock
1½ teaspoons curry powder

1 teaspoon salt
1 teaspoon Worcestershire Sauce
1½ cups cooked lamb, diced
3 cups cooked Uncle Ben's Rice

In heavy skillet, sauté onion, celery, and garlic in melted fat until tender. Add gravy or stock and seasonings. (If stock is used, thicken with 2 tablespoons flour blended in ¼ cup cold water.) Cook, covered, over low heat for 15 minutes. Add lamb and heat thoroughly. Serve in a border of hot rice with chutney. Makes 4 servings.

KIDNEYS IN SHERRY SAUCE
McCormick & Co., Inc.

12 lamb kidneys
4 strips bacon
1 tablespoon McCormick or Schilling Instant Minced Onion
1 tablespoon flour

1 teaspoon salt
⅛ teaspoon McCormick or Schilling Black Pepper
2 cups broth
1 tablespoon McCormick or Schilling Sherry Extract

Scald kidneys 3 minutes; rinse in cold water. Skin, quarter, and remove white portion from kidneys. Cut bacon strips into 4 or 5 pieces; fry until golden brown. Add minced onion and kidneys, and brown lightly, about 2 minutes. Stir in flour, salt, and pepper. Add broth; cover and simmer 25 minutes, or until kidneys are tender. Just before serving, stir in the sherry extract. Makes 6 servings.

LAMB KIDNEY STEW
Paul Masson Vineyards

8 lamb kidneys
½ teaspoon salt
A little pepper
2 tablespoons fat
2 tablespoons butter
1 or 2 shallots (or ¼ onion),
 finely chopped

1½ tablespoons flour
½ cup canned tomatoes or
 1 tablespoon tomato paste
1 glass Paul Masson Pale
 Dry Sherry
¼ cup stock
½ teaspoon chopped
 parsley

Remove fat from kidneys and peel off skin. Cut each in quarters and season with salt and pepper. Put fat in hot saucepan, add kidneys and sauté very quickly, about 2 or 3 minutes. Drain well in a colander. Put butter in saucepan, add shallots (or onion); cook a few minutes. Add flour and continue cooking until flour is golden brown. Add tomato and stock, and cook, stirring constantly until thickened. Cook slowly 10 minutes longer; add sherry. Add kidneys, bring just to a boil. Serve sprinkled with parsley. If desired, the sauce may be strained before adding kidneys.

PORK

GLAZED SMOKED PORK BUTT
The Seven-Up Company

2 small boneless smoked
 pork shoulder butts
6 whole cloves
2 bay leaves

1 medium onion, sliced
1 cup brown sugar
1 7-ounce bottle 7-Up
1 small lemon, sliced

Place pork in a deep pan and add water to cover. Add cloves, bay leaves, and onion. Cook over low heat until meat is tender, allowing about 45 minutes per pound cooking time. Remove from water and place on a rack in a shallow pan. Moisten brown sugar with a few tablespoons of 7-Up and spread over meat. Anchor lemon slices on top of meat with picks. Baste meat with a few spoons of 7-Up, and bake in a 350° oven for ½ hour, basting every 10 minutes with remaining 7-Up. Makes 6 to 8 servings.

FRUITED PORK ROLLS
California Packing Corporation

1½ to 2 pounds thinly cut pork steak
1½ cups soft stale bread crumbs
1 cup chopped apple
1½ teaspoons instant minced onion or 2 tablespoons chopped raw onion

½ cup Del Monte Seedless Raisins
½ teaspoon salt
⅛ teaspoon thyme
2 tablespoons water or broth
1 tablespoon shortening
1 cup chicken broth

Trim any excess fat from meat; pound meat and then cut into 5 or 6 serving pieces. Combine bread crumbs, apple, onion, raisins, salt, thyme, and water. Center each piece of meat with the stuffing. Roll up and fasten each piece with string. Brown rolls in heated shortening. Add broth, cover, and cook slowly until meat is very tender, about 45 to 50 minutes. Skim any excess fat from pan drippings; thicken remaining juices slightly with a little corn starch mixed with water, if desired. Makes 5 or 6 servings.

HAWAIIAN PORK
The Procter & Gamble Company

1½ pounds lean shoulder pork, cut in 1-inch pieces
¼ cup Crisco
¼ cup water
2 tablespoons corn starch
½ teaspoon salt
¼ cup brown sugar
⅓ cup vinegar

1 cup pineapple juice
1 tablespoon soy sauce
½ cup green pepper, chopped
1 medium onion, thinly sliced
2½ cups pineapple chunks or tidbits

Brown pork in shortening. Add water. Cover and cook about 1 hour over low heat. Combine corn starch, salt, sugar, vinegar, pineapple juice, and soy sauce in saucepan and cook, stirring constantly, until slightly thickened. Pour sauce over hot pork. Allow to stand 10 minutes. Stir in green pepper, onion, and pineapple. Cook about 5 minutes. Serve over hot rice. Makes 6 servings.

ROAST PORK ROSE
Hunt Foods, Inc.

1 3- to 6-pound loin or rib pork roast
2 8-ounce cans Hunt's Tomato Sauce
½ cup cider vinegar
½ cup brown sugar

½ cup dark corn syrup
½ cup water
2 tablespoons corn starch
1 teaspoon salt
¼ teaspoon pepper

Have butcher loosen backbone from ribs. Place roast in open roasting pan with fat side up. Roast at 325°, 40 minutes per pound. Combine remaining ingredients in saucepan; cook over low heat, stirring until thickened. Thirty minutes before roast is done, remove pan drippings. Slice roast halfway down between rib bones so baste can penetrate meat. Baste generously with sauce. Baste with additional sauce 2 or 3 times. Serve remaining sauce with meat.

BAKED PORK CHOPS
Hunt Foods, Inc.

6 pork chops
1 teaspoon salt
⅛ teaspoon pepper
Oil for skillet
2 8-ounce cans Hunt's Tomato Sauce

½ cup water
½ cup finely chopped celery
2 tablespoons brown sugar
1 teaspoon prepared mustard
Juice of ½ lemon

Sprinkle chops with salt and pepper. Brown in hot, greased skillet. Place in shallow, greased baking dish. Combine remaining ingredients. Pour over chops. Cover and bake in 350° oven 1 hour, or until chops are tender. Makes 6 servings.

GOURMET CHOPS WITH RICE
Pet Milk Company

4 pork chops, ½-inch thick
¼ teaspoon pepper
½ teaspoon salt
1 tablespoon hot shortening
1 can beef consommé
½ teaspoon thyme
½ cup finely cut celery

½ cup sliced onion
1 4-ounce can mushroom stems and pieces
1 tablespoon dried parsley flakes
½ cup Pet Evaporated Milk

Sprinkle both sides of chops with salt and pepper. Brown slowly on both sides in shortening in a 10-inch skillet. Drain off fat and stir in consommé, thyme, celery, and onion.

Cover and simmer chops in consommé mixture for 30 minutes, Meanwhile, drain and save juice from mushrooms. Stir mushroom liquid into flour until mixture is smooth. Remove skillet from heat and move chops to one side of skillet. Gradually stir flour mixture into consommé mixture. Cook, stirring all the time, until thick. Stir in drained mushrooms, parsley flakes, and evaporated milk. Arrange chops in sauce. Cover and cook over low heat 5 minutes. Serve with hot rice. Makes 4 servings.

PORK CHOPS WITH PEANUT BUTTER DRESSING

Best Foods, Division of
Corn Products Company

¼ cup Skippy Creamy Peanut Butter
¼ cup (½ print) margarine
¾ cup water
¼ cup minced onion
3 cups day-old bread cubes
1 cup diced celery
4 pork chops

Melt peanut butter and margarine over very low heat. Add water gradually and blend thoroughly. Add onion. Add peanut butter mixture to bread cubes and celery, and mix thoroughly. Place dressing around pork chops and bake in a 350° oven for 1½ hours. Makes 4 servings.

BAKED PORK CHOPS AND APPLES

Grocery Store Products Co.

4 1-inch pork chops
1½ teaspoons Kitchen Bouquet
1 teaspoon salt
⅛ teaspoon pepper
2 tablespoons flour
1 cup water
1 tablespoon vinegar
2 tablespoons brown sugar
½ cup seedless raisins
2 apples

Brush pork chops with Kitchen Bouquet. Brown in frying pan over moderate heat. Remove to shallow baking dish and sprinkle chops with salt and pepper. Stir flour into fat in frying pan. Add water, vinegar, sugar, and raisins. Cook, stirring constantly, until sauce thickens and boils. Core apples and cut in slices as for pie. Arrange on top of chops. Pour sauce over apples and chops. Bake in 375° oven, until chops are tender, about 45 minutes, basting once or twice. Serve immediately. Makes 4 servings.

STUFFED PORK CHOPS

The Campbell Soup Company

¼ cup chopped dried apricots
½ cup water
1 cup dry bread cubes
¼ teaspoon salt
Dash black pepper

¼ cup chopped celery
2 tablespoons butter or margarine, melted
4 double pork chops, cut with pocket
1 cup medium beef gravy

In a covered saucepan, simmer apricots in water for 5 minutes. Drain off liquid and save it; blend 1 tablespoon apricot liquid with apricots, bread cubes, seasonings, celery, and butter. Trim excess fat from chops; stuff with apricot stuffing. Brown chops well on both sides in hot skillet; pour beef gravy and remaining liquid from apricots over chops. Cover; simmer about 45 minutes, or until chops are tender. Serve with Campbell's Bean with Bacon Soup. Makes 4 servings. (See illustration 3.)

SPANISH-STYLE PORK CHOPS

Thomas J. Lipton, Inc.

6 pork chops
2 tablespoons flour
1 tablespoon shortening
1 can (2 cups) tomatoes
1 package Lipton Dehydrated Onion Soup

1 green pepper, chopped
½ cup chopped celery
2 tablespoons chopped parsley
½ teaspoon salt
⅛ teaspoon pepper

Dredge chops in flour. Melt shortening in skillet and brown chops on both sides. Combine tomatoes, onion soup, green pepper, celery, parsley, salt, and pepper; pour over chops. Cover and cook until well done. Makes 6 servings.

BARBECUED SPARERIBS
The Chun King Corp.

3 pounds spareribs, cut into 2-rib sections
Water to cover
2 tablespoons corn starch
⅔ cup brown sugar, firmly packed

⅔ cup Chun King Soya Sauce
¼ cup cider vinegar
¼ teaspoon ground ginger
2 cloves garlic, crushed

Place spareribs in saucepan; cover with water and bring to boiling. Reduce heat and simmer 45 minutes. Drain. Dip each piece into an uncooked sauce made of the remaining ingredients, coating thoroughly. Broil about 5 minutes, or until richly browned, brushing occasionally with the sauce. Turn ribs and broil about 3 minutes, brushing with sauce. Makes 4 to 6 servings.

SPARERIBS WITH SAUERKRAUT AND PARSLEY DUMPLINGS
American Skultuna Inc.

2 to 3 tablespoons fat or oil
3 pounds spareribs
1 tablespoon caraway seeds

1 green pepper, chopped
1 cup white wine or boiling water

Have butcher chop through ribs at large end and cut ribs in 4 serving pieces. Heat fat in base pot of Skultuna Steamer for Split-Level Cookery®. Add meat and brown on all sides about 10 minutes. Add caraway seeds, green pepper, and wine. Blend well. Cover and simmer for 1 hour.

Remove meat from base pot. Place sauerkraut in base pot and blend with sauce. Place meat over sauerkraut; if necessary, add a few tablespoons water. Cover base pot, and continue to simmer for 15 minutes. Meanwhile, prepare a recipe for dumplings, place in inset pot over base pot, and cook with meat and sauerkraut an additional 15 minutes, or until dumplings are fluffy and tender.

To serve, place spareribs over sauerkraut in deep, warm serving dish. Serve dumplings in separate dish. Makes 4 servings.

Sauerkraut:

2 pounds or 1 27-ounce can sauerkraut
1 cooking apple, grated

¼ cup raisins
1 teaspoon white pepper (optional)

Blend ingredients and place in base pot of steamer; cover with the meat.

HAM-BANANA ROLLS WITH CHEESE SAUCE
United Fruit Company

Rolls:

4 thin slices boiled ham
Prepared mustard
4 firm Chiquita Bananas

1½ tablespoons butter or margarine, melted
Cheese sauce (see below)

Spread each slice of ham slightly with mustard. Peel bananas. Wrap a slice of the prepared ham around each banana. Brush tips of bananas with butter or margarine. Place rolls in a greased shallow baking dish, and pour Cheese Sauce over them. Bake in a 350° oven 30 mintues, or until bananas are tender, easily pierced with a fork. Serve hot with the Cheese Sauce. Makes 4 servings.

Cheese Sauce:

1½ tablespoons butter or margarine
1½ tablespoons flour

¾ cup milk
1½ cups grated sharp American cheese

Melt butter or margarine in saucepan; add flour and stir until smooth. Stir in milk slowly. Add cheese and cook, stirring constantly, until sauce is smooth and thickened. Makes about 1 cup sauce.

RUBY RED GLAZED PINEAPPLE-HAM
Dole Corporation

1 whole ham	1 can Dole Pineapple Slices
⅓ cup currant jelly	1 bottle maraschino cherries

Cook whole ham according to your favorite method. Whip ⅓ cup currant jelly and spread over scored surface of ham. Use sections of picks to affix pineapple slices and maraschino cherries, then return ham to preheated 400° oven for 15 minutes. (See illustration 8.)

FESTIVE HAM
Grocery Store Products Co.

1 4- to 5-pound boneless, skinless ham	¼ cup brown sugar
⅔ cup apricot purée	2 teaspoons Kitchen Bouquet

Place ham on rack in shallow roasting pan and cover. Bake in preheated 350° oven for 1 hour. Combine apricot purée, brown sugar, and Kitchen Bouquet, and brush mixture over entire surface of ham. Bake until glazed, about 20 minutes. Serve with Quick Apricot Sauce (see page 174). Makes 15 to 16 servings.

GLAZED HAM ANGOSTURA
The Angostura-Wuppermann Corp.

1 3-pound canned ham	3 tablespoons lemon juice
2 cups water	4 teaspoons Angostura Aromatic Bitters
½ cup honey	

Arrange ham, with water, in shallow baking pan. Bake 20 minutes in 325° oven. Mix honey, lemon juice, and bitters, and spread over ham. Continue baking about 20 minutes, basting with liquid from pan. Serve on heated platter, garnish with pineapple slices.

CHERRY-GLAZED HAM STEAK
National Red Cherry Institute

2 pounds (about 6) sweet potatoes
¾ cup brown sugar, firmly packed
1 tablespoon corn starch

1 can (1 pound) red sour pitted cherries (water pack)
4 tablespoons butter or margarine
1 1½-inch thick ham slice

Cook unpared sweet potatoes in boiling water 15 minutes. Peel; halve lengthwise. (If small, leave whole.) Mix together brown sugar and corn starch in skillet. Drain cherries; add enough water to liquid to make 1 cup. Add to skillet with butter; add sweet potatoes. Cook uncovered, over low heat, basting occasionally, until potatoes are tender and glazed, about 30 minutes. Add drained cherries last 5 minutes cooking time. While potatoes are cooking, prepare ham. Slash fat edges of ham; stud with cloves, if desired. Broil or pan-broil 12 to 15 minutes on each side for cook-before-eating ham, 8 to 10 minutes on each side for fully-cooked ham. To serve, spoon sweet potatoes and cherries around ham. Makes 6 servings.

HAM PATTIES ON PINEAPPLE
Grocery Store Products Co.

1 3-ounce can chopped Broiled-in-Butter Mushrooms
1 tablespoon Cream of Rice Cereal
1½ cups chopped cooked ham

1 egg
1 tablespoon brown sugar
¼ teaspoon dry mustard
$\frac{1}{16}$ teaspoon ground cloves
8 slices canned pineapple

Place contents of can of mushrooms in small saucepan and bring to boil. Sprinkle in Cream of Rice and cook until beginning to thicken, about ½ minute. Remove from heat and let cool while putting enough cooked ham through food chopper to make 1½ cups. Combine ham with the mushroom mixture. Add egg, brown sugar, mustard, and cloves, and mix thoroughly. Drain pineapple and arrange slices on greased baking sheet. Drop heaping spoonful of ham mixture onto each slice and pat out into patty shape. Bake in moderately hot oven until cooked through and lightly browned, about 30 minutes. Serve immediately with buttered garden vegetables. Garnish with wedges of crisp, fresh cucumber. Makes 4 servings.

GRANDMA'S HAM FRITTERS
The Angostura-Wuppermann Corp.

⅔ cup sifted flour
1 teaspoon baking powder
⅓ cup milk
2 eggs
1 tablespoon Angostura Aromatic Bitters

2 cups cooked ground ham
½ cup crushed pineapple, well drained
Fat for deep frying

In mixing bowl, sift flour with baking powder. Add milk, eggs, bitters, and mix until smooth. Fold in ham and pineapple. Drop by teaspoonsful into deep hot fat at 350° and fry until golden brown. Drain on paper towel. Makes 20 to 30 small fritters.

SAUSAGE-STUFFED APPLES
National Biscuit Company

4 large cooking apples	1 teaspoon salt
½ pound sausage meat	½ teaspoon pepper
1 small onion, chopped	1 egg
1 packet Premium Saltine Crackers, crumbled	

Core apples and scoop out pulp leaving ½-inch shell. Save pulp. Cook sausage meat, draining off fat as it accumulates. When sausage is nearly cooked, add chopped onion. Crumble crackers into bowl. Chop apple pulp; add to crackers with sausage meat, onion, salt, pepper, and egg. Mix together. Stuff apples and bake in 375° oven only until apples are tender. Makes 4 servings. (See illustration 5.)

CASSOULET
Hunt Foods, Inc.

¼ pound link sausages	1 8-ounce can Hunt's Tomato Sauce
1 medium onion, sliced	½ cup hot water
1 clove garlic, minced	½ teaspoon salt
2 tablespoons butter or margarine	1 teaspoon sugar
2 8-ounce cans lima beans, drained	Pinch of thyme
1 cup cooked and cubed beef, lamb, or veal	½ cup coarse dry bread crumbs
	2 tablespoons chopped parsley

Cut sausages into chunks; separate onion into rings. Cook both with garlic in 1 tablespoon butter until sausage is lightly browned, and onion is soft. In 1½-quart casserole, put layers of drained beans, then meat, then onion mixture; repeat layers. Combine tomato sauce, water, salt, sugar, and thyme. Heat to boiling and pour over layers. Bake in 350° oven 45 minutes or longer. Heat remaining tablespoon butter in saucepan. When bubbly, mix in crumbs and parsley. Sprinkle around edge of casserole; return to oven until crumbs are golden brown. Makes 4 servings.

9 Holiday meals are important occasions, richly deserving the special planning and extra effort that American women lavish upon them. This picture shows one of our all-time favorites—roast turkey with all the trimmings—a memorable contribution to festive fun. Photo courtesy of Best Foods, Division of Corn Products Company.

10 Spaghetti is a buffet supper standby. Offer your guests—or your family—a choice of sauces, an innovation guaranteed to encourage second helpings. Photo courtesy of Buitoni Foods Corp.

11 Pastas vary endlessly in appearance, and for that reason, lend themselves readily to creative cooking. Here are the pastas assembled for a family portrait, from the simple noodle to the complex wagon wheel. Photo courtesy of Buitoni Foods Corp.

12 This casserole will have strong appeal for the man in the family because of its hearty combination of meat and vegetables edged with mashed potatoes. It's called Shepherd's Pie (p. 81). You'll find it perfect for Saturday night suppers, buffet dinners, or whenever your family gets together. Photo courtesy of American Lamb Council.

13 There is no more classic American dish than a pot of baked beans. Sophisticated Baked Beans (p. 144) takes liberties with past practices, but the results will please the most rigid adherent to traditional recipes. Photo courtesy of The Seven-Up Company.

14 Curried Chicken 'N' Rice (p. 103) is an elegant but uncomplicated main dish. Raisins and almonds add to its special taste and texture. Photo courtesy of The Campbell Soup Company.

15 A Whipped Potato Soufflé (p. 132) is a particularly handsome compliment to your guests. Try it with a mixed grill of mushrooms, chicken livers, cubes of pineapple, and beef or lamb broiled on skewers. Photo courtesy of The Borden Company.

16 A colorful pasta treat is the Italian Tri-Color (p. 129)—spinach ribbons, spaghetti, and Mari Twists. Cover with melted butter and sprinkle with grated Parmesan cheese. A green salad and vin rosé are the right accompaniment for this selection of pastas. Photo courtesy of Buitoni Foods Corp.

16

POULTRY and EGGS

Which comes first—the chicken or the egg? It doesn't matter, really, since most of us eat over half a pound of poultry a week and at least one egg a day.

The popularity of turkey, chicken, and duck in American homes can be traced to two principal motivations: economy and weight control. The young broiler-fryer chicken, extremely low in fat content, is probably the most popular of all fowl. Young turkey, duck, and goose are also relatively low in calories.

Dark meat is higher in fat content than white, but it also has more nutrients. For this reason, it is not advisable to eliminate one or the other from your diet.

Eggs are nature's most "regulated" food; they are almost always perfect in form and pure in content. Their versatility and adaptability are borne out by the hundreds of recipes for preparing and serving them that have been developed over the years. Eggs can be "built in" to almost any kind of dish—from appetizers to dessert.

The recipes that follow should prove mainstays in your menu-planning. And don't overlook the soufflés. They will serve you handsomely for special dinners and Sunday night suppers. At these times, they have a very unusual quality that only a handful of foods can claim, for in addition to proving your own culinary skill, they are the supreme compliment to your guests.

CHICKEN

CORN-CRISPED CHICKEN
Kellogg Company

1 broiler-fryer, cut in serving pieces
4 cups Kellogg's® Corn Flakes or 1 cup Packaged Kellogg's® Corn Flake Crumbs

1½ teaspoons salt
⅛ teaspoon pepper
½ cup evaporated milk, ½ cup buttermilk, or 1 cup sour cream

Wash chicken pieces and dry thoroughly. If using corn flakes, crush into fine crumbs. Combine corn flake crumbs with salt and pepper. Dip chicken pieces in evaporated milk, then roll in seasoned corn flake crumbs. Line shallow baking pan with aluminum foil. Place chicken pieces, skin side up, in pan; do not crowd. Bake in 350° oven about 1 hour, or until tender. No need to cover or turn chicken while cooking. For less crisp crust, cover lightly with foil during first 45 minutes of baking. Makes 4 to 5 servings.

CHICKEN IN THE PINK
Hunt Foods, Inc.

3 broilers, halved
2 8-ounce cans Hunt's Tomato Sauce
½ cup lemon juice
¾ cup vegetable oil
2 tablespoons sugar

½ teaspoon salt
½ teaspoon pepper
1 tablespoon finely minced onion
1 clove garlic, finely minced
3 bay leaves

Wipe chickens and place in 13 x 9 x 2-inch baking pan. Combine remaining ingredients. Pour over chicken, completely covering halves. Let stand 2 to 3 hours, turning occasionally. Pour off sauce and save for basting. Bake in a 350° oven about 90 minutes, or until chicken is tender, basting every 10 minutes with sauce. Makes 6 servings.

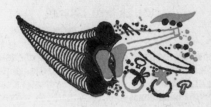

CHICKEN CERISE
National Red Cherry Institute

1 can (1 pound) red sour pitted cherries (water pack)	⅛ teaspoon each, allspice, cinnamon, and dry mustard
1 broiler-fryer chicken, cut in pieces	1 9-ounce can crushed pineapple
3 tablespoons butter or margarine	1 chicken bouillon cube
1 tablespoon flour	¼ teaspoon red food coloring
¼ teaspoon salt	3 cups hot cooked rice
1 teaspoon sugar	

Drain cherries; reserve liquid. Sprinkle chicken with salt, pepper, and paprika. Melt butter in skillet; add chicken and brown well on all sides. Remove chicken. Blend flour, salt, sugar, and spices in drippings in skillet. Gradually stir in cherry liquid; add crushed pineapple, bouillon cube, and red food coloring. Add chicken. Cover; simmer 40 minutes, or until chicken is tender. Add drained cherries last 5 minutes of cooking time. To serve, place chicken in center of serving platter; spoon some of the sauce over chicken. Surround with hot cooked rice. If desired, sprinkle rice with finely chopped parsley and toasted slivered almonds. Serve with remaining sauce. Makes 4 servings.

MING'S DIAMOND CHICKEN
Diamond Walnut Growers, Inc.

3 chicken breasts
10 tablespoons vegetable oil
6 teaspoons corn starch
1½ cups Diamond Walnuts
1 teaspoon salt
1 cup button mushrooms
1 cup chicken stock
1½ cups sliced bamboo shoots

2 cups snow peas or 1 cup each celery and green peppers, sliced
Pepper to taste
¾ teaspoon Ac'cent
1 teaspoon granulated sugar
4 teaspoons soy sauce
2 tablespoons water

Skin and bone chicken and slice wafer-thin. Cut into diamond shapes. Mix 2 tablespoons oil with 2 teaspoons corn starch, and cover chicken slices with it. Heat 2 tablespoons oil in skillet and sauté walnuts until slightly brown. Remove nuts from pan and set aside. In hot pan, add remaining oil, the salt, and the chicken. Stir until the chicken meat turns white. Add stock, mushrooms, bamboo shoots, and snow peas. Cover and cook for 1 minute. Mix pepper, Ac'cent, sugar, soy sauce, remaining corn starch, and water. Add to pan and stir gently until sauce thickens. Add walnuts and mix slightly before serving. Makes 8 servings. Ming's Diamond Chicken will freeze well, wrapped in Saran Wrap.

CHICKEN AND CHEESE PIE
Pet Milk Company

Crust:

Pastry for 9-inch pie crust
¼ teaspoon paprika
⅓ cup grated process American cheese

¼ cup sesame seeds, toasted

Mix ingredients in a 1½-quart bowl. Roll out on lightly floured board to fit 9-inch pie pan.

Filling:

2 cups grated process American cheese
¼ teaspoon garlic salt
2 teaspoons Worcestershire Sauce
½ cup Pet Evaporated Milk

3 cups cooked noodles, well drained
2 5-ounce cans chicken, cubed
½ cup stuffed olives, sliced
⅓ cup almonds, cut up

Put 2 cups American cheese, garlic salt, and Worcestershire Sauce into a 1½-quart bowl. Stir in evaporated milk gradually, mixing until smooth. Stir in noodles, chicken, olives, and almonds. Pour into prepared shell. Just before serving garnish with paprika or sliced olives and bake near center of 375° oven 25 to 30 minutes. Makes 6 servings.

CHICKEN-VEGETABLE CASSEROLE
The Campbell Soup Company

2 medium potatoes, peeled and cut in 1-inch cubes (about 2 cups)
2 medium carrots, sliced (about 1 cup)
1 small onion, sliced and separated into rings
¼ cup chopped green pepper
1 tablespoon chopped parsley
¾ teaspoon salt

1 cup water
1 10½-ounce can Campbell's Condensed Cream of Chicken Soup
Dash pepper
⅛ teaspoon whole rosemary, crushed
⅓ cup liquid from vegetables
2 5-ounce cans Swanson's Boned Chicken or Turkey
2 slices buttered bread

In saucepan, combine potatoes, carrots, onion, green pepper, parsley, salt, and water. Cover; cook 10 to 15 minutes, or until vegetables are just tender crisp. Drain, reserving ⅓ cup liquid. Combine soup, pepper, rosemary, and vegetable liquid in a buttered 1-quart casserole; blend. Fold in vegetables and chicken. Trim crusts from bread; cut each slice into 4 triangles. Place on top of chicken mixture. Bake, uncovered, in 400° oven about 20 minutes, or until bubbly. Makes 4 generous servings.

CHICKEN ROSE WITH TARRAGON
Paul Masson Vineyards

1 3½-pound chicken, cut in 4 pieces	1½ cups Paul Masson Vin Rosé Sec
Seasoned flour	½ cup chicken consommé
2 ounces butter	½ teaspoon dried tarragon
½ pound fresh mushrooms, sliced	

Shake the chicken pieces in a bag containing seasoned flour. Melt butter in a heavy skillet; when it is hot, brown the chicken pieces in it on both sides. Then place them in a casserole. In the same skillet, adding more butter if necessary, sauté mushrooms for 5 to 6 minutes. Then add to the mushrooms, wine, and consommé, taking up the brown in the skillet by stirring over a low flame. Pour the mushrooms and the liquid over the chicken pieces. Sprinkle with tarragon, which has been rubbed between the palms of the hand. Cover the casserole, and cook for 1 hour in a 375° oven.

CHICKEN NEWBURG
The Borden Company

6 tablespoons butter	1 8-ounce package Borden's Process Swiss Cheese, shredded
1 medium onion, chopped	
½ cup (4-ounce can) sliced mushrooms, drained	4 cups diced chicken or turkey, cooked
3 tablespoons flour	¼ cup sherry (optional)
3 cups Borden's Light Cream	

Melt butter in large skillet or blazer pan of chafing dish over low flame. Add onions and mushrooms; sauté until onions are tender. Blend in flour. Add light cream and cheese. Cook over low heat or place blazer pan over hot water. Cook, stirring constantly, until cheese is melted and mixture thickens slightly. Add chicken or turkey and sherry. Cover and cook until chicken or turkey is thoroughly heated, about 10 minutes. Serve over toasted frozen waffles. Makes 8 1-cup servings.

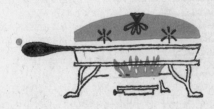

CURRIED CHICKEN 'N' RICE
The Campbell Soup Company

½ cup chopped celery
½ cup chopped onion
¼ cup slivered almonds
2 tablespoons butter or margarine
¾ cup rice
¼ cup raisins

1 teaspoon curry powder
1 13½-ounce can chicken broth
1 5-ounce can Swanson's Boned Chicken
Salt and pepper to taste

In a heavy skillet, cook celery, onion, and almonds in butter until vegetables are transparent and almonds are lightly browned. Stir in rice, raisins, and curry powder. Add chicken broth; bring to a boil. Cover and simmer 15 minutes over low heat. Add chicken; cover and continue to cook about 5 minutes more, or until rice is tender and chicken is hot. Season to taste. Makes 4 servings. (See illustration 14.)

SWEET-AND-PUNGENT CHICKEN LIVERS
Uncle Ben's, Inc.

2 large green peppers
1 pound chicken livers
½ teaspoon salt
Few grains pepper
2 tablespoons butter or margarine
4 canned pineapple slices
⅔ cup canned pineapple syrup

2 tablespoons corn starch
2 teaspoons soy sauce
2 tablespoons vinegar
⅓ cup sugar
1 cup chicken bouillon
1 cup Uncle Ben's Converted Rice, cooked

Wash peppers; remove seeds and cut each in 6 pieces. Cook in boiling salted water 8 to 10 minutes. Drain. Quarter chicken livers; sprinkle with salt and pepper. Sauté in butter or margarine 10 minutes; remove and keep hot. Cut each pineapple slice in 6 pieces; place in pan in which livers were sautéed. Add ⅓ cup pineapple syrup and peppers. Cover; simmer 10 minutes. Mix corn starch to smooth paste with remaining pineapple syrup; add soy sauce, vinegar, sugar, and bouillon. Add to pepper and pineapple mixture. Cook, stirring constantly, until thickened. Place chicken livers on rice; pour sauce over all. Makes 4 servings.

CHICKEN LIVERS AND GREEN RICE
Uncle Ben's, Inc.

1 cup milk
2 tablespoons butter
2 tablespoons flour
½ teaspoon salt
½ cup sharp grated cheese
1 cup freshly boiled spinach
2 cups Uncle Ben's Converted Rice, cooked

1 pound chicken livers
4 tablespoons butter
1 tablespoon minced onion
1 cup whole canned tomatoes
1 teaspoon salt

Make cheese sauce of milk, butter, flour, salt, and cheese. Combine with rice and spinach. Pack in greased ring mold and keep warm. Sauté chicken livers in butter; add onion and tomatoes that have been well drained. Salt. Cook over low fire until livers are done, about 20 minutes. Unmold rice on warm platter and place livers in center of mold. Makes 6 servings.

ROCK CORNISH HEN

ROCK CORNISH DELUXE
Grocery Store Products Co.

3 1-pound Rock Cornish Hens	¾ cup muscatel or chicken broth
3 tablespoons butter	2 tablespoons corn starch
¼ cup minced onion	¼ cup cold water
1 6-ounce can sliced Broiled-in-Butter Mushrooms	1 teaspoon Kitchen Bouquet
	1 cup commercial sour cream

Cut hens in half using sharp kitchen shears. Melt butter in skillet, add hens, skin side down, and the onion. Sauté until hens are a good brown color and the onion is tender, about 10 minutes. Drain mushrooms and add mushroom broth and wine to hens. Lower heat; cover and simmer 30 minutes. Remove hens from skillet and place on warm serving platter. Combine corn starch, cold water, and Kitchen Bouquet, and stir into pan drippings. Cook, stirring constantly, until gravy thickens and is smooth. Stir in sour cream and mushrooms and heat gently until piping hot. Do not allow to boil. Serve in gravy boat or pour directly over hens on serving plates. Makes 6 servings.

Note: Three 1-pound squab chickens or 2 packages frozen chicken breasts may be substituted for Rock Cornish Hen.

TURKEY

TURKEY WITH CORN STUFFING
Grocery Store Products Co.

1 8- to 10-pound ready-to-
  cook turkey
⅓ cup margarine
⅔ cup finely diced onion
⅔ cup finely diced celery
1½ teaspoons salt

½ teaspoon marjoram
6 cups corn bread cubes
4 tablespoons soft fat
2 teaspoons Kitchen Bou-
  quet

In 9-inch skillet, melt margarine over moderate heat. Add onion, celery, salt, and marjoram, and sauté until just tender, about 5 minutes. Combine with corn bread which has been cut into ½-inch cubes. Stuff turkey cavity lightly with stuffing. Close vent by inserting poultry pins from one side of opening to other, then lacing string around the pins. Truss legs and wings into position. Place turkey on rack in shallow roasting pan, breast side up. Blend together soft fat and Kitchen Bouquet, then rub over entire surface of turkey. Roast in preheated 325° oven, until meat thermometer inserted into thickest part registers 190° for meat and 165° for stuffing, about 3 hours. Makes 8 to 10 servings.

TURKEY DIVAN
The Angostura-Wuppermann Corp.

1 package frozen broccoli
4 tablespoons butter or margarine
3 tablespoons flour
½ teaspoon salt
1½ cups milk
1 egg yolk
¼ cup grated Parmesan or ½ cup American cheese
1 teaspoon Angostura Aromatic Bitters
1 egg white, stiffly beaten
4 large or 8 small slices turkey, cooked

Cook broccoli until just tender; drain. Melt butter or margarine, and stir in flour and salt. Add milk gradually, while stirring over low heat, until sauce thickens. Beat in egg yolk quickly. Stir in grated cheese and bitters. Fold in beaten egg white. Reserve 4 flowerets of broccoli, and divide remainder among 4 individual baking dishes. Cover with ⅓ of the sauce. Arrange slices of turkey in each dish, and pour remaining sauce over this. Bake in 400° oven about 10 minutes until thoroughly hot. Garnish with broccoli.

CREAMED TURKEY ROYAL
Grocery Store Products Co.

2 tablespoons butter
2 tablespoons flour
⅛ teaspoon mace
⅛ teaspoon ginger
1 6-ounce can Broiled-in-Butter Mushroom Crowns
1½ cups rich milk or light cream
1 chicken bouillon cube
2 cups cubed turkey, cooked
½ cup slivered blanched almonds

Melt butter in top of double boiler. Stir in combined flour, mace, and ginger. Cook over moderate heat, stirring constantly, for about 2 minutes. Drain mushroom broth into saucepan, add milk, and bring to boil. Dissolve bouillon cube in hot broth mixture and add to fat-flour mixture. Cook, stirring constantly, until sauce is thick and smooth. Add cubed turkey, drained mushroom crowns, and almonds, mixing well. Heat until piping hot. Serve with hot fluffy rice, toast points, or noodles. Makes 4 servings.

DUCK

HONEY-GLAZED DUCKLING WITH TANGERINE SAUCE
Grocery Store Products Co.

2 4-pound ready-to-cook Long Island ducklings	2 teaspoons Kitchen Bouquet
¼ cup honey	

Clip off wing tips; wash ducks carefully inside and out with cold water and dry with a cloth. Close vents by tying string around poultry pins which have been inserted from one side to the other. Pin neck fat over the neck with another pin. Place ducks on a rack in a shallow baking pan, breast side up. Roast in a 325° oven until tender and brown, about 2 hours. About 15 minutes before ducks are done, brush all over with a mixture of ¼ cup honey and Kitchen Bouquet to give an even glaze. Garnish with tangerine sections and water cress. Makes 6 to 8 servings.

Tangerine Sauce:

2 tablespoons butter	3 tablespoons corn starch
3 tablespoons minced onion	1 teaspoon salt
1 6-ounce can concentrated frozen tangerine juice	1 teaspoon ginger
2¼ cups water	Dash bitters
2 tablespoons lemon juice	2 small tangerines, peeled and sectioned
¼ cup honey	

Melt butter in saucepan. Add onion and cook 2 minutes, stirring frequently. Add concentrated juice, 2 cups water, lemon juice, and ¼ cup honey; bring to boil. Combine and add remaining ¼ cup water, corn starch, salt, ginger, and bitters to boiling mixture and bring to boil again stirring constantly. Add tangerine sections and remove from heat. Serve with roast ducks. If you prefer, use condensed frozen orange juice and orange sections.

ROAST DUCKLING WITH SWEET POTATO STUFFING
Grocery Store Products Co.

1 4- to 5-pound ready-to-cook Long Island duckling
2 pounds sweet potatoes
3 tablespoons melted fat
1½ teaspoons salt
½ teaspoon celery salt
¼ teaspoon pepper
1 cup canned crushed pineapple, drained
1 cup corn bread crumbs, lightly packed
2 tablespoons honey
1 teaspoon Kitchen Bouquet
4 oranges, sliced

Prepare duckling for roasting. Cook and peel sweet potatoes; mash through sieve or food mill. To 3 cups mashed potatoes, add melted fat, seasonings, pineapple, and corn bread crumbs, tossing lightly with fork to blend well. Mix thoroughly and lightly stuff cavity of duck. Fold back skin at neck and fasten with small skewer. Close vent by lacing string around small skewers inserted from side to side. Roast in a 325° oven for about 1½ to 2 hours. About 30 minutes before duckling is done, brush all over with a mixture of Kitchen Bouquet and honey. Return to oven and continue roasting. Serve on platter garnished with sliced oranges. Accompany with Mushroom-Giblet Gravy (see page 112). Makes 4 servings.

DUCKLING MONTMORENCY
National Red Cherry Institute

1 4- to 5-pound ready-to-
cook duckling
4 teaspoons corn starch
4 tablespoons sugar
¼ teaspoon each, salt, dry
mustard, and ginger

1 can (1 pound) red sour
pitted cherries (water
pack)
1 tablespoon slivered orange
rind
½ cup orange juice
¼ teaspoon red food coloring

Sprinkle cavity of duck with salt and pepper. Stuff, if desired. Place on rack in shallow baking pan. Do not add water; do not cover; do not baste. Roast in a 325° oven 30 to 35 minutes per pound. During last 15 minutes roasting time, prepare sauce. Mix together corn starch, sugar, salt, mustard, and ginger in saucepan. Drain cherries; add cherry liquid to corn starch mixture with orange rind and orange juice. Stir in red food coloring. Place over medium heat and cook, stirring constantly, until mixture comes to a boil; boil ½ minute. Add drained cherries; heat to serving temperature. Serve with roasted duck. Makes 4 servings.

BRAISED DUCKLING WITH CRANBERRY SAUCE
Grocery Store Products Co.

1 4- to 5-pound ready-to-
cook Long Island duckling
1 tablespoon Kitchen Bou-
quet
1 teaspoon salt
½ cup duck broth or red
wine

1 cup whole cranberry
sauce, freshly cooked or
canned
½ cup currant jelly
1 tablespoon cognac

With sharp knife, cut duck skin along center of breast from neck to vent. Run knife between layer of skin and flesh, pulling skin away from flesh at the same time. Cut skin where necessary but try to keep flesh intact. Cut duckling into serving-size pieces or quarters, using poultry shears or a sharp knife. Put pieces of skinned duckling into mixing bowl. Mix Kitchen Bouquet and salt, and sprinkle over duck pieces. Toss gently with fork to coat pieces evenly.

Meanwhile, cook duck giblets and skin in 2 cups water, covered, until tender, about 45 minutes. Pour broth into suitable container. When fat rises to top, skim off. Cook duck in ¼ cup duck fat in heavy skillet or Dutch oven until nicely browned, turning frequently. Add duck broth or red wine, cover and cook over low heat until tender, about 45 minutes. Heat cranberry sauce and currant jelly in saucepan, mixing well. Remove from heat and stir in cognac. Serve duckling with sauce poured over it. Makes 4 servings.

ORANGE DUCK EN CASSEROLE
Grocery Store Products Co.

1 4- to 5-pound ready-to-cook Long Island duckling	1 3-ounce can sliced Broiled-in-Butter Mushrooms
2 teaspoons Kitchen Bouquet	1 6-ounce can frozen concentrated orange juice
⅓ cup duck fat	¼ cup currant jelly
⅓ cup flour	8 small white onions
1 teaspoon salt	8 small carrots
1 cup duck broth	

With sharp, pointed knife, cut skin along breast of duck from neck to vent. Loosen layer of fat and skin by running knife underneath, close to flesh. Peel skin back as it is loosened, cutting where necessary, but keeping flesh intact. Cook duck skin, fat, neck, and giblets in 3 cups boiling salted water for about 45 minutes. Strain broth. Allow fat to rise and pour it off. Cut skinned duck in serving-size pieces and place in bowl. Sprinkle with Kitchen Bouquet. Toss lightly with fork to coat evenly. Heat ⅓ cup duck fat in large frying pan or Dutch oven. Brown pieces of duck on all sides over moderate heat. Remove browned duck from pan. Stir in flour and salt. Add 1 cup duck broth and contents of can of mushrooms. Cook, stirring constantly, until sauce thickens. Add orange juice and jelly. Bring to boil and cook 1 minute. Add pieces of browned duck, peeled onion, and carrots. Cover tightly and cook over moderate heat until duck and vegetables are tender, about 45 minutes. Or arrange in casserole dish and bake, covered, in 350° oven for about 1 hour. Serve immediately. Makes 4 servings.

GRAVY AND STUFFING

MUSHROOM-GIBLET GRAVY
Grocery Store Products Co.

Duck or other giblets	1 teaspoon salt
2 cups water	1 teaspoon Kitchen Bouquet
½ teaspoon salt	1 3-ounce can sliced Broiled-
¼ cup duck fat	in-Butter Mushrooms
¼ cup flour	Duck giblets, minced

Cook duck giblets, covered, in 2 cups water and ½ teaspoon salt, until tender, about 40 to 45 minutes. When done add sufficient water to broth to make 2 cups, and remove the giblets. Mince and save. Then, drain fat from roasting pan and measure ¼ cup into a saucepan. Blend in flour. Pour 2 cups giblet broth into the roasting pan and stir to blend with drippings. Add gradually to the fat-flour mixture, stirring constantly until gravy thickens. Add salt, Kitchen Bouquet, contents of can of mushrooms, and minced giblets. Bring to boil again. Serve immediately.

BRAZIL NUT STUFFING
Brazil Nut Association

¼ cup chopped onion
½ cup diced celery
½ cup coarsely chopped
  Brazil nuts

Butter
8 ounces stuffing

Sauté onion, celery, and Brazil nuts in butter; cook until onion is tender, but do not brown. Add to stuffing; place in 1-quart casserole and cover. Bake in 375° oven last 45 minutes of chicken baking time. Garnish with sliced Brazil nuts. Makes 8 servings.

HOLIDAY STUFFING
McCormick & Co., Inc.

1½ cups butter
3½ cups chopped celery
5 tablespoons McCormick
  Minced Onion
1 tablespoon McCormick
  Poultry Seasoning
2 teaspoons McCormick
  Season-All
½ teaspoon McCormick
  Black Pepper

½ teaspoon salt
8 cups white bread cubes
4 cups whole wheat bread
  cubes
4 cups corn bread cubes
2 eggs, lightly beaten
⅔ cup slivered toasted almonds
4 chicken bouillon cubes
1½ to 2 cups water

Melt butter in skillet. Add celery and onions; sauté until tender but not brown. Sprinkle poultry seasoning, Season-All, salt, and pepper over bread cubes. Add celery and onion mixture, eggs and almonds. Toss. Dissolve bouillon cubes in water; pour over bread mixture and toss lightly until well blended. Stuff bird. Put remaining stuffing in a buttered casserole. Cover. Bake 40 minutes at 300°. Remove cover and allow to brown. Makes enough for a 10- to 12-pound bird, plus an extra casserole.

WILD RICE STUFFING
The Chun King Corp.

¼ cup chopped onions
½ cup chopped celery
2 tablespoons butter
2 cups Nokomis Wild Rice, cooked

¼ teaspoon sage
¼ teaspoon thyme
½ teaspoon salt

Sauté onions and celery in butter until tender. Add wild rice and seasonings. Mix thoroughly. Makes sufficient stuffing for 4-pound fowl. May be prepared in advance. If so, wrap in Saran Wrap and store in refrigerator.

Note: One-half cup cooked mushrooms or ½ cup toasted, chopped Brazil nuts may be added.

WILD RICE-SAUSAGE STUFFING
The Chun King Corp.

½ pound bulk pork sausage
½ cup chopped onions
½ cup diced celery
1 can Nokomis Pre-Cooked Wild Rice

1 teaspoon salt
2 teaspoons poultry seasoning
1 cup crumbled corn bread

In skillet, brown pork sausage. Add onions and celery and cook until soft. Add remaining ingredients and mix well. Enough stuffing for 4-pound roasting chicken.

CORN BREAD STUFFING
Best Foods, Division of
Corn Products Company

4½ cups dry corn bread pieces	1½ teaspoons sage
7½ cups dry bread cubes	⅔ cup Mazola Corn Oil
2 cups chopped apples	1 cup chopped celery
2 teaspoons salt	1 cup chopped onion
½ teaspoon pepper	2 eggs
1½ teaspoons thyme	1½ cups milk
	1¼ cups water

Combine and mix breads, apple, and seasonings. Pour corn oil into fry pan. Put in celery and onion, and cook slowly about 5 minutes. Pour hot oil and vegetable mixture over seasoned bread and apple mixture. Toss and mix to coat bread crumbs with oil. Beat eggs slightly and mix with milk and water. Pour over bread mixture. Toss lightly. Makes about 12 cups. Stuff loosely into neck and body cavities of turkey. Close cavities with skewers or thread.

Note: A 12-pound ready-to-cook turkey will require about 6 cups stuffing. The remaining stuffing may be baked in a separate pan in a 350° oven 30 to 40 minutes.

This stuffing may be frozen. Wrap in Saran Wrap for maximum protection.

EASY WHIPPED POTATO STUFFING
The Borden Company

8 slices white bread, cubed	1 cup finely chopped celery
½ cup Borden's Homogenized Milk	½ teaspoon poultry seasoning
2 tablespoons dehydrated parsley flakes	Dash black pepper
1 small package instant minced onion	1 envelope Borden's Instant Whipped Potatoes

Combine bread cubes, milk, vegetables, and seasonings; mix lightly. Prepare potatoes according to directions on envelope. Add whipped potatoes to bread mixture; stir lightly with a fork until well blended. Use as stuffing for duck or chicken. Makes enough stuffing for a 5-pound duck.

Variation

WHIPPED POTATO PATTIES. Prepare stuffing as above; shape into 3-inch patties. Brown patties in hot butter in a skillet. Makes about 14 to 16 patties. A fine fowl or meat stretcher.

CHESTNUT STUFFING FOR TURKEY, GOOSE, OR CAPON
Paul Masson Vineyards

1 pound lean pork
1 pound fat pork
1 pound chestnuts
1 cup fresh bread crumbs
¼ teaspoon poultry seasoning
1 glass Paul Masson Pale Dry Sherry

Cut 1 pound lean pork and 1 pound fat pork in small pieces and run together through a meat grinder, using finest blade. Put in a bowl and add 1 teaspoon salt mixed with ¼ teaspoon poultry seasoning. Add 1 pound chestnuts (which have been shelled and boiled) and 1 cup fresh bread crumbs. Toss all together lightly and add sherry. Fill cavity of bird loosely—never pack it firmly. This amount is sufficient for a 10- to 12-pound bird.

To prepare chestnuts for stuffing: Cut a small ⅓- to ½-inch cross on the rounded top of each chestnut, using a very sharp knife. Put in a hot oven or under broiler for 8 to 10 minutes. When cool enough to handle, remove shells and inside skin; put chestnuts in a saucepan with enough water or white stock to cover well. Add 1 teaspoon salt and 2 stalks celery and boil gently for 25 minutes. Leave chestnuts in liquid to cool or until ready to use them.

EGGS

CREAMED EGGS
Poultry and Egg National Board

¼ cup butter or margarine
3 tablespoons flour
1 teaspoon salt
⅛ teaspoon ground pepper
⅛ teaspoon paprika
1 teaspoon grated onion

2 cups milk
6 hard-cooked eggs, sliced
or chopped
1 tablespoon finely chopped
parsley

Melt butter or margarine; add flour and seasonings. Blend well and cook over low heat until bubbly. Add milk all at once; cook, stirring constantly, until thickened throughout. Add eggs and parsley; heat thoroughly. Serve hot on toast or waffles, in noodle nests, or over corn bread. For brunch serve over sliced tomatoes or cooked asparagus on toast. Makes 4 servings.

Note: One cup cooked vegetables, diced cooked meat, or shredded dried beef may be added to cream sauce just before adding eggs.

Variation

SCALLOPED EGGS. Spoon Creamed Eggs into 9-inch pie pan. Cover with ½ cup fine bread crumbs, buttered. Bake in 400° oven until crumbs are brown and sauce is bubbly, 20 minutes. Makes 4 servings.

ZESTY BAKED EGGS
Poultry and Egg National Board

⅓ cup salad dressing or mayonnaise
¼ teaspoon salt
⅛ teaspoon ground pepper
½ teaspoon paprika

½ teaspoon Worcestershire Sauce
½ cup milk
1 cup grated sharp cheese
8 eggs

Combine salad dressing or mayonnaise and seasoning. Gradually add milk, stirring until smooth. Add cheese and cook over low heat until cheese is melted, about 5 minutes. Pour 2 tablespoons of the sauce into each of 4 individual greased baking dishes. Break 2 eggs into each dish and top with remaining sauce. Place in pan of hot water. Bake in 350° oven until eggs are desired consistency, 12 to 15 minutes. Makes 4 servings.

BANANAS PAN-FRIED WITH HAM AND EGGS
United Fruit Company

2 tablespoons butter or margarine
1 slice ham, cut ¼- to ½-inch thick

2 firm Chiquita Bananas
2 eggs

Melt butter or margarine in large skillet. Cut ham into 2 pieces, and place in skillet. Peel bananas and fry slowly with ham about 8 minutes, turning both bananas and ham frequently to brown evenly. Carefully break 1 egg at a time into saucer; slip each egg into skillet containing bananas and ham. Fry over low heat about 3 minutes longer, or until eggs are set, the ham is browned, and bananas are tender. Makes 2 servings.

Variation

BANANAS PAN-FRIED WITH SAUSAGE OR BACON AND EGGS. Sausage or bacon may be used in place of ham, but should be fried separately.

TOAST CUPS A LA EGGS
McCormick & Co., Inc.

1 cup thick white sauce
½ teaspoon salt
⅛ teaspoon McCormick or Schilling White Pepper
⅛ teaspoon McCormick or Schilling Dry Mustard
Dash McCormick or Schilling Red Pepper

¼ cup grated cheese
6 hard-cooked eggs, chopped
4 slices crisp bacon, crumbled
8 slices white bread

To the hot white sauce, add the remaining ingredients except bread. Blend. Cut crusts from bread. Place each slice of bread in a muffin tin to form a shell. Toast in the oven until lightly browned. Fill each shell with egg mixture. Makes 4 servings.

WESTFIELD OMELET
The Welch Grape Juice Company, Inc.

6 eggs, separated
¼ teaspoon salt
1 tablespoon sugar
6 tablespoons water

2 tablespoons butter, margarine, or salad oil
Welch's Grape Jelly

Beat egg whites until stiff. Beat yolks until light and thick. Add salt, sugar, and water to yolks and beat until well blended. Fold egg yolk mixture gently into beaten egg whites. Warm butter, margarine, or salad oil at low heat in heavy skillet. Add mixture to pan. Cook until well puffed and golden. Place omelet in 350° oven for about 15 minutes. Remove. Spread with grape jelly. Fold, serve at once. Makes 6 servings.

BEER OMELET ROYALE
McIlhenny Company

6 eggs
⅓ cup beer
½ teaspoon salt
½ teaspoon Tabasco

3 teaspoons chopped truffles
½ cup grated Cheddar cheese
2 to 3 tablespoons butter

Break eggs into mixing bowl. Combine beer, salt, Tabasco, and truffles; add to eggs. Beat with rotary beater only until well blended; do not beat until frothy. Melt butter in pan, 1 tablespoon for each omelet. Pan is hot enough when drop of water spatters in pan. Pour part of egg mixture into pan.

With left hand palm down on handle, move pan in back-and-forth motion. Stir with fork. This motion should be continued about 7 times. Sprinkle with part of cheese. Omelet should be ready to turn out. Tip pan and roll omelet out onto hot dish. Makes 2 to 3 omelets.

PUFFY WHEAT GERM OMELET
Kretschmer Wheat Germ Corp.

¼ cup Kretschmer Wheat Germ
½ cup milk
4 eggs, separated
½ teaspoon salt

1 tablespoon butter or margarine
¼ pound processed American cheese, shredded
¼ pound fully-cooked Canadian bacon, diced

Add wheat germ to milk; let stand while preparing rest of mixture. Beat egg whites until stiff but not dry. Beat egg yolks and salt together until thick and lemon-colored. Fold yolks and wheat germ–milk mixture into beaten egg whites. Heat butter or margarine in 10-inch fry pan with heat proof handle until pan is hot enough to make drops of water sizzle when dropped into pan. Pour egg mixture into pan and spread gently until level. Cook over low heat until puffy and lightly browned on bottom and sides, about 10 minutes. Place in 325° oven until done (a knife inserted in center comes out clean when done), about 10 minutes. Sprinkle cheese and bacon over omelet a few minutes before removing from oven. Fold omelet slightly off center and turn out on platter. Serve with vegetable sauces. Makes 3 to 4 servings.

SPICY OMELET
The Angostura-Wuppermann Corp.

5 eggs, separated
5 tablespoons milk
½ teaspoon salt
1 teaspoon Angostura Aromatic Bitters
5 tablespoons butter
2 tablespoons flour

1 cup milk
¼ teaspoon salt
Dash paprika
½ pound fresh mushrooms or 1 6-ounce can sliced mushrooms

Beat yolks, add milk, salt, and bitters. Beat egg whites stiffly and fold into egg yolk mixture. Put 1 tablespoon butter into skillet and heat until butter is barely browned. Pour egg mixture into skillet and bake at 400° until brown on top, about 8 minutes. In saucepan, melt 2 tablespoons butter, stir in flour. Add milk gradually, stirring constantly, until mixture is smooth and thick. Add seasonings. Sauté mushrooms in remaining 2 tablespoons of butter and add to white sauce. When omelet is baked, pour mushroom mixture over top before removing from skillet. Fold omelet over and turn out of pan. Makes 6 servings.

RUM OMELET
McCormick & Co., Inc.

6 eggs
½ teaspoon salt
⅛ teaspoon McCormick or Schilling Black Pepper
4 tablespoons confectioners' sugar

6 tablespoons cold water
2 tablespoons butter
1 tablespoon McCormick or Schilling Rum Extract

Beat eggs slightly. Add salt, pepper, 2 tablespoons of the sugar, and water; mix until smooth and creamy. Melt 1 tablespoon butter in large skillet. Pour in egg mixture. Cook slowly over medium heat. When eggs have cooked through, fold over omelet to make a roll. Place on a fireproof platter. Spread with remaining butter and sprinkle with remaining sugar. With a match, light rum extract; pour over omelet. Serve immediately.

NEW-WAY SOUFFLE
Best Foods, Division of
Corn Products Company

Basic Soufflé:

4 tablespoons flour
¼ teaspoon salt
Dash of pepper
½ cup Hellmann's or Best Foods Real Mayonnaise

4 tablespoons milk
1 to 1¼ cups of mixture suggested below (see Variations)
4 egg whites

Gently stir flour, salt, and pepper into mayonnaise. (Beating or overmixing will cause curdling but will not affect final product.) Add milk slowly. Stir in selected mixture. Beat egg whites until stiff. Gently fold mayonnaise mixture into egg whites until thoroughly blended. Pour into a greased 7-inch casserole and bake in a 325° oven 40 to 50 minutes. Serve at once. Makes 4 to 6 servings.

Variations

FISH SOUFFLÉ. One 7-ounce can tuna or salmon, drained and flaked; 2 tablespoons chopped parsley; ¼ teaspoon grated onion; 1 teaspoon lemon juice.

MEAT SOUFFLÉ. One cup cooked ground ham or luncheon meat, dash dry mustard, ¼ cup grated cheese (optional).

CHEESE SOUFFLÉ. One cup grated cheese, dash of cayenne pepper, dash of Tabasco.

CORN-BACON SOUFFLÉ. One cup well-drained kernel corn; dash of curry powder; 3 slices crisp bacon, crumbled.

ONION-CHEESE SOUFFLÉ. One cup cooked chopped onion, ¼ cup grated Parmesan cheese, ⅛ teaspoon Tabasco; increase salt to 1 teaspoon.

BEEF SOUFFLÉ. One cup (½ pound) ground round steak, uncooked; ¼ cup minced green pepper; 1 tablespoon finely minced onion; ⅛ teaspoon Tabasco.

GREEN PEA SOUFFLÉ. One and one-quarter cups cooked green peas, 1 tablespoon minced onion, ¼ teaspoon marjoram; increase salt to ½ teaspoon.

MUSHROOM SOUFFLÉ. Sauté 1¼ cups chopped fresh mushrooms in 1 tablespoon margarine 3 minutes. Add to soufflé mixture with 1 tablespoon minced onion, ¼ cup chopped celery; increase salt to ½ teaspoon.

BROCCOLI SOUFFLÉ. One cup cooked broccoli, mashed; ¼ cup grated cheese; ¼ teaspoon grated onion; ¼ teaspoon paprika.

CLAM SOUFFLÉ. One cup cooked minced clams, 1½ teaspoons lemon juice, 1 teaspoon grated onion.

CHICKEN SOUFFLÉ. One cup cooked minced chicken, 2 tablespoons chopped parsley, dash of nutmeg.

DEVILED EGGS SPANISH STYLE
Poultry and Egg National Board

⅓ cup chopped onion
⅓ cup chopped celery
⅓ cup butter or margarine
3 tablespoons flour
1 teaspoon sugar
1 teaspoon salt
¼ teaspoon ground pepper

¼ teaspoon garlic salt
1 1-pound, 13-ounce can tomatoes
6 hard-cooked eggs, deviled
½ cup buttered fine bread crumbs

Cook onion and celery in butter or margarine over low heat until onion is transparent but not brown. Blend in flour and seasonings. Add tomatoes all at once. Cook until thickened, stirring constantly. Pour into shallow 1½-quart baking dish. Arrange deviled eggs in sauce. Top with crumbs. Bake in 425° oven until sauce is bubbly around edges, 10 to 15 minutes. Serve over toast, rice, spaghetti, or noodles. Makes 6 servings.

ITALIAN EGG PIE
Poultry and Egg National Board

Pastry for 9-inch pie crust
4 eggs
¼ cup milk
1 6½- or 7-ounce can tuna, flaked, or 1 cup flaked cooked fish

½ pound Mozzarella cheese, grated
¼ teaspoon salt
¼ teaspoon ground pepper
½ teaspoon basil
½ teaspoon oregano

Prepare pie crust. Line a 9-inch pie pan; trim edge and flute. Beat eggs and milk together until blended. Add remaining ingredients and stir well. Spoon into unbaked crust. Bake in a 425° oven until brown, 30 to 35 minutes. Serve hot cut in wedges. Makes about 6 servings.

GOLDEN EGG SALAD CASSEROLE
Poultry and Egg National Board

6 hard-cooked eggs,
chopped
2 tablespoons diced pi-
miento
½ cup diced celery
¼ pound soda crackers,
finely crushed
1 cup mayonnaise or salad
dressing

¼ cup milk
¼ to ½ teaspoon salt
¾ teaspoon garlic salt
¼ teaspoon ground pepper
2 tablespoons melted butter
or margarine

Blend chopped eggs, pimiento, celery, 1 cup of the cracker
crumbs, mayonnaise or salad dressing, milk, and seasoning.
Spread in greased 1-quart shallow casserole or 9-inch pie
pan. Top with remaining cracker crumbs blended with the
butter or margarine. Bake in 400° oven until golden brown,
about 25 minutes. Serve hot. Makes 6 servings.

QUICHE LORRAINE
Best Foods, Division of
Corn Products Company

1 unbaked 8- or 9-inch pastry shell
½ pound (2 cups) grated or
thinly sliced Swiss cheese
3 eggs

1½ teaspoons Argo Corn
Starch
¼ teaspoon salt
⅛ teaspoon pepper
1 cup light cream

Sprinkle cheese over pastry. Beat eggs. Combine corn
starch, salt, and pepper; add small amount of cream, stir
well to mix, then gradually stir in rest of cream. Add to
beaten eggs and mix. Pour over cheese. Bake in 375° oven
for about 35 minutes, or until set and crust is delicately
browned. Serve hot. Makes 6 servings.

PaSTA, POTATOES, and RICE

Pasta, potatoes, and rice may rightly be called the food axis of the world. These three form the basic diet of great multitudes on every continent; they are prominent in the diet of all cultures. All three are economical and easy to prepare, and for this reason, conventional recipes have been avoided in the pages that follow. Instead, some exciting new ideas have been included—ideas worth returning to again and again.

PASTA

SESAME MACARONI
Buitoni Foods Corp.

1 8-ounce package Buitoni Magherite Macaroni	½ cup sesame seed
	¼ cup butter

Cook macaroni. Meanwhile, toast sesame seeds in a pie tin in a moderate oven about 15 minutes, or until the seeds are light brown. Add butter and seeds to macaroni, reserving a few; cover, and shake well to thoroughly mix. Remove to platter, and sprinkle with a few remaining seeds.

MACARONI AND CHEESE
Kretschmer Wheat Germ Corp.

¼ cup butter or margarine
3 tablespoons flour
2 cups milk
½ teaspoon salt
1 7-ounce package elbow macaroni, cooked
½ pound American cheese, shredded

1 teaspoon dehydrated minced onions
2 teaspoons Worcestershire Sauce
1 teaspoon dry mustard
2 tablespoons chopped pimientoes
⅔ cup Kretchmer Wheat Germ

Melt butter or margarine; blend in flour and salt. Stir in milk and cook until smooth and thickened, stirring constantly. Stir in remaining ingredients, except ⅓ cup wheat germ. Pour mixture into buttered individual or 1½-quart casserole. Sprinkle with remaining wheat germ. Bake in 350° oven until hot and bubbly around edges, about 25 minutes. Makes 6 servings.

AMERICAN LASAGNE
The Dow Chemical Company

8 ounces lasagne noodles, or any wide noodles
2 8-ounce cans tomato sauce
2 cups creamed cottage cheese
½ teaspoon basil
1 teaspoon salt

¼ teaspoon Worcestershire Sauce
¼ cup finely chopped onion
½ pound process American cheese, thinly sliced
¼ cup grated Parmesan or Romano cheese
½ cup buttered bread crumbs

Cook noodles in boiling salted water until tender; drain and rinse. Mix tomato sauce with the cottage cheese, basil, salt, Worcestershire Sauce, and onion. Arrange alternate layers of noodles, American cheese, and sauce mixture in buttered 2½-quart casserole. This preparation may be done in the morning, then overwrap the casserole with Saran Wrap and refrigerate. When ready to put into the oven, remove Saran Wrap and top with crumbs mixed with grated cheese. Bake in 375° oven for about 25 minutes or until bubbly. Makes 6 to 8 servings.

SPAGHETTI WITH CHEESE BALLS
The Borden Company

Spaghetti:

1 clove garlic, finely chopped
2 tablespoons finely chopped green pepper
½ cup chopped celery
¼ cup finely chopped onion
½ teaspoon salt
¼ teaspoon oregano
⅛ teaspoon pepper
¼ cup butter, melted
2¼ cups tomato purée
½ teaspoon sugar
1 4-ounce can (½ cup) sliced mushrooms
1 8-ounce package spaghetti

Combine garlic, green pepper, celery, onion, salt, oregano, and pepper, and sauté in butter for 5 minutes. Add tomato purée, sugar, and mushrooms. Simmer for 15 minutes. Meanwhile cook spaghetti; drain. Put spaghetti on warm platter. Pour sauce over spaghetti. Serve with Cheese Balls. Makes 4 servings.

Cheese Balls:

1½ cups fresh bread crumbs, lightly packed
4 tablespoons evaporated milk
¼ teaspoon salt
⅛ teaspoon nutmeg
2 eggs
½ pound Borden's Chateau Cheese Food, shredded
2 teaspoons finely chopped parsley
¼ cup dry bread crumbs

Soak bread crumbs in evaporated milk for 5 minutes. Add salt, pepper, and nutmeg to 1 egg which has been slightly beaten. Add egg mixture, cheese, and parsley to the fresh bread crumbs. Mix well. Shape into 12 1½-inch balls. Roll balls in slightly beaten egg, then in dry bread crumbs. Fry in deep fat heated to 350° until golden brown, about 1 minute. Drain on absorbent paper. Serve with spaghetti. Makes 12 1½-inch balls.

SPAGHETTI WITH SHRIMP SAUCE
Hunt Foods, Inc.

1 onion, chopped
1 clove garlic, minced
¼ cup minced parsley
¼ cup vegetable oil
2 8-ounce cans Hunt's Tomato Sauce
1 can water
½ teaspoon salt
½ teaspoon sugar
Pinch of sweet basil or dash of cayenne
2 cups shrimp, cooked or canned
Salt, if needed
1 8-ounce package spaghetti, cooked

Cook onion, garlic, and parsley lightly in oil. Stir in tomato sauce, water, and seasonings. Simmer 30 minutes. Add shrimp. Simmer gently 10 minutes longer. Serve over hot spaghetti. Makes 3 to 4 servings.

Note: Two cups canned minced clams or drained flaked tuna may be substituted for the shrimp.

ITALIAN TRI-COLOR
Buitoni Foods Corp.

½ pound butter
1 package Buitoni 20% Protein Tagliatelle Verdi (spinach ribbons)
1 package Buitoni 20% Protein Thin Spaghetti
2 packages Buitoni Mari Twists
1 tablespoon chopped parsley
1 3½-ounce shaker grated Parmesan cheese

Unwrap butter and let stand at room temperature to soften. Cook Tagliatelle Verdi, spaghetti, and Mari Twists according to package directions; drain. In a large, warm, rectangular serving dish or casserole, arrange the Tagliatelle Verdi in a band to the left. Arrange spaghetti in a band in the center. Place Mari Twists to the right. Top Tagliatelle Verdi and spaghetti with the softened butter. Sprinkle Tagliatelle Verdi with parsley and dust spaghetti generously with the grated cheese. Serve immediately and pass more grated cheese. Makes 12 servings. (See illustration 16.)

POTATOES

FRENCH FRIED POTATOES
The Procter & Gamble Company

2 pounds potatoes   Crisco for deep frying

Pare potatoes and cut into ¼-inch strips, cubes, or lattice slices. Rinse with cold water and dry thoroughly. Fry until tender and golden brown in deep shortening heated to 365°. Drain on absorbent paper. Serve hot. Makes 4 servings.

COUNTRY FRIED POTATOES
Best Foods, Division of
Corn Products Company

5 medium potatoes   1 teaspoon salt
¼ cup Mazola Corn Oil   ⅛ teaspoon pepper

Wash and pare potatoes. Cut in thin slices. Heat corn oil in large skillet over medium heat about 3 minutes. Add potatoes and fry about 10 minutes, or until brown on 1 side. Turn potatoes with broad spatula to complete cooking and brown other side. Season and serve. Makes 4 servings.

BROILER FRENCH FRIES
Best Foods, Division of
Corn Products Company

4 medium potatoes
⅓ cup Mazola Corn Oil

1 teaspoon salt

Wash and pare potatoes. Cut lengthwise into slices ¼-inch thick. Soak in salted cold water (2 tablespoons salt to 1 quart water) 20 minutes. Preheat broiler. Drain potatoes and dry thoroughly with towel. Brush potatoes with corn oil. Place on broiler rack 3 to 4 inches from heat. Broil 8 to 10 minutes. Turn potatoes and brush again with corn oil. Broil about 5 minutes longer, or until tender and golden brown. Salt and serve. Makes 4 servings.

HOLIDAY CREAMED POTATOES
The Angostura-Wuppermann Corp.

3 tablespoons butter
3 tablespoons flour
1½ cups milk
½ teaspoon salt
Dash pepper

1 teaspoon Angostura Aromatic Bitters
2 cups cooked, cubed potatoes
1 3-ounce package cream cheese

Melt butter, blend in flour, and gradually add milk to make the sauce. Cook, stirring constantly, until thickened. Add seasoning and bitters. Place cooked potatoes in baking dish, cover with sauce. Dot top with pieces of cream cheese and heat in 350° oven until cheese melts and top is browned, about 15 minutes. Makes 4 servings.

WHIPPED POTATO SOUFFLE
The Borden Company

1 envelope Borden's Instant Whipped Potatoes
½ cup Borden's Light or Heavy Cream or ½ cup Borden's Sour Cream
½ teaspoon salt

Dash nutmeg
2 portions (5 tablespoons) Borden's Gruyere Cheese, shredded
3 eggs, separated

Prepare potatoes according to directions on envelope. Combine whipped potatoes, cream, seasonings, and cheese; blend well. Add egg yolks, one at a time, beating well after each addition. Beat egg whites until stiff but not dry; fold into whipped potato mixture. Turn into a buttered 1½-quart casserole. With the back of a spoon, make a shallow path about 1-inch from edge of dish all the way around. (This will form a crown when baked.) Bake in a 375° oven about 35 minutes, or until soufflé is puffed and lightly browned. If serving is delayed, keep soufflé in oven with heat turned down to 250°. Makes 4 to 6 servings. (See illustration 15.)

WHIPPED ORANGE POTATOES
The Borden Company

1 envelope Borden's Instant Whipped Potatoes
2 tablespoons butter

2 tablespoons milk
1 teaspoon grated orange rind

Prepare potatoes according to directions on envelope. Combine whipped potatoes with remaining ingredients;

blend well. Fill pastry tube with whipped orange potatoes. Use to flute edges of individual ham, veal, or chicken casseroles. Bake until lightly browned. Good when used to edge planked ham or veal steaks. Makes enough to top 6 individual casseroles.

YAMS AND SWEET POTATOES

BAKED STUFFED YAMS WITH PEANUTS
Louisiana Yam Commission

6 Louisiana Yams, baked
¼ cup butter
½ cup sherry

½ cup brown sugar, firmly packed
½ cup chopped peanuts

Slice off small portion of each yam and scoop pulp into a mixing bowl. Blend with butter, sherry, sugar, and nuts, reserving a few nuts for the top. Whip until fluffy; pile lightly back into shells. Return to a hot oven about 10 minutes before serving.

BAKED STUFFED YAMS WITH CHIPPED BEEF
Louisiana Yam Commission

½ cup dried beef, chopped
¼ cup hot milk
4 Louisiana Yams, baked
2 tablespoons finely chopped onion

3 tablespoons butter
½ cup grated Cheddar cheese

Combine dried beef and milk in mixing bowl. Cut yams in half lengthwise and scoop out centers. Combine yams, beef-milk mixture, butter, and onion. Beat until light and fluffy. Fill yam shells with mixture. Sprinkle cheese on top. Bake in 350° oven for 20 minutes.

CANDIED YAMS WITH CITRUS AND SPICE
Louisiana Yam Commission

2 cups sugar
¾ cup water
3 tablespoons butter
½ teaspoon grated orange rind
½ teaspoon grated lemon rind
3 sticks cinnamon

¼ teaspoon nutmeg
6 medium Louisiana Yams, cooked, peeled, and cut in half lengthwise
6 lemon slices
1 small apple, cored and sliced

Combine sugar, water, butter, rinds, cinnamon, and nutmeg. Heat to boiling point over medium heat; cook 5 minutes. Meanwhile, arrange yams, lemon slices, and apple in a 1½-quart casserole. Pour syrup mixture over other ingredients. Bake in moderate oven 30 minutes, basting occasionally with syrup.

SWEET POTATO FRITTERS
General Foods Corporation

2 medium sweet potatoes or yams
⅓ cup honey
1 teaspoon lemon rind
1 tablespoon lemon juice
3 tablespoons water
½ cup sifted all-purpose flour

¼ teaspoon double-action Calumet Baking Powder
¼ teaspoon salt
½ cup milk
1 egg, beaten
1⅓ cups Baker's Angel Flake Coconut (or 1 cup Baker's Fine-Grated Coconut)

Cook potatoes in salted water until just tender. Peel and slice thinly. Combine honey, lemon rind, lemon juice, and water. Place potato slices in this mixture and put in refrigerator to marinate for at least 1 hour. Sift together flour, baking powder, and salt. Combine milk and egg, and add slowly to flour mixture, stirring to make a fairly smooth batter. Dip potato slices in batter and then in coconut. Fry in hot deep fat at 365° until golden brown. Serve hot. Makes 4 or 5 servings. Wrap in Saran Wrap and refrigerate if prepared in advance.

RICE

FRIED RICE
The Chun King Corp.

½ cup chopped onions
2 tablespoons butter
1 egg, beaten
2 cups cooked rice

½ cup cooked pork, diced (or shrimp or chicken, cooked)
2 tablespoons Chun King Soya Sauce

Sauté onions in butter until golden. Add egg and scramble mixture. Stir in rice, meat, and soya sauce and cook over low heat for 5 minutes. Makes 4 servings.

GREEN RICE
Uncle Ben's, Inc.

1 cup Uncle Ben's Converted Rice, uncooked
2 tablespoons butter or margarine

½ cup minced parsley
Other ingredient as desired (see below)

Prepare rice by directions on carton, adding butter during the cooking. Add minced parsley and any other desired ingredient. Toss with fork and serve with creamed chicken, crabmeat, or shrimp. Makes 4 to 6 servings.

Try any of the following ingredients as desired: toasted slivered almonds, chopped roasted peanuts, grated Parmesan cheese, sautéed mushrooms or onions, dash of onion or garlic salt or powder, chopped pimiento, caraway seed, chopped or sliced olives (stuffed or ripe), dash of curry powder, celery salt, ground cumin, or diced crisp bacon.

SPANISH RICE PRONTO
Hunt Foods, Inc.

¼ cup vegetable oil
1 medium onion, thinly sliced
½ green pepper, chopped
1⅓ cups (4⅝-ounce package) precooked rice
1½ cups hot water

1 teaspoon salt
Dash of pepper
½ teaspoon prepared mustard
2 8-ounce cans Hunt's Tomato Sauce

Heat oil in saucepan or skillet. Add onion, green pepper, and rice. Cook and stir over high heat until lightly browned. Add water, salt, pepper, mustard, and tomato sauce. Mix well. Quickly bring to a boil, then reduce heat. Simmer, uncovered, 5 minutes. Makes 4 servings.

Variations

WITH GROUND BEEF. Make Spanish Rice Pronto, browning ½ pound ground beef along with the rice.

WITH MUSHROOMS. Make Spanish Rice Pronto, browning 1 cup (¼ pound) sliced fresh mushrooms (or a 4-ounce can) with the rice.

WITH CHEESE. Make Spanish Rice Pronto as directed. Just after simmering, stir in ½ cup sharp grated cheese. Sprinkle another ½ cup grated cheese on top just before serving.

WITH FRANKS. Make Spanish Rice Pronto, browning 4 sliced frankfurters with the rice.

WITH LEFTOVER MEATS. Make Spanish Rice Pronto, browning 1 cup or 1½ cups leftover beef or pork with the rice.

EAST INDIAN FRIED RICE
Grocery Store Products Co.

2 cups well-seasoned chicken broth
1 teaspoon Kitchen Bouquet
1 cup rice, long grain or converted

3 tablespoons cooking oil
1 cup thinly sliced onion
½ teaspoon curry powder
1 tablespoon peanut butter

Heat chicken broth and Kitchen Bouquet to boiling in small saucepan. Add rice. Cover tightly and cook over low heat until rice is tender, about 25 minutes. Meanwhile place oil in frying pan over moderate heat. Add onion and cook, stirring frequently, about 10 minutes. Stir in curry powder and peanut butter, mixing well. Add cooked rice. Continue cooking about 5 minutes until flavors are blended, stirring to mix well. Serve as is for a vegetable. Or turn out on platter and garnish liberally with thin slices of unpeeled cucumber and quartered hard-cooked eggs for an unusual luncheon dish. Makes 4 servings.

BROWN RICE WITH RAISINS
Grocery Store Products Co.

1½ cups water
1 teaspoon Kitchen Bouquet
1 teaspoon salt
⅛ teaspoon turmeric
¼ teaspoon grated lemon rind

1 1-inch stick cinnamon
¾ cup raisins
1 5-ounce package pre-cooked rice
2 tablespoons butter

Combine water, Kitchen Bouquet, salt, turmeric, lemon rind, and cinnamon in 2-quart saucepan. Bring to boil and stir in raisins and rice. Cover tightly, remove from heat and place in warm place for 10 minutes. Remove cover and stir in butter. Makes 4 servings.

SPRING HARVEST RICE RING
Uncle Ben's, Inc.

¼ cup butter or margarine
1½ cups Uncle Ben's Converted Rice, uncooked
½ cup chopped onion

3½ cups hot water
1½ teaspoons salt
½ pound cheese, sliced
¼ cup bread crumbs

Melt butter or margarine in heavy skillet. Add uncooked rice and onion, and stir over low heat until golden brown. Add water and salt. Cook, covered, over low heat until water is absorbed and rice is tender, about 25 minutes. Sprinkle bread crumbs in well-buttered ring mold. Alternate layers of cooked rice and sliced cheese in mold, packing tightly. Bake at 350° for 10 minutes. Unmold on hot serving platter and fill with creamed vegetables or Harvest Sauce (see page 176). Makes 6 to 8 servings.

CHATEAU-RICE BROIL
The Borden Company

1 cup precooked rice
1 cup boiling water
12 slices Borden's Chateau Cheese Food

6 slices tomato
6 slices bread
Thyme

Add rice to boiling water. Remove from heat. Cover bread slices with rice. Add 2 slices cheese. Cover with tomato slices. Sprinkle on thyme. Place under broiler until cheese melts, 3 to 5 minutes. Cut into serving-size pieces. Serve hot. Makes 6 servings.

WILD RICE EN CASSEROLE
The Chun King Corp.

1 tablespoon shortening
1 pound veal, cut in 1-inch cubes
1 teaspoon salt
1½ cups Nokomis Wild Rice, cooked
1 can cream of mushroom soup

¼ cup chopped onions
½ cup chopped celery
½ teaspoon Worcestershire Sauce
2 tablespoons sherry
¼ cup cheese, grated

Melt shortening and brown veal. Add the remaining ingredients, except cheese. Pour into a greased 1½-quart casserole. Sprinkle cheese on top. Bake in 350° oven for about 50 minutes. Makes 4 servings.

RICE-CHEESE CROQUETTES
Best Foods, Division of
Corn Products Company

2 tablespoons butter or margarine
3 tablespoons Argo Corn Starch
½ teaspoon salt
⅛ teaspoon pepper
1 cup milk
2 cups rice, cooked

1½ cups grated cheese
Few grains cayenne
2 teaspoons grated onion
½ teaspoon dry mustard
1 cup fine dry bread crumbs
1 egg, beaten
1 tablespoon water
Mazola Corn Oil for frying

Melt butter or margarine. Add corn starch, salt, and pepper, and blend well. Gradually add milk, mixing until smooth. Cook over medium heat, stirring constantly, until mixture thickens and comes to a boil. Boil 2 minutes, stirring constantly. Add rice, cheese, cayenne, onion, and dry mustard. Mix well. Chill; shape into round balls or croquettes. Roll croquettes in bread crumbs, then in egg and water which have been beaten together, then roll in crumbs again. Croquettes may be prepared in advance and fried just before serving. Meanwhile, heat corn oil in heavy skillet or kettle to 375°, or until 1-inch square of bread browns in 30 to 40 seconds. Corn oil should be at least 1-inch deep but should not fill skillet or kettle more than ⅓ full. Drop croquettes into hot corn oil and fry about 2 minutes, turning once, or until golden brown. Drain on absorbent paper. Serve hot, plain, or with parsley white sauce. Makes 4 servings, 2 croquettes each.

Note: For tiny, appetizer-size croquettes, use a sharp Cheddar cheese. Makes about 2 dozen.

VeGeTABLeS

Every housewife recognizes the values that vegetables add to meals in health, variety, and color. Here's a twist, however, that may not be so widely known: the skins and shells of many vegetables provide attractive, dramatic serving dishes when filled with combinations of meats, rice, and other vegetables.

The larger the vegetable, the greater the possibility of using it as a salad bowl or a casserole. Filled food shells may be prepared in advance, covered with Saran Wrap, and stored until ready for baking or serving.

Try the following combinations: potato skins filled with mashed potatoes and topped with melted American cheese; egg plant filled with Frikadeller (p. 66) and rice; squash with Squash Fluff (p. 159); tomatoes filled with tuna salad; avocados with cottage cheese and mixed green vegetables; and cucumbers with cream cheese and chopped nuts.

Note: Fruit shells can serve equally well; try pineapple filled with Waikiki Whip (p. 196) or a hot creamed tuna; melons filled with melon balls, mandarin oranges, and berries; Sausage-Stuffed Apples (p. 94); and a coconut shell filled with Minted Tea (p. 295).

An unusual topping for cauliflower, asparagus, or broccoli: blend ¼ cup finely-mashed bread crumbs with 2 tablespoons mayonnaise. Toast in a skillet for 3 minutes, stirring constantly, and spread on the vegetables. Delicious also with potatoes au gratin or soup. For a variation, add chopped Brazil nuts to the toasted bread crumbs and fill large fresh mushrooms with the mixture. Sauté slowly in butter or margarine, and serve as a vegetable course or as a garnish with steak or any roast.

ARTICHOKE HEARTS IN TOMATOES
American Dehydrated Onion
& Garlic Association

1 1-pound can stewed tomatoes	Salt
2 teaspoons instant minced onion	1 8½-ounce can artichoke hearts
⅛ teaspoon garlic powder	Grated Parmesan cheese (optional)
¼ cup sauterne or Chablis	

Combine tomatoes, onion, garlic, and wine in a saucepan; simmer 10 minutes. Add salt to taste and drained artichoke hearts; simmer 5 minutes longer. Serve with a sprinkling of grated Parmesan cheese, if desired. Makes 4 to 5 servings.

HOT ARTICHOKE-CRABMEAT CASSEROLE
General Foods Corporation

1 9-ounce package Birds Eye Artichoke Hearts	1 teaspoon salt
¼ cup butter	1 tablespoon chopped onion
⅓ cup flour	⅛ teaspoon dry mustard
1⅓ cups milk	1 cup (6 ounces) frozen crabmeat, thawed
½ cup chopped celery	¼ cup dry bread crumbs
¼ cup chopped green pepper	1 tablespoon butter, melted

Cook artichoke hearts as directed on the package. Meanwhile, melt ¼ cup butter over low heat; then blend in flour. Add milk gradually, cook over low heat about 10 minutes, stirring constantly. Add celery, green pepper, salt, onion, and mustard, and remove from heat.

Arrange artichoke hearts and crabmeat in 1½-quart casserole or 6 individual baking dishes. Add sauce mixture. Combine dry bread crumbs and melted butter, and sprinkle over top of casserole. Bake in 350° oven about 35 minutes for casserole or 15 minutes for individual baking dishes. Makes 6 servings.

MARINATED ASPARAGUS SPEARS
Sunkist Growers, Inc.

1 package frozen or 1 30-ounce can asparagus spears, drained
½ cup salad oil
1 teaspoon mayonnaise
1 teaspoon sugar
½ teaspoon dry mustard
¼ cup Sunkist Fresh Lemon Juice

½ teaspoon paprika
Salt to taste
Freshly ground black pepper
2 teaspoons chopped pimiento
1 teaspoon minced green onion tops
Shredded lettuce
Sunkist Lemon Quarters

Cook asparagus spears according to package directions. Blend remaining ingredients (except lettuce and lemon quarters) for marinade and pour over asparagus. Chill for ½ hour. Serve on bed of shredded lettuce. Garnish with lemon quarters. Makes 4 servings.

BAKED BEANS HAWAIIAN
Burnham & Morrill Co.

1 tin sliced pineapple

1 large container B & M Oven Baked Beans

Ring a casserole with slices of pineapple. Fill casserole with baked beans. Heat in a medium oven until piping hot and bubbly. Serve with brown bread.

BAKED BEAN AND SAUSAGE BAKE
Burnham & Morrill Co.

1 medium onion
½ pound link sausage

1 medium container B & M
Oven Baked Beans
2 tablespoons pickle relish

Slice the onion and separate into rings. Place in bottom of a shallow baking dish with the sausage arranged on the top. Bake in a 375° oven about 15 minutes. Drain off excess fat. Combine the beans with the pickle relish and add to the onion and sausage. Return to the oven for 20 minutes, or until thoroughly heated.

SOPHISTICATED BAKED BEANS
The Seven-Up Company

2 1-pound cans beans with
pork and molasses
1 medium onion, minced
¼ cup light molasses
3 tablespoons pickle relish
1 tablespoon Worcestershire
Sauce

2 teaspoons mustard
¼ teaspoon pepper
1 7-ounce bottle 7-Up
1 2-ounce can sliced mushrooms

Stir beans with all ingredients except mushrooms. Pour into a casserole and bake in a 325° oven for 1½ hours. Stir in mushrooms and continue baking for ½ hour. Makes 6 to 8 servings. (See illustration 13.)

SWEET-SOUR BEETS
Sunkist Growers, Inc.

1 19-ounce can sliced beets, drained
2 tablespoons Sunkist Fresh Lemon Juice
¼ cup sugar
1 teaspoon salt
½ teaspoon caraway seeds
10 whole cloves
Few drops red food coloring
1 tablespoon corn starch
¼ cup water
Sunkist Lemon Quarters

Drain and reserve liquid from beets. Set beets aside. Combine next 6 ingredients with beet liquid. Blend corn starch and water together to form smooth paste. Blend into mixture in saucepan. Bring rapidly to boiling. Reduce heat and cook 3 to 5 minutes, or until thickened. Add the sliced beets and cook until heated thoroughly. Let each person season with squeeze of fresh lemon juice. Makes 6 servings.

BROCCOLI WITH BRAZIL NUT SLICES
Brazil Nut Association

½ cup shelled Brazil nuts
¼ cup butter
2 tablespoons lemon juice
¼ teaspoon Tabasco
Cooked broccoli for 4 servings

Cover Brazil nuts with cold water. Bring to boil slowly; simmer 5 minutes. Drain. Slice nuts lengthwise. Melt butter; stir in lemon juice and Tabasco. Combine nuts and butter sauce. Pour over broccoli. Makes 4 servings.

Note: If desired Brazil nut slices may be toasted in 350° oven 12 minutes after slicing. An excellent topping for brussel sprouts or green beans as well as for broccoli.

BROCCOLI WITH EGG SAUCE
Grocery Store Products Co.

1 bunch broccoli
2 tablespoons butter
2 tablespoons flour
½ teaspoon salt
½ teaspoon paprika
¾ cup milk

1 3-ounce can sliced Broiled-in-Butter Mushrooms
1 cup diced process American cheese, 4 ounces
2 hard-cooked eggs, sliced

Wash and trim broccoli, splitting stalks evenly so they will cook faster. Cook broccoli until barely tender. Meanwhile melt butter in saucepan. Stir in flour, salt, and paprika. Add milk and contents of can of mushrooms. Cook, stirring constantly, until sauce thickens and boils. Add cheese and continue stirring until cheese is melted and smooth. Add sliced hard-cooked eggs and heat thoroughly. Drain cooked broccoli and arrange on hot serving platter. Pour sauce over stalks and serve immediately for hot luncheon dish. Makes 4 servings.

BROCCOLI WITH MUSHROOM-CHEESE SAUCE
Grocery Store Products Co.

1 large bunch broccoli
3 tablespoons fat
3 tablespoons flour
½ teaspoon salt
½ teaspoon dry mustard
1 cup chicken broth

⅔ cup milk
1 3-ounce can sliced Broiled-in-Butter Mushrooms
½ cup finely diced American cheese

Prepare broccoli for cooking. Steam or cook until barely tender in small amount of boiling salted water. Meanwhile melt fat in saucepan over moderate heat. Stir in flour, salt, and mustard. Add broth, milk, and contents of can of mushrooms. Cook, stirring constantly, until sauce thickens and boils. Add cheese and stir until smooth. Serve immediately over cooked broccoli. Makes 4 servings.

OLD-COUNTRY STUFFED CABBAGE ROLLS
Hunt Foods, Inc.

1 pound ground beef
¼ pound ground pork
2 teaspoons salt
½ teaspoon pepper
¾ cup cooked rice
1 small onion, grated
2 8-ounce cans Hunt's Tomato Sauce

12 large cabbage leaves
2 tablespoons vegetable oil
¼ cup brown sugar
¼ cup lemon juice or vinegar

Combine first 6 ingredients with one can tomato sauce. Cover cabbage leaves with boiling water for 3 to 4 minutes, drain. Place equal portions of meat mixture in center of each leaf. Roll up, fold ends over, tucking them in securely, and fasten with toothpicks. Brown in hot oil in heavy skillet. Mix remaining can of tomato sauce with brown sugar and lemon juice. Pour over rolls. Simmer, covered, 1 to 1½ hours, basting occasionally. Makes 6 servings.

SPICED CARROTS
Sunkist Growers, Inc.

1 12-ounce can sliced carrots
1 tablespoon Sunkist Fresh Lemon Juice
1 tablespoon sugar

2 tablespoons butter, melted
4 whole cloves
Salt and pepper to taste
Sunkist Lemon Quarters

Heat carrots in liquid from can. Drain. Heat together lemon juice, sugar, melted butter, and cloves. Pour over drained carrots. Let each person season to taste with salt, pepper, and a squeeze of lemon juice. Makes 4 servings.

CREAMED CARROTS
Best Foods, Division of
Corn Products Company

8 to 10 carrots
4 tablespoons butter or margarine
2 tablespoons Argo Corn Starch

1 teaspoon salt
¼ teaspoon pepper
2 cups milk
Parsley (optional)

Wash and scrape or pare carrots. Cut into slices or strips. Cook covered in small amount of water. Meanwhile melt butter or margarine in a saucepan. Add corn starch, salt, and pepper, and blend well. Remove from heat; gradually add milk, mixing until smooth. Cook over medium heat, stirring constantly, until mixture thickens and comes to a boil. Boil 1 minute, continuing to stir. Drain carrots. Add to sauce. Mix and serve. Garnish with parsley, if desired. Makes 6 to 8 servings.

MUSHROOM-CARROT PIE
Grocery Store Products Co.

Pastry for single crust 9-inch pie
2 6-ounce cans sliced Broiled-in-Butter Mushrooms
½ cup coarsely chopped onion
2 tablespoons butter

2 eggs
1 cup light cream
1 teaspoon salt
⅛ teaspoon pepper
1/16 teaspoon mace
1 cup coarsely shredded carrot
2 sprigs parsley, chopped

Make pie shell using your own recipe. Meanwhile drain mushrooms reserving broth for future use. Sauté onion in butter until just tender, about 5 minutes. In large mixing bowl beat eggs lightly, stir in light cream and seasonings which have been blended together. Add mushrooms, cooked onion, carrot, and parsley, and mix well. Pour into unbaked pie shell. Bake in preheated 350° oven until custard sets and a knife inserted comes out clean, about 45 minutes. Makes 6 to 8 servings.

BAKED CELERY AND MUSHROOMS
Grocery Store Products Co.

3 cups diagonally sliced celery
3 tablespoons fat
2 tablespoons finely diced onion
3 tablespoons flour
⅔ cup milk
1 3-ounce can chopped Broiled-in-Butter Mushrooms

½ teaspoon salt
⅛ teaspoon pepper
⅛ teaspoon rubbed marjoram
2 ounces process American cheese
¼ cup buttered bread crumbs

Cook celery until barely tender in boiling salted water. Meanwhile melt fat over moderate heat. Add onion and cook for about 1 minute. Stir in flour. Add milk, contents of can of mushrooms, and seasonings. Cook, stirring constantly, until sauce thickens. Drain celery and combine with mushroom sauce. Pour into lightly oiled 1-quart baking dish. Top with thinly sliced cheese and sprinkle with buttered bread crumbs. Bake in 325° oven until lightly browned, about 20 minutes. Serve immediately. Makes 4 to 6 servings.

CORN WITH MUSHROOMS
Green Giant Company

2 tablespoons butter
2 tablespoons chopped onion
⅔ cup chopped mushrooms

1 12-ounce can Niblets Brand Corn
½ cup cream
Salt and pepper

Melt butter and cook onions and mushrooms for 5 minutes, or until tender, in top pan of chafing dish over direct heat, or in a skillet. Add drained corn. Toss mixture gently while warming it through. Add cream, salt, and pepper. Turn lamp low and keep hot over water pan. Garnish with chopped parsley. Makes 6 servings. (See illustration 19.)

REAL CORN SOUFFLE
Stokely-Van Camp, Inc.

1 1-pound can Stokely-Van Camp's Golden Cream Style Corn	1 tablespoon butter or margarine, melted
1 cup milk	1 tablespoon sugar
	3 large eggs, separated

Cook corn and milk together vigorously for about 10 minutes. Stir in butter or margarine, sugar, and beaten egg yolks. Beat egg whites (but not too stiff) and fold into corn mixture. Pour into a lightly greased 2-quart casserole. Bake, uncovered, in a 350° oven for 35 minutes. Leave oven door closed. Makes 8 to 10 servings.

CORN-AND-CHEESE TART
Green Giant Company

Pastry	¼ cup grated Swiss cheese
1 12-ounce can Niblets Brand Corn	5 eggs
Salt and pepper	1½ cups cream
	4 slices crisp bacon

Line a 9-inch pie pan with pastry. Combine drained corn, salt, pepper, and cheese. Spread evenly over pie shell. Add lightly beaten eggs to cream. Pour over corn mixture. Crumble bacon and spread over top. Bake 25 minutes at 400°; then for 20 minutes at 350°. Makes 6 servings. (Corn-and-Cheese Tart will serve 10 to 12 as appetizers.)

CORN FRITTERS
General Foods Corporation

1 10-ounce package Birds
  Eye Whole Kernel Corn,
  thawed
3 tablespoons corn liquid
  and sweet or sour milk
2 tablespoons butter,
  melted

½ cup sifted flour
¾ teaspoon Calumet Baking
  Powder
1 teaspoon salt
⅛ teaspoon pepper
2 eggs, well beaten

Drain corn in strainer, pressing slightly against sides.
Measure liquid and add milk to make 3 tablespoons. Chop
corn, if desired. Combine corn and melted butter. Sift
flour once; add baking powder, salt, and pepper, and sift
again. Add to corn mixture and mix thoroughly. Add the 3
tablespoons liquid and stir until smooth. Then add eggs and
blend gently. Pan fry in ½-inch hot fat until golden brown,
2 to 3 minutes on each side. Serve hot with Log Cabin Syrup.
Makes 5 servings, or 10 to 12 fritters.

GREEN BEANS CHINESE
Green Giant Company

6 thick bacon slices, cut in
  quarters
3 tablespoons chopped
  onion
1 clove garlic, chopped

2 16-ounce cans Green Giant
  Brand Kitchen-Sliced
  Green Beans
3 tablespoons soy sauce

Sauté bacon until slightly crisp. Add chopped onion and
garlic. Cook for 2 minutes. Add beans and soy sauce; season. Toss like a salad, until beans are heated through. Makes
5 to 6 servings. (See illustration 17.)

GREEN BEANS ROSEMARY
Green Giant Company

2 1-pound cans Green Giant
  Brand Whole or Kitchen-
  Sliced Green Beans
½ cup chopped green onion

¾ cup olive oil
1½ teaspoons rosemary
Juice of 1 lemon
Pinch dry mustard

Mix drained beans with onions. Combine oil, rosemary, lemon juice, and dry mustard. Season to taste. Cover and chill in refrigerator for at least 1 hour. Serve on a bed of greens. If desired, garnish with chopped parsley and a little rosemary. Makes 4 to 5 servings.

ITALIAN GREEN BEANS PIQUANT
General Foods Corporation

1 9-ounce package Birds Eye
  Italian Green Beans
2 slices bacon

¼ cup thinly sliced onion (1
  small onion)
2 teaspoons sugar
2½ tablespoons vinegar

Cook beans as directed on package; drain. Meanwhile, sauté bacon in skillet until crisp. Remove from skillet and crumble. Reserve about 1 tablespoon of the drippings in the skillet. Add onion rings and sauté until tender but not browned. Add sugar and vinegar; heat a few minutes to blend flavors. Combine mixture with the beans. Top with crumbled bacon. Serve hot. Makes 3 servings.

SAVORY BROILED EGGPLANT
Grocery Store Products Co.

1 medium eggplant, about
   1¼ pounds
¼ cup fat
2 teaspoons Kitchen Bouquet

1 teaspoon salt
¼ teaspoon pepper
1/16 teaspoon cayenne
1 cup grated American cheese

Peel eggplant and cut in ½-inch slices. Blend together the fat, Kitchen Bouquet, and seasonings. Brush slices with half of mixture and arrange on rack in broiling pan from preheated broiler. Broil under moderate heat at least 4 inches from heat for 10 minutes. Turn and brush slices with remaining mixture. Broil 5 minutes longer. Sprinkle tops with grated cheese and continue broiling until cheese is melted and lightly browned, about 5 minutes. Serve immediately. Makes 4 servings.

BAKED LIMA BEANS WITH CANADIAN BACON
Grocery Store Products Co.

4 cups (2 pounds) dried lima beans
4 quarts water
1 medium onion
½ pound salt pork
1 tablespoon salt
2 teaspoons dry mustard
½ teaspoon ginger
2 tablespoons Kitchen Bouquet

½ cup molasses
1½ pounds Canadian bacon, in 1 piece
2 teaspoons Kitchen Bouquet
2 tablespoons brown sugar
⅛ teaspoon cloves
⅛ teaspoon allspice

Soak beans overnight in water. In morning bring to boil. Cook slowly until skins of beans wrinkle when exposed to air, about 20 minutes. Drain beans, reserving water. Place whole onion in bottom of 3-quart baking dish. Add drained beans. Score salt pork in ¼-inch strips. Press pork, cut side down, into beans. Blend together salt, mustard, ginger, Kitchen Bouquet, and molasses. Add 1 cup of the bean liquid and pour over the beans. Cover and bake in 325° oven until beans are tender, about 2 hours. Occasionally remove cover and stir beans from bottom of pot, adding more bean liquid if necessary. An hour before the beans are done, place piece of Canadian bacon in oven in shallow roasting pan, still in wrapper. After 30 minutes, remove wrapping and spread meat with mixture of Kitchen Bouquet, sugar, and spices. Let bake another 30 minutes. Serve thinly sliced bacon with the beans. Makes 8 servings.

CHINESE VEGETABLES

Best Foods, Division of
Corn Products Company

1½ cups sliced celery	1 teaspoon salt
¾ cup French-cut green beans	1 teaspoon monosodium glutamate
1 5-ounce can water chestnuts, sliced	¾ teaspoon sugar
½ cup bean sprouts	⅛ teaspoon pepper
1 chicken bouillon cube	¾ teaspoon soy sauce
½ cup water or ½ cup liquid from vegetables	2 teaspoons Argo Corn Starch
	1 tablespoon cold water

Prepare vegetables. Dissolve chicken cube in water in a medium size saucepan over low heat. Add prepared vegetables and seasonings. Cover and steam 5 minutes. Blend corn starch with cold water; add to vegetables and cook just until broth thickens and becomes transparent. Makes 4 servings.

WESTERN LIMA BAKE
Hunt Foods, Inc.

1 pound dried lima beans
2½ teaspoons salt
3 tablespoons vegetable oil
½ pound ground beef
1 medium onion, finely chopped

2 8-ounce cans Hunt's Tomato Sauce
½ cup lima bean cooking liquid
½ teaspoon salt
Dash poultry seasoning

Wash beans, and soak overnight in 2 quarts water. Simmer, covered, in same water until tender, 1 to 1½ hours. Season beans with 2½ teaspoons salt after ½-hour of cooking. Drain and put in casserole, reserving ½ cup lima bean cooking liquid. Cook meat and onion in hot oil, stirring until lightly browned. Add tomato sauce and remaining ingredients. Mix and pour hot over beans. Bake in 350° oven 1 hour, or until bubbly hot. Makes 5 to 6 servings.

LIMA BEANS PANACHE
General Foods Corporation

2 tablespoons chopped onion
2 tablespoons butter
¾ cup water
½ teaspoon salt
1 bay leaf

1 10-ounce package Birds Eye Fordhook Lima Beans
1 9-ounce package Birds Eye Cut Green Beans
1 tablespoon lemon juice
2 teaspoons chopped chives

Sauté onions in butter in saucepan until lightly browned. Add water, salt, bay leaf, and lima beans. Then cook as directed on the package. Meanwhile, cook green beans as directed on the package. Drain and combine with lima beans. Add lemon juice and chives. Makes 6 to 8 servings.

CURRIED VEGETABLE CASSEROLE
Grocery Store Products Co.

2 cups medium white sauce
1 teaspoon curry powder
1 teaspoon Kitchen Bouquet
2 cups cooked carrots

2 cups cooked turnips
1 cup cooked green peas
1 cup chopped salted peanuts

To the white sauce, add curry powder and Kitchen Bouquet and blend together thoroughly. In a greased 1½-quart casserole, place 1 cup carrots, 1 cup turnips, and ½ cup peas. Then pour over vegetables 1 cup sauce and sprinkle in ½ cup peanuts. Add another layer of vegetables. Pour in remainder of sauce and top with ½ cup peanuts. Place in 350° oven and bake about 45 minutes. Makes 4 to 6 servings.

FRENCH FRIED ONIONS
The Procter & Gamble Company

2 pounds large onions
⅔ cup milk
½ cup flour

Salt and pepper
Crisco for deep frying

Peel onions and cut into ¼-inch slices and separate into rings. Dip onion rings in milk and then in seasoned flour. Fry, a few at a time, until lightly browned in deep shortening heated to 365°. Drain on absorbent paper. Serve hot. Makes 4 servings.

CREAMED ONIONS
Best Foods, Division of
Corn Products Company

2 pounds small white onions
¼ cup butter or margarine
2 tablespoons Argo Corn Starch

1 teaspoon salt
¼ teaspoon pepper
2 cups milk

Peel small onions; boil in water until tender. Meanwhile make the sauce. Melt butter or margarine in a saucepan. Add corn starch, salt, and pepper, and blend well. Remove from heat; gradually add milk, mixing until smooth. Cook over medium heat, stirring constantly, until mixture thickens and comes to a boil. Boil 1 minute, stirring constantly. Drain the cooked onions and add them to the sauce. Serve hot. Makes 4 to 6 servings.

PEAS SUPREME
General Foods Corporation

1 10-ounce package Birds Eye Green Peas
¼ cup slivered blanched almonds
3 tablespoons butter or margarine

1½ cups sliced fresh or canned mushrooms
¼ cup chopped onion (optional)
¼ teaspoon salt

Cook peas as directed on the package. Drain. Sauté almonds in butter until golden brown. Remove almonds, and sauté mushrooms and onions in butter remaining in skillet until mushrooms are tender. Combine peas, almonds, mushroom and onion mixture, and salt. Makes about 2⅓ cups, or 3 or 4 servings.

FRESH SPINACH WITH CALIFORNIA DIP
Thomas J. Lipton, Inc.

2 pounds fresh spinach
½ cup water
1 teaspoon salt

½ cup California Dip (see page 18)
2 tablespoons vinegar

Wash spinach thoroughly. Add to boiling salted water, cover and cook 7 to 10 minutes. Drain spinach. Mix California Dip and vinegar together. Spoon sauce over top of spinach when serving. Makes 6 servings.

LAULAUS
The Dow Chemical Company

3 pounds fresh spinach leaves
2 cups diced cooked chicken or cooked pork
1 cup drained flaked canned salmon

⅓ cup chopped onion
1 teaspoon salt
⅛ teaspoon pepper
3 tablespoons butter or margarine

Wash and stem spinach; lay leaves out flat in a pan. Cover with a small amount of boiling water. Cover pan and cook for about 1 minute, or until leaves wilt slightly. Drain leaves and keep them flat and whole. Place a 9-inch length of regular width Saran Wrap over table surface. Arrange an overlapping layer of drained spinach leaves in rectangle 7 x 8½-inches on the Saran Wrap. Place ¼ cup chicken and 2 tablespoons salmon on spinach leaves. Sprinkle with onion, salt, and pepper; dot with butter. Fold spinach leaves up around meat, making it into a bundle about 2½ x 3-inches. Fold Saran Wrap into a neat package around spinach bundle. Repeat 7 times. Freeze. Makes 8 laulaus.

To defrost: Unwrap bundles and place in electric fry pan

or heavy skillet. Add ½ cup water. Cover and let laulaus cook until tender, about 15 minutes at moderate heat.

SQUASH FLUFF
National Biscuit Company

2 tablespoons butter or margarine, melted
1 small onion, chopped
1 stack pack Ritz Crackers,
 finely rolled (about 1⅔
 cups crumbs)

1 cup milk
½ teaspoon salt
½ teaspoon pepper
2 cups cooked squash, fresh
 or frozen
4 eggs, beaten

Sauté onions in butter or margarine. Mix the cracker crumbs, milk, salt, pepper, and squash. Fold in beaten eggs. Pour into well-greased individual baking dishes or a 2-quart casserole. Bake in 350° oven 30 minutes for individual or 1 hour for large casserole. Makes 4 servings.

SQUASH WITH ORANGE AND BROWN SUGAR
General Foods Corporation

1 12-ounce package Birds
 Eye Cooked Squash
2 tablespoons butter or margarine
2 tablespoons brown sugar

2 tablespoons orange juice
¼ teaspoon grated orange
 rind
¼ teaspoon salt
Nutmeg

Place frozen block of squash in top of double boiler. Add remaining ingredients. Cover and heat over boiling water until completely thawed and hot throughout, about 25 minutes. Stir often. Before serving, sprinkle with nutmeg. Makes 3 servings.

Note: Squash with Orange and Brown Sugar may be heated gently in a saucepan about 10 minutes, or baked in a 350° oven about 45 minutes, if preferred.

17 Soy sauce, bacon, and onions transform a dish of plain green beans into an exotic specialty. See Green Beans Chinese (p.151). Photo courtesy of Green Giant Company.

18 The elements of tossed salads—from greens to ham, cheese, and shrimp. There are hundreds of possible combinations with the ingredients pictured here. Oil and vinegar dressing is unfailingly correct, and is the basis for countless variations. Photo courtesy of Best Foods, Division of Corn Products Company.

19 Corn with Mushrooms (p. 149) is a chafing dish novelty that will brighten a buffet or dinner table. Serve with meat or a cheese omelet. Photo courtesy of Green Giant Company.

20 A mousse served with vichyssoise and a tray of cold vegetables is an ideal meal for late summer dining. This ham mousse uses the original container in which the ham was packed as a simple, attractive mold. Photo courtesy of Knox Gelatine, Inc.

21 Here is a complete summer meal, which needs only assorted breads to complete the picture. Tuna in the center, flanked by rows of assorted vegetables, sandwich meats, and anchovies. It is called Salade Nicoise (p. 190). Photo courtesy of Green Giant Company.

22 The Cranberry Crown Salad (p. 197), in two beautiful layers of berries, turkey, and water chestnuts, is the epitome of grandeur in molded food. Photo courtesy of Ocean Spray Cranberries, Inc.

23 Two unusual, extremely effective party suggestions: Fruit Relish Ring with Shrimp Salad (p. 192) in the foreground, and Della Robbia Dessert Salad (p. 285). Together or separately they are conversation pieces for any special occasion. Photo courtesy of Standard Brands, Inc.

24 Summer holds no better promise than this magnificent combination of fresh fruit—strawberries, pineapple, oranges, apples, and grapes— tossed with dressing, and served as a main course or as a side dish. Photo courtesy of Best Foods, Division of Corn Products Company.

ACORN SQUASH WITH BRAZIL NUTS
Brazil Nut Association

3 acorn squash
¼ cup sugar
½ teaspoon salt
½ teaspoon cinnamon
¼ teaspoon nutmeg

¾ cup chopped Brazil nuts
1 tablespoon grated orange rind
3 tablespoons butter or margarine

Wash and halve squash lengthwise; remove seeds and stringy portion. Place squash, cut side down, in a greased shallow baking pan. Bake in a 375° oven 30 minutes. While squash is baking, put remaining ingredients in a small mixing bowl; cut in butter with two knives or pastry blender. Remove squash from oven; turn right side up. Divide nut mixture among the squash halves. Return to oven and bake approximately 30 minutes longer, or until squash is tender. Makes 6 servings.

BROILED TOMATOES
Best Foods, Division of
Corn Products Company

4 whole ripe tomatoes
4 tablespoons Mazola Margarine, melted
Salt and pepper
½ cup fine dry bread crumbs

1 teaspoon finely minced onion
1 teaspoon finely minced green pepper

Wash tomatoes; remove stem end and cut in half crosswise. Dip cut surface in melted margarine. Then dip in seasoned crumbs. Sprinkle tops with mixture of minced onion and green pepper. Place in shallow pan and broil slowly until tomato is tender and top is nicely browned. Tomatoes may be baked in 375° oven 15 to 20 minutes if preferred. Makes 4 servings, extremely low in calories.

WHIPPED POTATO-STUFFED TOMATOES
The Borden Company

6 large firm tomatoes
Salt and pepper to taste
1 envelope Borden's Instant Whipped Potatoes
1 small package instant minced onion

2 teaspoons fresh or dehydrated parsley
2 teaspoons dehydrated celery flakes
2 tablespoons melted butter

Wash tomatoes; remove a thin slice from blossom end of each. Scoop out pulp and juice from each. Sprinkle inside of each tomato shell with salt and pepper. Turn upside down and let drain 10 minutes. Prepare potatoes according to directions on envelope. Add onions, parsley, and celery flakes; blend well. Lightly fill tomato shells with whipped potato mixture; sprinkle with paprika. Brush tomatoes with melted butter. Place in baking dish. Bake in 375° oven about 20 to 25 minutes, or until tomatoes are tender and potato filling lightly browned. Makes 6 servings.

WAX BEANS MEXICANA
Green Giant Company

2 1-pound cans Green Giant Brand Wax Beans
¼ cup butter
¼ cup finely chopped onion
¼ teaspoon salt

⅛ teaspoon Tabasco
1 teaspoon Worcestershire Sauce
1 teaspoon prepared mustard
2 tablespoons chili sauce

Heat wax beans with juice in saucepan until thoroughly heated. Melt butter in small saucepan; add onion. Cook over low heat until onion is tender but not brown. Add remaining ingredients; mix well; heat. Serve over the wax beans. Makes 6 servings.

ReLISHES and SaUCES

Relishes and sauces are extras that make an occasion of the simplest foods. Today, more and more American cooks are discovering that the art of fine sauces, so long the province of the French, the Italians, and the Chinese, is surprisingly easy to master. One exposure to the magic of hollandaise served on vegetables, or to a cut of meat garnished with a tempting fruit relish, is enough to convince anyone that the time and effort involved in their preparation is well spent. Here is a collection of piquant recipes that will add a new dimension to your favorite menus.

RELISHES

STEAK SPREAD
McIlhenny Company

½ teaspoon Tabasco
2 tablespoons butter

1 3-ounce package Roquefort or bleu cheese

Cream all ingredients together until blended. Spread over broiled steak or on toast rounds. Makes ⅓ cup.

JELLIED SHERRY MEAT GARNISH
Knox Gelatine, Inc.

1 envelope Knox Unflavored
   Gelatine
2 tablespoons sugar
¾ cup water

¼ cup orange juice
2 tablespoons lemon juice
¾ cup sweet sherry

Mix together gelatine and sugar in saucepan. Stir in water. Place over low heat, stirring constantly, until gelatine is dissolved. Remove from heat; stir in remaining ingredients. Pour into a 2-cup mold; chill until firm. Serve with turkey, chicken, ham, or beef. Makes 6 servings.

COLORFUL PEAR GARNISH
McCormick & Co., Inc.

To 1 30-ounce can pear halves add ¼ teaspoon McCormick or Schilling Pure Mint and/or Peppermint Extract and several drops McCormick or Schilling Green Food Color. (Amount of food color depends on shade desired.) Allow pears to stand several hours or overnight. Excellent as a garnish with meat.

Note: For an interesting variation, use 1½ teaspoons McCormick or Schilling Brandy Extract and several drops McCormick or Schilling Red Food Color in place of the mint extract and green food color.

BAKED CRANBERRY-WALNUT RELISH
Ocean Spray Cranberries, Inc.

4 cups (1 pound) Ocean
   Spray Fresh Cranberries
2½ cups sugar

1 cup coarsely broken walnuts, toasted
1 cup orange marmalade
   Juice of 1 lime or lemon

Wash cranberries and drain. In shallow pan, stir cranberries with sugar. Cover tightly. Bake in 350° oven for 1 hour. Spread walnuts in separate shallow pan; toast until light golden brown, about 12 minutes. Stir together baked cranberries, walnuts, marmalade, and lime or lemon juice until well mixed. Chill. A natural mate for roast beef.

GLAZED FRUIT WITH BRAZIL NUTS
Brazil Nut Association

1 29-ounce can cling peach or pear halves	½ teaspoon grated lemon rind
2 tablespoons lemon juice	½ cup chopped Brazil nuts
	2 tablespoons brown sugar

Drain fruit syrup into saucepan; boil rapidly until reduced to 1 cup. Remove from heat; add lemon juice and rind. Put peach or pear halves in shallow baking dish, hollow side up; sprinkle with nuts and brown sugar. Spoon over syrup. Bake in 350° oven 25 to 30 minutes, basting occasionally. Serve as a meat garnish. Makes 4 to 6 servings.

Note: Also delicious as a dessert with ice cream, or on a fruit salad plate.

SPICED PINEAPPLE RELISH
Dole Corporation

1 20-ounce can Dole Crushed Pineapple	1 tablespoon white vinegar
	¼ cup cinnamon red hots

Drain off ½ cup of juice from pineapple; place remaining juice and pineapple in saucepan and add vinegar. Heat gently and add cinnamon red hots. Let simmer until thoroughly blended and cooked down. Chill, covered with Saran Wrap. Serve with pork, ham, lamb, or turkey. This is an excellent addition to a relish tray of grape preserves and cranberry relish.

BRANDIED SPICED PEACHES
McCormick & Co., Inc.

1 30-ounce can peach halves
McCormick or Schilling
Whole Cloves
1 cup brown sugar
⅓ cup vinegar
1 cup water

1 cup canned peach syrup
2 inches McCormick or
Schilling Stick Cinnamon
5 teaspoons McCormick or
Schilling Brandy Extract

Drain peaches, reserving the syrup; insert 3 cloves in each half. Combine sugar, vinegar, water, syrup, and cinnamon in a deep saucepan and simmer for 15 minutes over low heat. Cool spiced syrup and stir in extract; pour over peaches. Chill overnight. (If you have canned spiced peaches, just add brandy extract to syrup and let stand overnight.)

BRANDIED APPLE FRITTERS
McCormick & Co., Inc.

4 medium tart, firm, juicy
apples
2 tablespoons McCormick
or Schilling Brandy Extract
2 tablespoons water
1 egg, separated
½ cup milk

1 tablespoon sugar
1 cup flour
½ teaspoon salt
1½ teaspoons baking pow-
der
Confectioners' sugar

Pare, core, and slice apples in circles or cut into sections. Mix together brandy extract and water, and pour over apples; cover tightly with Saran Wrap. Let set while making batter. Combine well-beaten egg yolk with milk and sugar. Sift together flour, salt, and baking powder; add to egg mixture. Fold in stiffly beaten egg white. Dip brandied apples in this batter and fry in deep fat at 375° about 3 minutes. Sprinkle with confectioners' sugar.

BROILED BANANAS
United Fruit Company

4 firm Chiquita Bananas   Salt
Butter or margarine, melted

Peel bananas. Place on broiler rack or into pan containing rack. Brush bananas well with butter or margarine and sprinkle lightly with salt. Broil 3 to 4 inches from heat about 5 minutes on each side, or until bananas are browned and tender, easily pierced with a fork. Serve hot as a vegetable. Makes 4 servings. (See illustration 29.)

Variations

BROILED BANANAS WITH CURRY SAUCE. Top broiled bananas with a hot curry sauce.

BROILED BANANAS WITH APPLESAUCE. Cover each banana with about ¼ cup applesauce or apple butter. Top with plain, whipped, or sour cream.

BANANA FRITTERS
United Fruit Company

Melted fat or salad oil   ¼ cup flour
2 to 3 firm Chiquita Bananas   Fritter Batter (see below)

To deep-fry, have deep kettle ½ to ⅔ full of melted fat or oil. To shallow-fry, have 1½ to 2 inches of melted fat or oil in frying pan. Heat fat to 375°, or until a 1-inch cube of bread will brown in about 40 seconds. Peel bananas and cut each crosswise into 3 or 4 diagonal pieces. Roll in flour. Dip into Fritter Batter, completely coating the banana pieces with the batter. Fry in the hot fat about 6 minutes, or until well-browned. Drain on a rack. Serve hot with main course, or serve as a dessert with a hot fruit sauce, syrup, or sweetened whipped cream. Makes 6 to 12 fritters.

Fritter Batter:

1 cup sifted flour
2 teaspoons baking powder
1¼ teaspoons salt
¼ cup sugar

1 egg, well beaten
⅓ cup milk
2 teaspoons melted shortening

Sift together flour, baking powder, salt, and sugar into mixing bowl. Combine egg, milk, and shortening. Add to dry ingredients and mix until batter is smooth.

BAKED BANANAS IN THE PEEL
United Fruit Company

4 firm Chiquita Bananas
Salt

1½ tablespoons melted butter or margarine

Cut off the tips of both ends of each banana. Remove a lengthwise section of the peel about 1-inch wide, extending from end to end. Brush exposed portion of the pulp with butter or margarine and sprinkle lightly with salt. Place in baking dish. Bake in a 375° oven 15 to 20 minutes, or until peels are dark and bananas are tender, easily pierced with a fork. Serve hot as a vegetable. Makes 4 servings.

MEAT, FISH, AND VEGETABLE SAUCES

MEDIUM WHITE SAUCE
Best Foods, Division of
Corn Products Company

2 tablespoons butter or margarine	½ teaspoon salt
1 tablespoon Argo Corn Starch	⅛ teaspoon pepper
	1 cup milk

Melt butter or margarine in a saucepan. Add corn starch, salt, and pepper, and blend well. Remove from heat; gradually add milk, mixing until smooth. Cook over medium heat, stirring constantly, until mixture thickens and comes to a boil. Boil 1 minute, stirring constantly. Makes about 1 cup sauce.

Variations

THIN WHITE SAUCE. Decrease butter or margarine measurement to 1 tablespoon and decrease corn starch to 1½ teaspoons.

EGG SAUCE. To 2 cups Medium White Sauce, add 4 chopped hard-cooked eggs. Serve over asparagus, broccoli, or spinach.

PARSLEY SAUCE. To 2 cups Medium White Sauce, add 2 tablespoons chopped parsley. Serve with croquettes, fish cakes, or plain boiled potato.

CHEESE SAUCE. To 2 cups Medium White Sauce, add ½ cup grated cheese and stir until cheese is melted. Serve on vegetables or croquettes.

CREAMED DISHES. To 2 cups Medium White Sauce, add 1 to 1½ cups cooked diced meat, flaked fish, or vegetables.

SCALLOPED DISHES. To 2 cups Medium White Sauce, add 1 to 1½ cups cooked meat, fish, or vegetables. Pour into quart casserole and top with ¼ cup buttered, seasoned bread crumbs. Bake in 375° oven 25 to 30 minutes.

CURRY SAUCE
Best Foods, Division of
Corn Products Company

½ cup Hellmann's or Best
   Foods Real Mayonnaise
2 tablespoons flour
1 cup milk

¼ teaspoon salt
Dash pepper
¼ teaspoon curry powder
⅛ teaspoon ginger

Blend mayonnaise and flour to smooth paste. Add milk gradually and cook over hot water until thickened. Add seasonings and serve. Makes 1⅓ cups.

HORSERADISH SAUCE
McIlhenny Company

⅔ cup evaporated milk
½ cup soft bread crumbs
½ cup horseradish

⅛ teaspoon Tabasco
¼ teaspoon salt
1 tablespoon lemon juice

Spoon 3 tablespoons of the evaporated milk over bread crumbs. Add horseradish, Tabasco, and salt; let stand. Chill remaining evaporated milk in freezer tray until ice crystals form around edges. Turn milk into chilled bowl and whip until stiff. Add lemon juice and continue whipping until very stiff. Fold in horseradish mixture. Serve immediately with cold ham, tongue, or beef. Makes 2 cups.

CAPER SAUCE
Knox Gelatine, Inc.

1 2¼-ounce bottle capers
1 cup mayonnaise

2 teaspoons lemon juice
⅛ teaspoon Tabasco

Drain liquid from capers into mayonnaise. Add lemon juice and Tabasco; stir until smooth. Add capers; serve with veal.

CHEESE SAUCE
The Borden Company

2 tablespoons butter
2 tablespoons flour
½ teaspoon salt
¼ teaspoon dry mustard
Dash of pepper
⅛ teaspoon Worcestershire
   Sauce

½ cup evaporated milk
½ cup water
1 cup shredded Chateau
   Cheese Food, firmly
   packed

Melt butter in saucepan. Combine flour, salt, dry mustard, and pepper; blend into melted butter. Stir in Worcestershire Sauce. Gradually stir in evaporated milk and water. Cook over medium heat, stirring constantly, until thickened. Add cheese and continue to heat and stir until cheese is melted. Makes 1½ cups.

SOUR CREAM SAUCE
National Biscuit Company

Add 2 tablespoons white vinegar and finely chopped dill (or crumbled dry dill) to 1 container sour cream to suit your taste. Serve with Stuffed Veal Shoulder (see page 70).

MEXICAN BARBECUE SAUCE FOR HAM STEAKS
The Seven-Up Company

1 small onion, minced
2 tablespoons margarine
1 7-ounce bottle 7-Up
¼ cup catsup
1 teaspoon dry mustard

1 teaspoon salt
⅛ teaspoon chili powder
⅛ teaspoon pepper
4 whole cloves

Brown onion in margarine and stir in remaining ingredients. Heat to boiling; reduce heat and simmer 10 minutes.

Spoon out cloves and discard. Brush sauce over ham steaks as they grill. Makes about 1¼ cups.

BURGUNDY BARBECUE SAUCE
Paul Masson Vineyards

1 cup minced onions
2 cups chili sauce
Juice of 1 lemon
1 teaspoon chili powder
1 tablespoon Worcestershire Sauce
1 teaspoon salt

½ cup drippings or butter
1 cup water
1 clove garlic, finely minced
1 teaspoon dry mustard
Pepper to taste
½ cup Paul Masson Burgundy

Sauté onions in butter to a golden brown. Add remaining seasonings, omitting wine, and simmer for 30 minutes. Add wine just before serving. Makes about 2 cups, enough for saucing 4 to 5 pounds of meat.

BARBECUE SAUCE FOR LAMB
American Lamb Council

1 cup catsup
1 cup water
¼ cup vinegar
2 tablespoons sugar
4 teaspoons Worcestershire Sauce

Several dashes Tabasco
2 teaspoons dry mustard
Clove of garlic, mashed or minced with 2 teaspoons salt

Combine and serve. Delicious with Lamb Riblets with Spaghetti (see page 80). Makes 8 servings.

DILL SAUCE
American Skultuna Inc.

2 tablespoons butter or margarine	2 tablespoons chopped fresh dill
2 tablespoons sifted flour	1½ tablespoons cider or wine vinegar
2 cups lamb stock or 1 bouillon cube dissolved in 2 cups hot water	½ to 1 tablespoon sugar
	1 egg yolk, well beaten

Melt butter or margarine; add flour and stir until well blended. Add 2 cups stock; stir while adding. Cook slowly for 10 minutes. Add remaining ingredients except egg yolk. Remove from heat. Mix 2 tablespoons sauce with egg yolk. Blend with remaining sauce. Serve with Swedish Boiled Lamb (see page 77).

SPICY RAISIN SAUCE
California Packing Corporation

1 cup Del Monte Seedless Raisins	¼ teaspoon cloves
1¾ cups water	¼ teaspoon dry mustard
⅓ cup brown sugar, packed	¼ teaspoon salt
1½ tablespoons corn starch	1 tablespoon butter or margarine
¼ teaspoon cinnamon	1 tablespoon vinegar

Boil raisins in 1¾ cups water for 5 minutes. Blend brown sugar with corn starch, cinnamon, cloves, dry mustard, and salt. Add to raisins and cook, stirring, until clear and thickened. Blend in butter or margarine and vinegar. Serve hot with broiled or baked ham. Makes about 1½ cups.

QUICK APRICOT SAUCE
Grocery Store Products Co.

1½ cups apricot jam
2 tablespoons lemon juice
1 tablespoon vinegar

1 teaspoon Kitchen Bouquet
⅛ teaspoon allspice
½ teaspoon dry mustard

In a saucepan, blend together all ingredients. Heat over low heat until jam is slightly melted and sauce is smooth. Serve with Festive Ham (see page 91). Makes 1⅔ cups.

BURGUNDY SAUCE
Paul Masson Vineyards

2 tablespoons butter
¼ cup flour
1 chopped onion
1 diced carrot
2 or 3 chopped shallots (if available)
1 piece of garlic crushed (optional)
Chicken or veal bones

2 glasses Paul Masson Pinot Noir
2 cups meat stock (or water)
Mushroom trimmings
3 sprigs parsley
1 bay leaf
A little thyme
1 teaspoon salt
6 peppercorns

Melt butter in saucepan; add onion and carrot, and cook until golden brown. Add the shallots, garlic, bones, and flour. Mix well, put in hot oven, and cook 5 to 10 minutes, or until flour is golden brown. Remove from oven, add wine, meat stock, and remaining ingredients; bring to a boil and cook slowly for 1 hour. Strain through a fine sieve; bring to boil and season to taste. Serve with baked, boiled, or fresh ham.

SMORGASBORD SAUCE
McIlhenny Company

½ cup sour cream
1 teaspoon horseradish
¼ teaspoon salt

¼ teaspoon sugar
¼ teaspoon Tabasco

Combine ingredients. Chill. Serve with salmon, lobster, sliced roast beef, asparagus, cucumbers, or green beans. Makes ½ cup.

TARTAR SAUCE
Best Foods, Division of
Corn Products Company

1 cup Hellmann's or Best Foods Real Mayonnaise
1 tablespoon chopped onion or chives
2 tablespoons chopped olives

1 tablespoon chopped sweet pickle
1 tablespoon chopped sour pickle
1 tablespoon chopped pimiento
1 tablespoon capers

Mix all ingredients together and serve cold with any hot or cold fish. Makes 1⅓ cups.

Note: This can be made into a hot sauce by reducing mayonnaise to ½ cup and adding to 2 cups hot medium white sauce.

SAUCE PIQUANTE
McIlhenny Company

2 tablespoons salad oil or
  bacon fat
¼ cup flour
1 cup chopped onion
1 cup chopped celery
1 cup chopped green pepper
1 cup water

1 6-ounce can tomatoes or
  2 8-ounce cans tomato
  sauce
1 6-ounce can tomato paste
1 teaspoon salt
¼ teaspoon Tabasco
½ teaspoon brown sugar

Put oil in skillet and gradually add flour. Stir constantly
while lightly browning the flour. Add onion, celery, and
green pepper; cook until soft. Stir in remaining ingredients.
Heat to a boil. Cover; reduce heat to simmer and cook
about 20 minutes. Makes about 4 cups.

HARVEST SAUCE
Uncle Ben's, Inc.

⅓ cup butter or margarine
½ cup flour
2 cups milk
1 teaspoon salt
Dash pepper
Dash marjoram and garlic
  (optional)

2 cups cooked vegetables
  (peas and carrots, or any
  other combination)
Several hard-cooked eggs
  (optional)

Melt butter or margarine in saucepan. Remove from
heat and stir in flour. Add milk slowly, stirring constantly.
Continue stirring and cook over low heat until thickened.
Add seasonings and vegetables. If desired, add several
chopped hard-cooked eggs. (For special effect grate yolks
and chop whites.) Serve with Spring Harvest Rice Ring
(see page 138).

EASY HOLLANDAISE
Best Foods, Division of
Corn Products Company

¾ cup Hellmann's or Best
 Foods Real Mayonnaise
⅓ cup milk
¼ teaspoon salt

⅛ teaspoon white pepper
1 tablespoon lemon juice
1 teaspoon grated lemon
 rind

Combine mayonnaise and milk. Cook over hot water 5 to
6 minutes, stirring constantly. Add seasonings, lemon juice,
and rind. Remove from hot water and serve over any desired vegetable. Makes about 1¼ cups.

SAUCE FOR BROCCOLI
Thomas J. Lipton, Inc.

1 box frozen broccoli
1 tablespoon butter
1 tablespoon flour
Broth from broccoli or ½
 cup water

1 teaspoon lemon juice
⅓ cup California Dip (see
 page 18)

Cook broccoli according to package instructions. Make a
sauce of the butter, flour, and broth; slowly add lemon juice
and California Dip. Heat to boiling, stirring constantly.
Pour sauce over broccoli and serve. Makes 4 servings.

CREAMY ALMOND SAUCE
California Almond Growers Exchange

1 cup commercial sour
 cream
1 tablespoon butter or margarine, soft
1 tablespoon lemon juice

Dash salt
Dash cayenne
¼ cup Blue Diamond Almonds, chopped or readydiced

Combine sour cream and butter, and warm gently over hot water. Do not allow to get too hot. Stir in lemon juice, salt, and cayenne. Spoon over cooked cauliflowerets and sprinkle with almonds. Serve at once. Makes 4 servings.

HOT BACON DRESSING

Best Foods, Division of
Corn Products Company

2 strips bacon, diced
1½ tablespoons chopped onion
1 tablespoon Argo Corn Starch
½ cup vinegar
½ cup water
1 tablespoon sugar
¼ teaspoon salt
Dash pepper

Cook diced bacon until crisp. Remove bacon and set aside. Add onions to fat in pan and cook slowly until tender but not brown. Add corn starch; mix well. Add vinegar and water. Bring to a boil, stirring constantly. Add sugar, salt, and pepper. Prepare dressing just before serving. Pour hot over shredded raw or cooked cabbage, cooked spinach, kale, or salad greens. Sprinkle with crisp bacon. Toss lightly and serve immediately. Makes 1 cup.

SAUCE POULETTE

The Campbell Soup Company

2 tablespoons minced onion
2 tablespoons butter
1 can Campbell's Cream of Chicken Soup
⅓ cup milk
2 tablespoons chopped parsley
1 to 2 teaspoons lemon juice
1 tablespoon sherry (optional)

Cook onion in butter until tender. Blend in soup, milk, parsley, lemon juice, and sherry. Heat slowly. Pour over asparagus, peas, or lima beans. Makes 4 to 6 servings.

CLAM-ONION SAUCE FOR SPAGHETTI
Thomas J. Lipton, Inc.

½ cup butter
½ cup olive oil
1 clove garlic, minced
3 tablespoons Lipton Dehydrated Onion Soup
½ teaspoon rosemary

½ teaspoon marjoram
2 10½-ounce cans minced clams
⅛ teaspoon pepper
½ cup chopped parsley

In skillet, heat butter and oil; then lightly brown minced garlic. Mix in dehydrated onion soup, herbs, and liquid from canned clams. Simmer 5 minutes. Stir in minced clams, pepper, and chopped parsley; heat. Serve over cooked spaghetti. Makes 6 to 8 servings.

DESSERT SAUCES

BUTTERSCOTCH SAUCE
The Nestlé Company

¼ cup light corn syrup
¼ cup evaporated milk

1 6-ounce package Nestlé's Butterscotch Morsels

Combine corn syrup and evaporated milk, and bring *just* to boil over moderate heat, stirring constantly. Remove from heat. Stir in butterscotch morsels until smooth. Serve warm over ice cream or warm cake. Makes 1 cup. (If sauce becomes too thick on standing, reheat over hot water.)

COFFEE-WALNUT SAUCE
Pan American Coffee Bureau

1 cup sugar
1½ cups strong coffee
2 tablespoons corn starch
3 tablespoons cold coffee

2 tablespoons butter
⅓ teaspoon salt
½ cup broken walnut meats

Melt sugar slowly in heavy skillet, stirring often. Add 1½ cups coffee, slowly and carefully (much steam will rise). Stir constantly. Dissolve corn starch in cold coffee; stir into warm mixture, and continue stirring over low heat until sauce boils and thickens. Add butter, salt, and walnuts. Serve warm on ice cream. Makes about 2 cups.

ORANGE SAUCE
Best Foods, Division of
Corn Products Company

½ cup sugar
1½ tablespoons Argo Corn
 Starch
¼ teaspoon salt
1¼ cups boiling water

2 tablespoons Mazola Margarine
2 tablespoons orange juice
2 teaspoons grated orange peel

Mix sugar, corn starch, and salt in small saucepan. Gradually add water. Cook over medium heat, stirring constantly, until sauce thickens and comes to a boil. Boil 2 minutes. Remove from heat. Add margarine, orange juice, and peel. Serve hot on cottage pudding, gingerbread, fruit betty, or steamed pudding. Makes about 1½ cups.

PINEAPPLE-MINT SAUCE
Best Foods, Division of
Corn Products Company

1 9-ounce can crushed pineapple

¾ cup Karo Syrup, Red Label

¼ teaspoon peppermint flavoring

Few drops green food coloring

Combine ingredients. Cover and chill thoroughly. Use as ice cream or pudding sauce. Makes 1½ cups.

PEACH SAUCE
California Packing Corporation

1 cup Del Monte Dried Peaches

1½ cups water

⅓ cup sugar

2 teaspoons corn starch

Few grains salt

¼ teaspoon grated lemon peel

1 teaspoon fresh lemon juice

Cut peaches into small pieces. Add the water and boil uncovered about 15 to 20 minutes until peaches are tender. Blend sugar, corn starch, and salt, and stir into peaches. Cook, stirring occasionally, until mixture boils and is thickened. Remove from heat; blend in lemon peel and juice. Serve on ice cream, pudding, tapioca, etc. Makes about 1½ cups.

CHERRIES IN THE SNOW
National Red Cherry Institute

½ cup sugar

4 teaspoons corn starch

¼ teaspoon salt

1 can (1 pound) red sour pitted cherries (water pack)

½ cup water

1½ teaspoons lemon juice

¼ teaspoon almond flavoring

¼ teaspoon red food coloring

Combine sugar, corn starch, and salt in a saucepan. Drain cherries; stir cherry liquid and water into dry ingredients. Cook, stirring constantly, until mixture comes to a boil. Boil ½ minute. Remove from heat; add cherries, lemon juice, almond flavoring, and red food coloring. Cool. Serve on ice cream, rice pudding, vanilla pudding, tapioca, farina, or angel food cake wedges. Makes 2½ cups.

HARD SAUCE

The Dow Chemical Company

½ cup softened butter
2 cups sifted confectioners' sugar
1 teaspoon vanilla

¼ cup chopped nuts
¼ cup chopped red and green maraschino cherries

Cream together butter, sugar, and vanilla. Blend in nuts and cherries. On Saran Wrap, shape mixture into roll about 2 inches in diameter. Freeze. Before serving cut roll into ¼-inch slices; serve with pudding. Makes 8 servings.

PEANUT BUTTER DESSERT SAUCE

Best Foods, Division of
Corn Products Company

¼ cup (½ print) margarine
1 teaspoon flour
½ cup water

⅓ cup Skippy Chunk-Style Peanut Butter
1½ cups sifted confectioners' sugar

Cook margarine, flour, and water over medium heat, stirring constantly, until margarine is melted. Add peanut butter and remove from heat. Stir in sugar. Beat with rotary beater until smooth. Serve hot or cold over ice cream. Makes 1½ cups.

SALaDS

The mold is long in style and great in opportunity. It is ideal for salads, the epitome of convenience in preparation and serving. It is perfect for refrigerating-in-advance, wrapped in Saran Wrap. There is probably no other method of preparation that lends such a "party look" to salads, yet requires so little time and effort.

Recipes for molded foods have been included as often as possible throughout *Food From Famous Kitchens*. In this chapter, you will find recipes for molded salads suitable for a multitude of meals: luncheons and suppers, large gatherings and small, simple family meals and extra-special company dinners.

Here is a seven-day selection of greens for simple salads. Serve them with a fine oil and vinegar dressing.

Romaine: ½ bunch, sliced.

Boston lettuce: ½ head, broken into small pieces.

Iceberg lettuce: ½ head, broken into small bites.

Watercress: 1 bunch, separated with stems trimmed.

Escarole: ½ head, broken into leaves of uniform size.

Spinach: 1 bunch with stems removed. Tear leaves in half.

Romaine: 1 head, sliced across in ½-inch pieces.

Watercress: ½ bunch.

Endive: 1 bunch, separated and broken into small pieces.

Bibb lettuce: ½ head, leaves can be left whole.

Red cabbage: ½ cup, shredded.

Leaf lettuce: 1 bunch, broken into serving pieces.

Escarole: ½ bunch, separated with long stems removed.

Watercress: ½ bunch, separated with long stems removed.

Boston lettuce: ½ bunch, served with leaves whole.

Spinach: 1 bunch, large leaves broken in half.

Watercress: ½ bunch, with stems removed.

Leaf lettuce: 1 bunch, with leaves torn 2 or 3 times.

Romaine: 1 head, with leaves in any suitable size.

Variations can be played on these basic themes with the addition of any sharp cheese, either grated or broken with a fork, and added to the dressing. Larger pieces should be tossed in with the greens. Crushed bacon or slivers of any leftover meat or fowl are superb garnishes.

Cucumbers, water chestnuts, hearts of palm, and canned artichoke hearts give salads an added texture. Serve them individually or in combinations. Top with slices of sweet red pepper, green pepper, pimiento, or anchovy fillets.

ITALIAN SALAD BOWL
Best Foods, Division of
Corn Products Company

½ clove garlic
¼ teaspoon prepared mustard
1 teaspoon salt
Few grains pepper
1½ tablespoons vinegar
¼ teaspoon Worcestershire Sauce
4 tablespoons Mazola Corn Oil
1 quart assorted salad greens

Drop garlic clove in wooden bowl. Add prepared mustard, salt, and few grains pepper. Blend thoroughly with fork. Add vinegar, Worcestershire Sauce, and corn oil. Beat with fork until thoroughly mixed. Add crisp and well-drained salad greens, broken into bite-size pieces. Toss lightly until all greens glisten. Serve at once. Makes 4 servings.

Note: Assortment of greens might include Italian salad greens; for example: dandelion, chicory, escarole, endive, and romaine. Cherry or plum tomatoes should be added for color.

CUCUMBER SLICES WITH CALIFORNIA DIP
Thomas J. Lipton, Inc.

2 large cucumbers
3 tablespoons vinegar
1 tablespoon sugar
½ cup California Dip (see page 18)

½ teaspoon salt
Sprinkling of pepper
1 tablespoon chopped parsley

Peel cucumbers and slice thin. Marinate cucumber slices with vinegar and sugar for ½ hour in refrigerator. Mix together California Dip, salt, and pepper. Drain liquid from cucumbers and add to the dressing. Pour dressing over cucumbers and mix. Sprinkle with chopped parsley before serving. Makes 6 servings.

CUCUMBER-ASPARAGUS SALAD
Green Giant Company

1 19-ounce can Green Giant Brand Asparagus Spears
½ cucumber, peeled, split, and thinly sliced

3 green onions, shredded lengthwise into 3-inch strips
¾ cup French dressing
1 tablespoon chopped green onion

Arrange asparagus in shallow serving dish. Distribute cucumber over the asparagus. Arrange green onion over all. Add chopped green onion to French dressing; pour over salad. Chill for 30 minutes before serving. Makes 4 servings.

GREEN BEANS VINAIGRETTE
Green Giant Company

½ cup olive oil
2 tablespoons wine vinegar
½ teaspoon salt
½ teaspoon black pepper

Basil
1 16-ounce can Green Giant Brand Whole or Kitchen-Sliced Green Beans

Combine oil, vinegar, salt, and pepper, and pinch of basil. Pour over drained beans. Let stand for ½ hour. Serve on bed of greens. Makes 4 to 5 servings.

FRUIT SALAD BOWL
Best Foods, Division of
Corn Products Company

Strawberries
Pineapple slices
Unpeeled apple slices
Sliced oranges

Water Cress
Lettuce
Fruit French Dressing

Prepare fruits and salad greens. Drain well. Chill. Arrange in large salad bowl or individual salad plates. Serve with Fruit French Dressing (see page 199). Allow about 2 tablespoons dressing per serving of salad. About one cup of salad dressing is needed for 8 servings of fruit salad.

SOUTH SEAS CHICKEN SALAD
McIlhenny Company

½ cup mayonnaise
¼ cup syrup from pineapple
½ teaspoon Tabasco
2 cups diced chicken, cooked

1 cup chopped celery
1 cup pineapple cubes, drained
¼ cup slivered toasted almonds

Blend mayonnaise, syrup from pineapple, and Tabasco. Toss chicken, celery, pineapple, and almonds with dressing until lightly coated. Add salt if needed. Chill. Serve on lettuce. Makes 4 to 6 servings.

BUTTONS AND BOWS SALAD
Grocery Store Products Co.

4 ounces bow-shaped macaroni
1 3-ounce can Broiled-in-Butter Mushrooms
1 cup green beans, cooked
¼ cup well-seasoned French dressing

½ cup sliced radishes
1 cup diagonally-sliced celery
2 tablespoons mayonnaise
1 tablespoon chili sauce
¼ teaspoon Worcestershire Sauce

Cook macaroni with a clove of garlic in boiling salted water until barely tender; drain well. Drain mushrooms. Combine mushrooms and macaroni in bowl; add beans and French dressing. Toss lightly to mix well. Cover and chill thoroughly. To serve, drain off any excess dressing, and add radishes and celery. Blend together and lightly mix in the mayonnaise, chili sauce, and Worcestershire Sauce. Add more salt if necessary. Serve immediately with crisp salad greens. Makes 4 servings.

TUNA-SLAW SALAD
Star-Kist Foods, Inc.

1 large head cabbage
1 teaspoon salt
⅛ teaspoon pepper
2 teaspoons minced scallions (green onions)
2 tablespoons pimiento

2 tablespoons minced green pepper
1 6½-ounce can Star-Kist Chunk Style Tuna
1 cup sour cream
1 tablespoon sugar
2 tablespoons wine vinegar

Slice off top ½ of cabbage; hollow out base to form "bowl." Chop cut-out cabbage and the top to make 3 cups slaw; add salt, pepper, scallions, pimiento, green pepper, and tuna. Toss combined sour cream, sugar, and vinegar with slaw. Heap in cabbage bowl.

TOSSED TUNA SALAD
Star-Kist Foods, Inc.

2 cups cooked green beans
Tart French dressing
1 6- to 7-ounce can Star-Kist Tuna
1 cup diced cucumber
1 cup sliced radishes
1 teaspoon salt
1 teaspoon Worcestershire Sauce
¼ cup mayonnaise
Lettuce

Marinate green beans in French dressing. Break tuna into chunks and combine with cucumber and radishes; add seasonings and toss lightly with mayonnaise. Drain beans and add to tuna mixture. (After draining beans, French dressing may be saved and used again if stored in Saran Wrap.) Serve on lettuce leaves. Makes 4 to 5 servings.

SPECIAL SALADS AND MOLDS

PARTY CHICKEN OR TURKEY SALAD
The Campbell Soup Company

1 5-ounce can Swanson's Boned Chicken or Turkey
1 teaspoon lemon juice
2 tablespoons mayonnaise
¼ teaspoon ground ginger
¼ cup chopped celery
1 tablespoon minced onion
4 pear halves, chilled and drained
Crisp salad greens
Grapes, chilled and seeded
Toasted almonds, slivered

Dice chicken; sprinkle with lemon juice. Blend mayonnaise and ginger; lightly mix with chicken, celery, and onion. Chill. To serve, arrange pear halves on greens. Fill each pear with chicken salad mixture; garnish with grapes and almonds. Makes 4 servings.

SEA AND GARDEN SALAD DINNER
Star-Kist Foods, Inc.

1 medium-large head of lettuce
4 hard-cooked eggs
3 tomatoes, peeled
4 thick slices bleu, American, or Swiss cheese
½ cucumber, sliced
10 radishes
1 large red or white onion, cut into rings
2 6½-ounce cans Star-Kist Chunk Style Tuna
Salad dressing

Tear lettuce into large chunks and place in salad bowl. Quarter eggs and tomatoes. Cut cheese into bite-size chunks. Add cucumber slices, radishes, and onion rings. Top with tuna. Toss with salad dressing. Makes 6 servings.

SALADE NICOISE
Green Giant Company

Salad greens
1 17-ounce can Green Giant Brand Peas with Onions
1 16-ounce can Green Giant Brand Kitchen-Sliced Green Beans
1 12-ounce can Green Giant Brand White Corn
1 19-ounce can Green Giant Brand Asparagus Spears
2 7-ounce cans solid white meat of tuna
6 hard-cooked eggs, sliced in quarters
24 anchovy fillets
2 large onions, thinly sliced
1½ cups ripe olives
18 slices salami
2 cups garlic-flavored French dressing

Arrange greens on large oval platter. Arrange vegetables separately, with strips of anchovy fillets and quarters of hard-cooked egg between each vegetable. Place tuna, removed from cans in one piece, toward center of platter. Surround tuna with salami slices, anchovy fillets, and any hard-cooked egg quarters remaining. Garnish with ripe olives. Spoon a little salad dressing over salad. Serve rest with it in a separate server. Excellent for buffet. (See illustration 21.)

CHICKEN-ALMOND MOUSSE
National Biscuit Company

2 cups chicken broth or bouillon
1 envelope unflavored gelatine
2 cups cooked diced chicken
1 cup blanched slivered almonds
1 small onion, chopped
¼ cup chopped green pepper

1 tablespoon chopped Dromedary Pimiento
½ teaspoon salt
¼ teaspoon pepper
1½ teaspoons curry powder, or to taste
26 Nabisco Vegetable Thins crushed, about 1 cup crumbs
1 cup commercial sour cream

Add gelatine to broth or bouillon, and heat until gelatine is dissolved. Cool. Combine remaining ingredients. When broth is thick enough to mound when dropped from a spoon, fold it into the chicken mixture. Turn into a greased 2-quart mold. Chill until firm. Unmold on platter; garnish with pimiento and parsley and surround with crackers. Makes 6 servings.

JELLIED TOMATO-OLIVE MOLD
The Seven-Up Company

1 envelope unflavored gelatine
½ 10½-ounce can undiluted bouillon or consommé
1 cup tomato juice

1 7-ounce bottle 7-Up
¼ teaspoon Worcestershire Sauce
1 cup stuffed olives, sliced

Dissolve gelatine in bouillon. Heat tomato juice to boiling and stir into gelatine mixture. Stir in 7-Up and Worcestershire Sauce. Chill until slightly thickened. Stir in olives. Pour into a 1-quart ring mold and chill until firm. Makes 6 servings.

VEAL-AND-VEGETABLE RING
National Biscuit Company

2 cans beef consommé	1 tablespoon lemon juice
1 consommé can water	3 cups cooked veal, cubed
2 envelopes unflavored gelatine	½ cup chopped scallions
	½ cup chopped celery
28 Triangle Thins	½ cup French dressing

Combine consommé, water, and gelatine. Heat until gelatine dissolves. Cool. Meanwhile, stand about 14 crackers around edge of ring mold. Crush other crackers and mix with remaining ingredients. When gelatine mixture is thick enough to mound when dropped from a spoon, fold it into veal mixture. Spoon into mold, being careful that crackers stand upright. Chill until firm. Unmold on platter and fill center of ring with a variety of crisp vegetables. Makes 6 servings.

FRUIT RELISH RING WITH SHRIMP SALAD
Standard Brands, Inc.

2 packages Royal Watermelon Gelatin	1½ pounds shrimp, cooked, shelled, deveined
2 cups boiling water	1 cup pistachio nuts
1 1-pound, 13-ounce can pear halves	French Mayonnaise
	Salad greens
1 cup pickled watermelon rind, well drained	

Dissolve gelatin in boiling water. Drain pear halves. Measure liquid and add enough cold water to make 2 cups;

add to gelatin. Refrigerate until slightly thickened. Then pour about ¼ inch of thickened gelatin into ring mold. Arrange pears in decorative design and refrigerate mold until gelatin is set. Dice watermelon rind and any remaining pears; fold into thickened gelatin and turn into mold. Refrigerate until set. Meanwhile, combine shrimp with celery, pistachio nuts (reserve a few for garnish), and enough French Mayonnaise to moisten. Chill. At serving time, unmold jellied ring onto large platter. Surround with greens and shrimp salad. Turn remaining dressing into small serving dish and set it in center of ring; top with reserved nuts. Makes 8 servings. (See illustration 23.)

French Mayonnaise: Combine 1 cup mayonnaise with ½ cup French dressing, 2 tablespoons chili sauce, 1 teaspoon grated onion, and ¼ teaspoon horseradish.

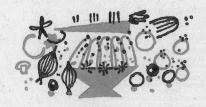

JEWEL SALAD
Best Foods, Division of
Corn Products Company

2 envelopes unflavored gelatine
½ cup water
½ cup light Karo Corn Syrup
¼ cup orange juice
1 teaspoon lemon juice

2 cups cranberry juice
⅛ teaspoon salt
½ cup sliced apples
½ cup drained orange sections
Salad greens

Soften gelatine in cold water. Place over boiling water and stir until dissolved. Remove from heat. Add corn syrup, orange juice, lemon juice, cranberry juice, and salt. Mix well. Chill until slightly thickened. Add sliced apple and orange sections. Turn into a 1-quart mold or 8 individual molds which have been lightly oiled with corn oil. Chill until firm. Unmold. Arrange on crisp salad greens. Serve with Pastel Cranberry Dressing (see page 201). Makes 8 to 12 servings.

HONEYDEW SURPRISE
The Dow Chemical Company

1 package lime gelatin
1 cup boiling water
1 cup chunk-style pineapple, drained
1 cup mandarin oranges
1 medium honeydew melon
Cottage cheese
Greens
French dressing

When dissolved gelatin is cold and somewhat thick, add pineapple and orange. Peel whole melon. Cut a slice from one end and remove seeds. Fill center with thick fruit gelatin. Wrap in Saran Wrap and refrigerate until gelatin is firm.

When ready to serve, slice; place each slice on bed of greens; spoon cottage cheese around edge of melon. Serve with French dressing.

CALCUTTA SALAD
Knox Gelatine, Inc.

Chutney Molds:

2 envelopes Knox Unflavored Gelatine
2 cups cold water
1 cup sugar
1 teaspoon salt
1 cup lemon juice
2 cups chutney

Soften gelatine in cold water. Place over moderate heat; stir until gelatine is dissolved. Stir in sugar, salt, and lemon juice. Chill to consistency of unbeaten egg white. Mix in chutney. Turn into 12 individual molds. Chill until firm. Makes 12 servings.

Salad:

Lettuce
Canned pineapple slice
Cottage cheese
Cream cheese
Milk
Cantaloupe wedges
Honeydew wedges
Strawberries
Mint leaves

For each salad, make a nest of lettuce leaves; fill with shredded lettuce. Place pineapple slice in center; mound with cottage cheese; top with Chutney Mold. Mix cream cheese with milk to spreading consistency. Force through pastry tube to decorate sides of mold. Alternate cantaloupe and honeydew wedges around mold. Cut 2 strawberries in half and place halves on melon wedges at bottom of cream cheese strips. Cut 1 strawberry in quarters lengthwise almost to bottom. Insert strip of mint and place on top of mold.

FRUITS OF WINTER SALAD
The Seven-Up Company

2 envelopes unflavored gelatine
¼ cup sugar
1 cup very hot water
1 cup orange juice
1 7-ounce bottle 7-Up
2 medium bananas, sliced
2 large eating oranges, peeled and cut up
1 medium red apple, cut up
1 cup seeded and halved grapes
¼ cup chopped walnut kernels

Mix gelatine with sugar and stir in very hot water. Cool slightly. Stir in orange juice and 7-Up. Add fruits and nuts; refrigerate until firm. For a layered salad, pour some of the mixture over grapes in mold. Let set in refrigerator and repeat with each layer of fruit and nuts. Makes 8 servings. (See illustration 25.)

WAIKIKI WHIP
Star-Kist Foods, Inc.

1 package lime jello
1 cup boiling water
1 20-ounce can pineapple tidbits, drained
1 cup sour cream
2 teaspoons white vinegar

Juice of ½ lemon
¼ teaspoon salt
2 6½-ounce cans Star-Kist Chunk Style Tuna
1 fresh lime, sliced
1 whole fresh pineapple

Dissolve lime jello in boiling water. Chill until syrupy. Whip jello into froth; fold in remaining ingredients. Serve in hollowed-out pineapple halves. Decorate with fresh lime slices. Makes 4 to 6 servings. (See illustration 38.)

RUBY RING MOLD
Knox Gelatine, Inc.

For Fresh Cranberries:

2 cups fresh cranberries
1 cup sugar, plus 2 tablespoons
1½ cups water

1 envelope Knox Unflavored Gelatine
¼ teaspoon salt

Combine cranberries, 1 cup of the sugar, and water in saucepan; bring to a boil. Reduce heat and simmer 10 minutes. Mix together remaining 2 tablespoons sugar, gelatine, and salt. Add to hot cranberry mixture; stir until gelatine is dissolved. Turn into 5-cup ring mold. Chill until firm.

For Canned Whole Cranberries:

2 envelopes Knox Unflavored Gelatine
1 cup cranberry juice cocktail or water

2 1-pound cans whole cranberry sauce
2 tablespoons lemon juice

Sprinkle gelatine on cranberry juice cocktail in saucepan to soften. Place over low heat, stirring constantly, until gelatine is dissolved. Stir into whole cranberry sauce. Add lemon juice. Turn into a 5-cup ring mold. Chill until firm.

CRANBERRY CROWN SALAD
Ocean Spray Cranberries, Inc.

Cranberry Layer:

1 envelope unflavored gelatine
½ cup sugar
Dash of cloves and cinnamon

1 cup water
2 cups Ocean Spray Fresh
  Cranberries, ground

Blend gelatine, sugar, and spices in saucepan; stir in water. Heat, stirring constantly, until gelatine dissolves. Add cranberries. Turn into 1½-quart mold. Chill until firm.

Second Layer:

1 envelope unflavored gelatine
½ cup cold water
½ cup mayonnaise
½ cup evaporated milk or
  top milk
1½ cups cooked turkey or
  chicken, chopped

1 5¼-ounce can water
  chestnuts, drained and
  thinly sliced
½ cup minced celery
½ teaspoon salt
¼ teaspoon poultry seasoning

Soften gelatine in cold water; heat slowly until gelatine is dissolved. Combine mayonnaise and milk; blend in dissolved gelatine. Stir in turkey or chicken, water chestnuts, celery, salt, and poultry seasoning. Spoon over firm cranberry layer. Chill thoroughly. Turn onto bed of crisp greens. Makes 6 servings. (See illustration 22.)

Note: For parties, double the quantity and mold in a fancy 3-quart mold for a festive salad.

SNOW-COVERED RASPBERRY SALAD
Stokely-Van Camp, Inc.

1 3-ounce package raspberry
gelatin
1 package Stokely-Van
Camp's Finest Frozen Red
Raspberries

1 cup hot water
½ cup whipping cream
5 large marshmallows
1 3-ounce package Philadel-
phia cream cheese

Dissolve gelatin in hot water. Add frozen red raspberries and juice. Chill until firm. Mix whipping cream, marshmallows, and cream cheese together until stiff. Spread over gelatin mixture and chill. Makes 6 servings.

DRESSINGS

BASIC FRENCH DRESSING
Best Foods, Division of
Corn Products Company

1 cup Mazola Corn Oil
½ to 1 cup vinegar
1 to 3 tablespoons sugar
1½ teaspoons salt

½ teaspoon paprika
½ teaspoon dry mustard
1 clove garlic, peeled and
sliced

Measure all ingredients into a bottle or jar. (Lemon juice may be used to replace all or part of the vinegar.) Cover tightly and shake well. Chill several hours, then remove garlic. Shake before serving. Makes 1⅓ to 1½ cups.

Variations

ZESTY FRENCH DRESSING. To the Basic French Dressing add 2 tablespoons catsup, 1 teaspoon Worcestershire Sauce, and 1 tablespoon lemon juice.

MYSTERY FRENCH DRESSING. Combine ingredients for Zesty French Dressing in a bowl. Add 1 unbeaten egg white. Beat with rotary beater until well blended. Store in refrigerator in container covered with Saran Wrap. Dressing thickens slightly on standing and keeps well. Mix thoroughly before serving. Makes about 1½ cups.

SPICY FRENCH DRESSING. Prepare spiced vinegar and use in preparation of basic recipe. To make spiced vinegar, heat and add 1 tablespoon mixed pickling spices. Tie spices in cheesecloth, if desired. Let spices stand until vinegar is cool. Strain or remove bag of spices.

FLORENTINE DRESSING. To the Basic Dressing add 4 table-spoons finely chopped raw spinach and ½ teaspoon onion juice.

CHEESE DRESSING. To the Basic Dressing add ¼ cup crumbled Roquefort or blue cheese.

FRUIT FRENCH DRESSING
Best Foods, Division of
Corn Products Company

¼ cup lemon juice
¼ cup maraschino cherry, canned sweet cherry, or plum juice

½ cup Mazola Corn Oil
1 to 2 tablespoons sugar
½ teaspoon salt
½ teaspoon paprika

Measure all ingredients into a bottle or jar. Cover tightly and shake well. Chill several hours. Shake thoroughly before serving. Makes 1 cup.

Variation
FRUIT CREAM DRESSING. Gradually fold ½ cup Fruit French Dressing into ½ cup heavy cream, whipped.

AVOCADO DRESSING
The Dow Chemical Company

1 cup whipping cream,
 whipped
⅓ cup sifted confectioners'
 sugar

⅔ cup mashed avocado
2 teaspoons grated orange
 rind
2 tablespoons lemon juice

Blend ingredients together. Freeze in ice cube tray. When frozen, wrap each cube in Saran Wrap and place in freezer bag. Before serving, defrost and serve on fruit salads. This recipe makes about 2⅔ cups dressing or 8 servings.

LOUIE SALAD DRESSING
Hunt Foods, Inc.

¾ cup Snider's Seafood
 Cocktail Sauce
1 cup mayonnaise

½ cup commercial sour
 cream

Blend above ingredients well; chill. Serve on crab, shrimp, lobster, or tuna salad.

BLUE CHEESE SALAD DRESSING
Paul Masson Vineyards

⅛ pound Wisconsin blue
 cheese
¼ cup Paul Masson Chablis
¾ cup sour cream

½ teaspoon salt
¼ teaspoon powdered cara-
 way
Dash of cayenne

Mix blue cheese with Chablis until smooth and creamy. Fold mixture into sour cream and season with remaining ingredients. Serve on head lettuce.

LIEDERKRANZ DRESSING
The Borden Company

2 3-ounce packages Bor- ¼ teaspoon celery seeds
den's Cream Cheese 4 tablespoons Madiera
1 4-ounce package Borden's
Liederkranz Cheese

Let cream cheese soften at room temperature. Beat until smooth and creamy. Stir in softened Liederkranz, celery seeds, and wine; blend well. Chill and serve over lettuce leaves or other salad greens. Makes 1½ cups.

PASTEL CRANBERRY DRESSING
Best Foods, Division of
Corn Products Company

¼ cup lemon juice ½ cup Mazola Corn Oil
1 3-ounce package cream 3 tablespoons sugar
cheese   ½ teaspoon salt
¼ cup cranberry juice ½ teaspoon paprika

Gradually beat lemon juice into cream cheese, mixing well. Add cranberry juice, corn oil, and seasonings, and beat with rotary beater until smooth and well blended. Chill thoroughly before serving. Makes about 1 cup. Serve with Jewel Salad (see page 193).

HONEY-SPICE DRESSING
McCormick & Co., Inc.

Mix together ½ cup French dressing, 1 tablespoon honey, ½ teaspoon McCormick Cinnamon, ¼ teaspoon McCormick Cloves, and ⅛ teaspoon McCormick Ginger; blend well. Excellent on fruit salads.

BREADS

There is a very special sense of accomplishment associated with the baking of bread. The feeling is perhaps a subconscious one, linked with the traditions of the past, with the role of the woman as "loaf-giver." And there is, too, a very special reward connected with baking—as the recipes in this section prove: the entrancing smell that fills the kitchen, the superb taste and texture of a homemade loaf. You are missing a great deal if you forego these pleasures —and so are your admiring family and friends!

MUFFINS

Best Foods, Division of
Corn Products Company

2 cups sifted flour
3 teaspoons baking powder
1 teaspoon salt
2 tablespoons sugar

1 egg, well beaten
1¼ cups milk
⅓ cup Mazola Corn Oil

Mix and sift dry ingredients. Make a well and add remaining ingredients all at once; stir only enough to dampen flour. Batter will be lumpy. Fill greased muffin pans ⅔ full. Bake in 400° oven 25 to 30 minutes. Makes 12 muffins.

Variations

CHEESE MUFFINS. Add 1 cup grated cheese to mixed and sifted ingredients. If desired, sprinkle tops of muffins with paprika before baking.

NUT MUFFINS. Add ½ cup coarsely chopped walnuts to mixed and sifted dry ingredients.

PEANUT BUTTER MUFFINS. Cut ½ cup peanut butter into mixed and sifted dry ingredients.

BLUEBERRY MUFFINS. Increase sugar to ⅓ cup. Add 1 cup fresh or drained canned blueberries to mixed and sifted dry ingredients.

SUGARED APPLE MUFFINS. Add 1 cup chopped apples to mixed and sifted dry ingredients. Combine ½ teaspoon cinnamon with 2 tablespoons sugar. Sprinkle over tops of muffins before baking.

JAM MUFFINS. Fill muffin cups ½ full. Place 1 teaspoon of jam or jelly in the center of the batter. Add more batter to fill cup ⅔ full.

QUICK CHERRY MUFFINS
National Red Cherry Institute

1 can (1 pound) red sour pitted cherries (water pack)	1 recipe plain muffins ½ teaspoon lemon rind 2 tablespoons sugar

Drain cherries; pat dry on absorbent paper. Prepare muffin recipe. Fold in well-drained cherries. Fill greased muffin pans ⅔ full. Mix together lemon rind and sugar. Sprinkle about ¾ teaspoon over each muffin. Bake according to muffin recipe directions.

MAYONNAISE MUFFINS
Best Foods, Division of
Corn Products Company

2 cups all-purpose flour
3 teaspoons baking powder
½ teaspoon salt
⅓ cup Hellmann's or Best
  Foods Real Mayonnaise

1 cup milk
1 teaspoon Best Foods Mustard-with-Horseradish

Sift all-purpose flour with baking powder and salt. Add mayonnaise and mustard-with-horseradish to milk and stir together. Add to flour. Mix only until flour is moistened —mixture will be slightly lumpy. Fill lightly greased muffin cups ⅔ full. Place tiny dot of mayonnaise on top of each muffin. Bake in 400° oven 15 to 20 minutes. Makes 10 to 12 2½-inch muffins.

HOT BREAD MIX
The Procter & Gamble Company

6 cups sifted enriched flour
3 tablespoons double-action
  baking powder

1 tablespoon salt
1 cup Crisco

Mix dry ingredients in large mixing bowl or on a large square of waxed or wrapping paper. Cut shortening into flour with 2 knives or pastry blender until mixture looks like coarse meal. Store mix in a covered container such as an empty 3-pound Crisco can. (No refrigeration needed.) For a richer mix use 1½ cups shortening.

QUICK BISCUITS
The Procter & Gamble Company

¾ cup milk

2½ cups Hot Bread Mix
(see above)

Add milk to Hot Bread Mix. Blend well. Place dough on floured board or pastry cloth. Knead lightly several times. Roll dough about ½-inch thick. Cut with a floured biscuit cutter. Bake on ungreased baking sheet in 425° oven 12 to 15 minutes. Makes 12 to 16 medium biscuits.

Variations

CHEESE BISCUITS. Add ⅓ cup shredded sharp cheese to dry ingredients. Stir. Add milk and mix enough to hold dough together.

RAISIN BISCUITS. Stir ½ cup raisins into Hot Bread Mix before adding milk.

HAM BISCUITS. Stir ½ cup finely diced cooked ham into Hot Bread Mix before adding milk.

BISCUIT FINGERS
Best Foods, Division of
Corn Products Company

2 cups sifted flour	¼ cup Mazola Margarine
3 teaspoons baking powder	½ cup milk
½ teaspoon salt	¼ cup water

Sift flour, baking powder, and salt into a bowl. Cut in margarine until coarse crumbs are formed. Add milk and water. Mix with fork just until dough is formed. Turn out onto floured cloth or board and knead gently 15 times.

Roll into an 8-inch square. Cut into fingers 1 x 4-inches each. Place on ungreased cooky sheet. Bake in 450° oven 15 to 20 minutes. Makes 16 biscuits.

BUTTERMILK BREAD
The Quaker Oats Co.

1½ cups Quaker or Aunt Jemima Enriched White Corn Meal
3 tablespoons enriched flour
1 teaspoon salt

1 teaspoon soda
2 cups buttermilk
1 egg
2 tablespoons drippings or butter

Sift together dry ingredients into bowl. Stir in buttermilk and egg. Melt drippings in skillet or baking pan and add to the batter. Pour batter into very hot skillet or baking pan. Bake in 450° oven 20 to 25 minutes. Cut in wedges or squares and serve hot. Makes 9 servings.

Variation

BUTTERMILK STICKS OR MUFFINS. Follow recipe for Buttermilk Bread. Pour batter into hot greased corn stick or muffin pans, and bake in a 450° oven 15 to 20 minutes.

GOLDEN CORN BREAD
The Quaker Oats Co.

1 cup Quaker or Aunt Jemima Enriched Yellow Corn Meal
1 cup sifted enriched flour
¼ cup sugar (optional)

½ teaspoon salt
4 teaspoons baking powder
1 egg
1 cup milk
¼ cup shortening, soft

Sift together dry ingredients into bowl. Add egg, milk, and shortening. Beat with rotary beater until smooth, about

1 minute. Do not overbeat. Bake in greased 8-inch square pan in a 425° oven 20 to 25 minutes. Cut in squares and serve warm with butter, or covered with creamed chicken, fish, or meat. Makes 9 servings.

Variation

CORN STICKS OR MUFFINS. Follow recipe for Golden Corn Bread. Pour corn bread batter into hot greased corn stick or muffin pans, and bake in a 425° oven 15 to 20 minutes.

CORN SKILLET BREAD
Thomas J. Lipton, Inc.

1½ cups all-purpose flour
4 teaspoons baking powder
2 tablespoons sugar
2½ teaspoons salt
2 teaspoons sage
1 teaspoon thyme
1½ cups yellow corn meal

1½ cups chopped celery
1 package Lipton Dehydrated Onion Soup
¼ cup chopped pimiento
3 eggs, beaten
1½ cups milk
⅓ cup salad oil

Sift flour, baking powder, sugar, and salt into bowl. Add sage, thyme, corn meal, celery, soup mix, and pimiento. Stir to blend. Combine eggs, milk, and salad oil; add and stir only to blend. Thoroughly oil 10- or 11-inch skillet with vegetable oil and pour in mixture. Bake in 400° oven 35 to 40 minutes. Serve hot with butter, or as a main dish with creamed meat or gravy.

CONTINENTAL PANCAKES
Poultry and Egg National Board

1 tablespoon fat
3 eggs
½ teaspoon salt
1 tablespoon sugar
⅓ cup sifted all-purpose flour

½ cup milk
Butter or margarine
Applesauce, or cooked sweetened berries
Confectioners' sugar

Place fat in deep skillet (10- to 12-inch diameter); place skillet in oven while ingredients are being mixed and oven is brought to 450°. Beat eggs and salt until light. Blend sugar and flour, add to egg mixture, and beat until batter is smooth. Add milk and beat thoroughly. Remove skillet from oven, and spread melted fat to grease bottom surface. Pour in all the batter. Return to oven and bake 15 minutes, or until pancake is puffy, well risen, and brown. Surface should be very irregular and pancake well risen at the sides. Remove from oven. Dot with butter or margarine and fruit. Roll or fold from opposite sides to center making 3 layers. Turn out on warm platter. Sprinkle with confectioners' sugar. Serve promptly. Makes 1 or 2 servings.

Note: A layer of thinly sliced apples or 3 slices of diced, cooked bacon may be placed over the batter just before putting it in the oven. Reduce salt to ¼ teaspoon. If desired, omit addition of butter, fruit, etc.

ORANGE PANCAKES AND SAUCE
Pet Milk Company

Pancakes:

1 egg
1 cup Pet Evaporated Milk

¼ cup frozen orange juice
   concentrate, thawed
1 recipe pancake batter

Mix egg, evaporated milk, and orange juice concentrate in a 1½-quart bowl. Add pancake batter all at once. Stir well, but do not overmix. Small lumps in batter disappear during baking. Using ¼ cup for each pancake, pour onto hot, lightly greased griddle or frying pan. Bake until bubbles appear on top and edges are cooked. Turn and bake until other side is brown. Makes about 12 pancakes.

Sauce:

¼ cup frozen orange juice
   concentrate, thawed
¼ cup butter or margarine

¼ cup Pet Evaporated Milk
½ cup sugar

Mix orange juice concentrate, butter or margarine, evaporated milk, and sugar in a 2-quart saucepan. Stir and heat until steaming hot, but do not boil. Serve warm sauce with pancakes. Makes 1 cup sauce.

GINGERBREAD WAFFLES
Penick & Ford, Ltd.

2 cups sifted all-purpose flour	1 egg, separated
1½ teaspoons baking soda	1 cup Brer Rabbit Molasses
1½ teaspoons ginger	½ cup sour milk or butter-milk
½ teaspoon cinnamon	⅓ cup butter, melted
½ teaspoon salt	

Sift together flour, baking soda, ginger, cinnamon, and salt. Beat egg yolk; add molasses, milk, and butter. Add to flour mixture; beat smooth. Beat egg white stiff; fold in. Bake according to manufacturer's directions for operating waffle iron. Serve hot. Makes 4 servings.

APRICOT-ALMOND COFFEE CAKE
California Packing Corporation

¾ cup Del Monte Dried Apricots	1½ cups sifted all-purpose flour
¼ cup shortening	2 teaspoons baking powder
¾ cup sugar	¾ teaspoon salt
1 egg	½ teaspoon cinnamon
	½ cup milk

Add 1 cup water to the dried apricots and boil slowly 15 minutes. Cool; drain and chop. Cream shortening and sugar together thoroughly. Add egg and beat well. Sift flour with baking powder, salt, and cinnamon. Add sifted dry ingredients alternately with milk to creamed mixture. Stir in chopped apricots. Turn into greased 9-inch square pan and spread topping over batter. Bake in 350° oven about 45 minutes. Serve warm. Makes 9 3-inch squares.

Topping:

½ cup brown sugar, packed
⅓ cup flour
¼ cup butter or margarine

⅓ cup chopped unblanched almonds

Blend brown sugar with flour, butter or margarine, and chopped almonds.

COFFEE DATE NUT LOAF
Pan American Coffee Bureau

2 cups sifted all-purpose flour
4 teaspoons double-action baking powder
1 teaspoon salt
⅔ cup sugar
⅓ cup broken walnut meats

¾ cup finely cut pitted dates
1 cup strong coffee
⅛ teaspoon baking soda
1 egg, well beaten
2 tablespoons shortening, melted

Mix and sift flour, baking powder, salt, and sugar. Stir in walnut meats and dates. Combine coffee, baking soda, egg, and shortening. Add all at once to dry ingredients. Stir only enough to dampen dry ingredients. Turn into greased loaf pan. Let stand 20 minutes. Bake in 375° oven 1 hour.

PRUNE BRAN MUFFINS
California Packing Corporation

1 cup cooked Del Monte
Prunes
2 eggs
1 cup milk
2 tablespoons light mo-
lasses
1½ cups all-bran cereal
⅓ cup melted shortening
or oil

1½ cups sifted all-purpose
flour
1 tablespoon baking powder
½ teaspoon soda
½ teaspoon salt
¼ cup sugar
Additional cooked and pitted
Del Monte Prunes for tops

Cut cooked prunes from pits into small pieces. Beat eggs lightly; stir in milk, molasses, bran, and melted shortening. Let stand 5 minutes, add prunes. Sift together flour, baking powder, soda, salt, and sugar. Stir lightly into bran mixture. Fill greased muffin pans ⅔ full. Top each with a half prune. Bake in 400° oven about 20 minutes. Makes 18 2½-inch muffins.

PINEAPPLE-NUT BREAD
Dole Corporation

2 cups sifted all-purpose
flour
½ cup sugar
1 teaspoon baking powder
½ teaspoon salt
1 cup raisins
½ cup coarsely chopped
walnuts

1 egg, beaten
1 teaspoon vanilla
2 tablespoons shortening,
melted
1 teaspoon soda
1 No. 1 flat can Dole
Crushed Pineapple, not
drained

Sift flour, sugar, baking powder, and salt into bowl. Add raisins and nuts. Combine egg, vanilla, and shortening; add to mixture. Dissolve soda in pineapple, and add. Stir just until blended. Pour into greased 8 x 4 x 4-inch loaf pan, and bake at 350° about 1 hour, or until done. Cool on rack. Serve buttered or spread with cream cheese.

CRANBERRY MUFFINS
Ocean Spray Cranberries, Inc.

2 cups Ocean Spray Fresh Cranberries, finely ground
1 cup sugar
2 cups sifted flour
3 teaspoons baking powder
½ teaspoon anise or ground ginger
½ teaspoon salt
¼ cup shortening, soft
1 egg
1 cup milk

Combine cranberries with sugar; let stand. Sift together dry ingredients; mix with cranberries. Stir in shortening, egg, and milk. Mix with fork just to moisten. Fill greased muffin tins ⅔ full. Bake in 400° oven 20 to 25 minutes.

FRUIT-NUT TEA BREAD
General Foods Corporation

3 cups sifted all-purpose flour
3 teaspoons double-action Calumet Baking Powder
1 teaspoon salt
1 cup granulated sugar
⅔ cup Baker's Angel Flake Coconut, toasted
⅔ cup chopped walnuts
1 tablespoon grated orange rind
1 egg
⅓ cup milk
1½ cups (3 to 4) mashed ripe bananas

Measure sifted flour; add baking powder, salt, and sugar, and sift together. Stir in toasted coconut, nuts, and grated orange rind. Beat egg until foamy; mix with milk and add mashed banana. Stir liquids into dry mixture and mix thoroughly, but do not beat. Pour into a greased 9 x 5 x 3-inch loaf pan. Bake in 350° oven 1 hour and 10 minutes. Cool. Cut in thin slices to serve. Toast if desired. Fruit-Nut Tea Bread improves in flavor if allowed to ripen for 2 or 3 days before serving.

APPLESAUCE-RAISIN BREAD
The Quaker Oats Co.

1½ cups sifted enriched
   flour
1 teaspoon baking powder
1 teaspoon soda
1½ teaspoons salt
1 teaspoon cinnamon
½ teaspoon nutmeg
⅔ cup brown sugar
2 eggs

1 cup thick, sweetened
   applesauce
1½ cups Quaker or
   Mother's Oats (quick or
   old-fashioned, uncooked)
1 cup raisins
½ cup chopped nutmeats
⅓ cup melted shortening

Heat oven to 350°. Sift together flour, baking powder, soda, salt, and spices. Add brown sugar, eggs, and applesauce. Beat until well blended. Stir in oats, raisins, nutmeats, and shortening. Pour batter into a greased, waxed, paper-lined 1-pound loaf pan. Bake in preheated 350° oven about 1 hour. Remove from pan; cool. Store 1 day before slicing. Makes 1 loaf.

BANANA BREAD
Kellogg Company

1½ cups sifted flour
2 teaspoons baking powder
½ teaspoon baking soda
½ teaspoon salt
¼ cup shortening, soft
½ cup sugar
1 egg

1 teaspoon vanilla flavoring
1½ cups mashed ripe ba-
   nanas
2 cups Kellogg's® Special
   K®
¼ cup chopped nutmeats

Sift together flour, baking powder, soda, and salt. Blend shortening and sugar. Add egg and vanilla; beat well. Stir in bananas and cereal. Add sifted dry ingredients together with nutmeats, stirring only until combined. Spread in greased 9½ x 5¼-inch loaf pan. Bake in 350° oven about

40 minutes. Cool thoroughly before slicing. Makes 1 loaf. (See illustration 27.)

YEAST BREADS

SWEET DOUGH
Kretschmer Wheat Germ Corp.

2 packages dry yeast
¼ cup warm, not hot, water
1 cup scalded milk
½ cup sugar
2 teaspoons salt
¼ cup shortening

4 cups (about) sifted enriched white flour
¾ cup Kretschmer Wheat Germ
2 eggs, beaten

Soften yeast in water. Combine milk, sugar, salt, and shortening. Cool to lukewarm. Mix flour and wheat germ and add 1 cup to milk mixture; mix well. Add softened yeast and eggs. Beat well. Add remaining flour and wheat germ to make a soft dough. Turn out on floured surface and knead until smooth and satiny, about 5 minutes. Place in greased bowl; turn dough over to grease surface. Cover with tea towel and let rise in warm place (80°-85°) until doubled, about 1½ hours. Punch down. Let dough rest 10 minutes. Shape into tea rings, rolls, or coffee cakes. Place on lightly greased cooky sheet or baking pans. Let rise until double, about 1 hour. Bake at 350°—30 minutes for coffee cakes, 25 minutes for pan rolls, or 20 minutes for individual rolls. Bake up all the dough and freeze the unused breads, covered with Saran Wrap. Makes 3 coffee cakes or about 3½ dozen rolls.

BATTERWAY BREAD
Red Star Yeast & Products Co.

2¾ cups warm water (110°-115°)
2 packages Red Star Special Active Dry Yeast
6½ cups sifted all-purpose flour

3 tablespoons sugar
1 tablespoon salt
2 tablespoons shortening, soft

Pour warm water into a large mixing bowl, and add yeast. Let stand a few minutes, then stir to dissolve. Add about half the flour, the sugar, salt, and shortening. Beat on medium speed in mixer or by hand until smooth, about 2 minutes. Stop mixer. Add the rest of the flour and stir in by hand until flour disappears, about 1 to 1½ minutes. (Beating in this recipe takes the place of kneading.) Scrape down batter from sides of bowl. Cover bowl with Saran Wrap and let rise in warm place until doubled, about 30 minutes. Meanwhile, grease 2 4½ x 8½ x 2¾-inch bread loaf pans. Stir down batter by beating hard for ½ minute. Put into the pans, spreading evenly. Batter will fill pans ½ full. Let rise in warm place until edges of batter reach tops of pans, 20 to 30 minutes. Brush with melted fat, if desired. Bake 40 to 50 minutes, or until well browned on sides and tops, in preheated 375° oven. Remove from pans and cool on rack.

Note: If desired, use 2 cups cooled, scalded milk with the first half of the flour. Dissolve the yeast in only ¾ cup warm water. For a warm rising place, put bowl or pan on rack over a bowl ½ full of hot water. Keep water hot.

BATTERWAY ROLLS
Red Star Yeast & Products Co.

1½ cups warm water (110°-115°)
2 packages Red Star Special Active Dry Yeast
4 cups sifted all-purpose flour

¼ cup sugar
1½ teaspoons salt
⅓ cup shortening, soft
1 egg at room temperature

Follow basic recipe for Batterway Bread (see above). Fill 1½ dozen large greased muffin cups ½ full. Let rise, and bake in preheated 425° oven 10 to 15 minutes.

BATTERWAY RYE BREAD AND ROLLS
Red Star Yeast & Products Co.

2½ cups warm water (110°-115°)
2 packages Red Star Special Active Dry Yeast
4 tablespoons brown sugar, packed
1 tablespoon salt

2 cups sifted rye flour
5 cups sifted all-purpose flour
4 tablespoons shortening, soft
1 to 2 tablespoons caraway seed

Follow recipe for Batterway Bread (see above). Fill 2 4½ x 8½ x 2¾-inch or 2 9 x 5 x 3-inch greased bread loaf pans, or 24 large greased muffin cups ½ full. Let rise. Make 3 slashes on tops of loaves ½-inch deep or 1 slash on top of each roll *just* before baking. Bake bread 40 to 50 minutes in preheated 375° oven; bake rolls 15 to 20 minutes in 400° oven.

BATTERWAY WHOLE WHEAT BREAD AND ROLLS
Red Star Yeast & Products Co.

2½ cups warm water (110°-115°)

2 packages Red Star Special Active Dry Yeast

2 cups unsifted whole wheat flour

4 cups sifted all-purpose flour

4 tablespoons honey or brown sugar

4 teaspoons salt

¼ cup shortening, soft

Follow recipe for Batterway Bread (see page 215). Fill 2 4½ x 8½ x 2¾-inch or 2 9 x 5 x 3-inch greased bread loaf pans, or 24 large greased muffin cups ½ full. Let rise. Bake bread 40 to 50 minutes in preheated 375° oven; bake rolls 15 to 20 minutes in 400° oven.

Note: For richer rolls or bread, use 2 cups warm water and 2 eggs. Add eggs after the yeast dissolves.

BATTERWAY PRUNE 'N' SPICE BREAD
Red Star Yeast & Products Co.

¾ cup warm water (110°-115°)

1 package Red Star Special Active Dry Yeast

3 cups sifted all-purpose flour

1 tablespoon sugar

1½ teaspoons salt

2 tablespoons shortening, soft

¼ teaspoon cinnamon

¼ teaspoon nutmeg or all-spice

⅛ teaspoon cloves, powdered

½ cup sweetened drained cooked prunes

1 egg at room temperature

Pour warm water into a mixing bowl, and add the yeast. Let stand a few minutes, then stir to dissolve. Blend in the egg. Blend the dry ingredients and the shortening. Add ⅔ of mixture and prunes to yeast mixture. Follow procedure outlined in Batterway Bread (see page 215) for mixing. Fill a greased 4½ x 8½ x 2¾-inch or 9 x 5 x 3-inch bread loaf pan. Tap pan on table to settle the batter. Let rise. Bake 40 to 50 minutes in preheated 375° oven.

HERB-CHEESE BREAD
Red Star Yeast & Products Co.

1 cup warm water (110°-115°)

1 package Red Star Special Active Dry Yeast

1 egg at room temperature

3 cups sifted all-purpose flour

2 tablespoons sugar

1 teaspoon salt

3 tablespoons shortening, soft

½ teaspoon basil

½ teaspoon oregano

Pour warm water into a mixing bowl, and add the yeast. Let stand a few minutes, then stir to dissolve. Blend in the egg. Blend the dry ingredients and the shortening. Add ½ of mixture to yeast mixture. Follow procedure outlined in Batterway Bread (see page 215) for mixing. Spoon into a 9 x 13 x 2-inch or 11 x 7 x 1½-inch greased oblong pan, or 2 8- or 9-inch greased square pans. Spread Topping evenly over the tops of the batter. Grease fingers and make dents with fingers in the Topping, pressing almost to the bottom of the pans. Tap the pans on the table. Let batter rise in warm place 20 to 30 minutes until doubled. Bake 30 to 35 minutes in preheated 375° oven.

Topping:

½ pound cheese, shredded

¼ cup minced onion

½ teaspoon oregano

½ teaspoon basil

Mix together and spread evenly over the tops of the batter.

BATTERWAY HOT CROSS BUNS
Red Star Yeast & Products Co.

1¼ cups warm water (110°-115°)
2 packages Red Star Special Active Dry Yeast
3½ cups sifted all-purpose flour
6 tablespoons sugar

½ teaspoon cinnamon
Rind of 1 lemon, shredded
1 teaspoon salt
¼ cup shortening, soft
1 egg
½ cup currants or seedless raisins

Follow procedure outlined in Batterway Bread (see page 215), adding currants after the first mixing. Fill 18 large, 24 medium, or 40 small greased muffin cups. Let rise. Bake 10 to 15 minutes in preheated 425° oven. Remove from oven 1 minute before end of baking time; brush with milk and sprinkle with sugar. Return to oven until glaze sets. Remove rolls to racks and make cross with thick confectioners' sugar icing.

Icing:

1 cup confectioners' sugar
¼ teaspoon salt

1 or 2 tablespoons hot milk or water

Blend and make cross on top of rolls.

BATTERWAY DROP DOUGHNUTS
Red Star Yeast & Products Co.

2 packages Red Star Special Active Dry Yeast
½ cup warm water (110°-115°)
¾ cup milk, scalded
¼ cup sugar
1 teaspoon salt

½ teaspoon mace
½ teaspoon nutmeg
3½ cups sifted all-purpose flour
2 eggs at room temperature
⅓ cup shortening, soft

Add the yeast to the warm water and let stand. Pour scalded milk over sugar, salt, and spices in a large bowl. Stir until dissolved and slightly cooled. Add half the sifted flour and beat until smooth. Beat in the eggs and the yeast mixture. Blend in the shortening with the remaining flour, beating until smooth. Scrape down batter from sides of bowl. Cover and let rise in warm place until doubled, about 30 minutes.

Stir down and let rest while fat is heating to 350° to 375°. Test to see if 1-inch cube of bread browns in 60 seconds. Drop batter from teaspoon into hot fat. Turn when edges show color, frying until golden brown, about 1½ minutes on each side.

Note: When cooking doughnuts, have fat 1½ to 2-inches deep in heavy pan for shallow fat frying. Keep temperature between 350° and 375°. Too hot fat forms crust before doughnuts are cooked through; too cool fat means doughnuts will soak up fat. Turn doughnuts when edges show golden brown color. Drain doughnuts on absorbent paper near a warm place. Sugar coat while still warm.

WALNUT CINNAMON ROLL BREAD
Diamond Walnut Growers, Inc.

1 cup buttermilk	1 package dry or com-pressed yeast
⅓ cup sugar	
1½ teaspoons salt	¼ cup warm water
¼ cup shortening, butter, or margarine	4 cups sifted all-purpose flour
	2 eggs

Heat buttermilk to lukewarm; pour into a large mixing bowl. Add sugar, salt, and shortening, and stir until sugar is dissolved. Sprinkle yeast into warm water and stir until dissolved; stir into buttermilk mixture. Gradually add 2 cups of the flour to the mixture and beat until smooth. Add eggs, one at a time, and beat well. Then beat in remaining flour. Cover with a cloth, and let set in a warm place for 1 hour.

Walnut-Honey Filling:

½ cup honey
¼ cup light brown sugar
¾ cup finely chopped Diamond Walnuts

2 teaspoons grated orange peel
1 teaspoon cinnamon
1 cup golden or dark raisins
1 tablespoon melted butter

Combine honey, brown sugar, chopped walnuts, orange peel, cinnamon, and raisins. Divide dough in half and roll out to make a 10-inch square; brush with butter; spread with half of the filling. Roll up, jelly-roll fashion, and cut into 1-inch slices; arrange, cut side down, in a greased 10-inch tube pan. Prepare remaining dough in the same manner and arrange slices overlapping on top of the first slices. Let rise until doubled in size, about 1½ to 2 hours. Bake at 350° 1 hour, or until golden brown. If top browns too quickly, cover very loosely with sheet of foil.

OATMEAL REFRIGERATOR ROLLS
The Quaker Oats Co.

2 packages or 2 cakes compressed or dry yeast
½ cup lukewarm water
1½ cups scalded milk
½ cup shortening
½ cup brown sugar
2 teaspoons salt

5 to 5½ cups sifted enriched flour
2 eggs, beaten
1½ cups Quaker or Mother's Oats (quick or old-fashioned, uncooked)

Soften yeast in lukewarm water. Pour scalded milk over shortening, sugar, and salt; stir occasionally until shortening melts. Cool to lukewarm. Stir in 1 cup of flour and the eggs; add softened yeast. Fold in rolled oats. Stir in enough flour to make a soft dough. Turn out on lightly floured board and knead until satiny, about 10 minutes. Round dough into ball; place in greased bowl and brush lightly with melted shortening. Cover and let rise in a warm place until double in bulk, about 1 hour. Punch down; brush with melted shortening. Cover with Saran Wrap and a damp cloth. Refrigerate overnight, or for as long as 3 or 4 days. Remove dough from refrigerator and punch down. Shape into rolls. Let rise and bake in a 400° oven 15 to 20 minutes. Makes 4 to 5 dozen rolls, or dough may be divided to make 1 coffee cake and 3½ dozen rolls.

OPERATION "SANDWICH"

Many busy mothers make the family's weekly supply of sandwiches at one time and freeze them until they are needed. To make an occasion of the proceedings, include children as special assistants to the chef.

Here's an intriguing sandwich that will add to the fun: you will need loaves of unsliced bread (corn, wheat, rye, white, fruit, oatmeal, relish, and New England brown breads are all excellent sandwich loaves), half a dozen cheeses (including a smoked cheese), and a wide assortment of meats and poultry (a good chance to use up leftovers). In addition, you will need an interest in experimentation and sense of adventure. Slice the loaves almost completely through (leave about ¼ inch uncut) and insert meat and cheese combinations between the slices. For a finishing touch sprinkle with any of the following: shredded green onions, parsley flakes, celery flakes, caraway, poppy, celery, cumin, or sesame seeds.

Place the loaves in a loaf pan or an oblong open casserole. Brush the tops of the loaves with butter or margarine and bake in a 350° oven from 10 to 15 minutes. These must be served at once while the cheese is soft and bubbly, and well blended with the slices of meat and poultry. Or they can be stored by wrapping each loaf in Saran Wrap and freezing or refrigerating until 30 minutes before heating.

DESSERTS

A dessert takes its cue from the meal that precedes it. An elaborate and filling dessert belongs at the end of a light meal where it can stand on its own merit, without competition from the dishes that came before it. Or it should be served with coffee to guests who arrive after dinner. Such special effort on your part deserves the place of honor on your table.

Conversely, a dessert that follows a heavy nourishing dinner should be light and delicate. Ice creams, sherbets, compotes of fruit, or soufflés are just the right contrast to a hearty meal.

This chapter contains recipes for cakes and pies, puddings and soufflés, ice creams and sherbets. The chapter entitled *Gifts From Your Kitchen* includes sections on cookies and steamed puddings, which are especially appropriate as presents on so many occasions. See the chapter on breads for a great variety of sweet loaves, adaptable as desserts, in many menus.

25 This gelatine fruit salad, served on a pedestal cake plate, has the look of something special. It contains oranges, bananas, apples, grapes, and walnut kernels. Its name: Fruits of Winter Salad (p. 195). **Photo courtesy of The Seven-Up Company.**

26 Soup concentrates take the problem out of sauces, and are amazingly adaptable—on meats, seafood, and vegetables. See **Relishes and Sauces (p. 163). Photo courtesy of The Campbell Soup Company.**

27 For breakfast, lunch, or dinner—and for between-meal snacks—there is nothing more versatile than fruit breads. They make wonderful sandwiches with butter, creamed cheese, or meat spreads, and are delicious served plain or toasted. Here, a Banana Bread (p. 213), made with cereal. **Photo courtesy of Kellogg Company.**

28 Cranberries make a wonderful year-round dessert, and this Cranberry-Orange Pie (p. 234), with its tart, spicy flavor, is a natural candidate for all-season honors. **Photo courtesy of Ocean Spray Cranberries, Inc.**

29 Broiled Bananas (p. 167) add a touch of imagination to simple luncheons or dinners. With the illustrated menu, serve a baked potato, if you wish, and assorted breads or muffins. **Photo courtesy of United Fruit Company.**

30 Lemon chiffon pie is appropriate for any and all occasions. This version—Mile-High Lemon Chiffon Pie (p. 236)—tops the chiffon with whipped cream and maraschino cherries. **Photo courtesy of Knox Gelatine, Inc.**

31 Pumpkin Chiffon Cake (p. 245) is the answer when you're looking for an extra-fancy dessert surprise. It's easier than it looks, and a lot of fun to serve. Your guests will be amazed and delighted by your inventiveness. **Photo courtesy of Best Foods, Division of Corn Products Company.**

32 Year after year, chocolate maintains its popularity over all other flavors. It may be served as simply or as elegantly as the occasion demands. See **Desserts (p. 223) for a fascinating variety of choice chocolate recipes. Photo courtesy of McCall's Magazine.**

PIES

PIE CRUST MIX
The Procter & Gamble Company

6 cups sifted enriched flour   1 pound (about 2⅓ cups)
1 tablespoon salt   Crisco

Mix flour and salt in a large mixing bowl or on a large square of waxed or wrapping paper. Cut shortening into flour with 2 knives or pastry blender until mixture is uniform and very fine. Store in container, such as an empty 3-pound Crisco can. (No refrigeration needed.) Makes 7 to 8 cups.

SINGLE PIE CRUST
The Procter & Gamble Company

3 tablespoons water   1½ cups Pie Crust Mix

Sprinkle water over mixture, a tablespoon at a time, tossing lightly with a fork. When all water has been added and mixed, work dough into a firm ball with the hands. Press the dough into a flat circle. Work with the dough until all edges are smooth. Roll on a lightly floured board or pastry cloth to ⅛-inch thickness. Use short light strokes moving away from the center to edge in all directions. If dough splits, work edge back into circle again with the hand. If necessary, dough may be rerolled several times.

Ease the rolled pastry into the pie plate, patting firmly to eliminate air under the pastry. Cut crust to extend ½-inch beyond edge of pie plate. Fold edge under on rim of plate and flute with fingers or fork. If shell is to be baked with no filling, prick bottom and sides thoroughly with fork before baking. Bake in 425° oven 12 to 15 minutes.

DOUBLE PIE CRUST
The Procter & Gamble Company

4 tablespoons water   2¼ cups Pie Crust Mix

Sprinkle water over mixture, a tablespoon at a time, tossing lightly with a fork. When all water has been added and mixed, work dough into a firm ball with the hands. Divide into 2 portions. Press the dough into a flat circle. Work with the dough until all the edges are smooth. Roll on a lightly floured board or pastry cloth to ⅛-inch thickness. Use short light strokes moving from the center to edge in all directions. If dough splits, work edge back into circle again with hand. If necessary, dough may be rerolled several times.

Roll half of dough 1½-inch larger than the top of pie plate. Fold dough over and lift onto pie plate. Gently ease the dough into the plate being careful not to stretch it. Trim edge even with plate. Roll remaining portion in similar manner and lift onto filled pie. Trim ½ inch beyond edge of plate. Fold top edge under and flute with fingers or fork. Prick or slit top crust to allow for escape of steam. Bake in 425° oven 12 to 15 minutes.

GRAHAM CRACKER CRUST
National Biscuit Company

20 square Nabisco Graham   ¼ cup butter or margarine,
   Crackers, finely rolled   soft
¼ cup sugar

Add softened butter or margarine and sugar to crumbs, blend thoroughly. Pour crumb mixture into 9-inch pie plate and press firmly against bottom sides of plate. (The easy way is to press crumbs into shape with an 8-inch pie plate.) Bake in 375° oven 8 minutes. Cool and fill.

WHEAT GERM CRUST
Kretschmer Wheat Germ Corp.

¾ cup (about 10) very fine graham cracker crumbs
¾ cup Kretchmer Wheat Germ
⅓ cup sugar
1½ teaspoons cinnamon
¼ teaspoon salt
½ cup butter or margarine, melted

Combine crumbs, wheat germ, sugar, cinnamon, and salt in mixing bowl. Mix in butter or margarine with pastry blender. Press mixture over bottom and sides of 9-inch pie pan. Bake in a 350° oven 8 to 10 minutes. Cool and fill.

COFFEE CHIFFON PIE
Pan American Coffee Bureau

1 tablespoon gelatine
¼ cup cold coffee
2 egg yolks
⅔ cup sweetened condensed milk
¼ teaspoon salt
1½ cups strong hot coffee
2 egg whites, stiffly beaten
1 tablespoon butter or margarine
1 cup corn flakes, rolled
1 tablespoon sugar or honey

Soften gelatine in cold coffee. Beat egg yolks slightly, and add condensed milk and salt. Dissolve gelatine mixture in hot coffee and stir gradually into egg-milk mixture. Place in refrigerator until mixture begins to set and fold into stiffly beaten egg whites. Pour into a deep pie pan or shallow serving dish with straight sides. Melt butter or margarine, stir in rolled corn flakes and sugar or honey. Sprinkle over top and return to refrigerator until ready to serve. Makes 6 servings.

PECAN PIE
Penick & Ford, Ltd.

1 cup sugar
¾ cup Brer Rabbit Molasses
¼ cup butter
3 eggs
1 cup pecan nut meats

Few grains salt
1 teaspoon vanilla extract
1 9-inch unbaked pastry shell
1 cup heavy cream

Mix sugar and molasses; add butter. Bring to boiling point. Beat eggs; gradually add syrup mixture. Add nut meats, salt, and vanilla. Pour into pastry shell. Bake in 375° oven 45 to 60 minutes. Cool. Whip cream; spread on pie.

BAVARIAN MINT PIE
The Nestlé Company

Choco-Nut Shell:

1 6-ounce package (1 cup) Nestlé's Semi-Sweet Chocolate Morsels

1 tablespoon shortening
1½ cups finely chopped nuts

Melt chocolate and shortening over hot, not boiling, water. Stir until smooth. Reserve 2 tablespoons of the mixture for Chocolate Triangles. Add nuts to the remaining mixture and stir until well blended. Spread evenly on bottom and sides, not over rim, of pie pan. Chill until firm.

Chocolate Triangles: Spread reserved 2 tablespoons semi-sweet mixture on waxed paper lined cooky sheet to form a 6 x 4-inch rectangle. Chill until firm. Invert carefully on second waxed paper lined cooky sheet. Gently peel off waxed paper. Cut in 2-inch squares, and cut each square diagonally to make triangles. Chill until ready to use.

Bavarian Mint Filling:

32 marshmallows
¾ cup milk
¼ teaspoon salt
¼ teaspoon peppermint extract

1¼ cups heavy cream, whipped
Few drops green food coloring

Combine first 3 ingredients and melt over hot water. Remove and let cool. Add peppermint extract and stir until blended. Fold whipped cream and food coloring into mixture. Pour into chilled Choco-Nut Shell, cover with Saran Wrap and chill several hours or overnight. Garnish by pressing the long side of the Chocolate Triangles into the top of the pie so that they stand.

COFFEE CREAM PIE
The Nestlé Company

Nut Shell:

1 egg white
⅛ teaspoon salt
¼ cup sugar

1½ cups finely chopped nuts

Preheat oven to 400°. Combine egg white (saving yolk for later use) and salt; beat until stiff but not dry. Gradually beat in sugar until stiff and satiny. Add and blend well ½ cup chopped nuts. Press on bottom and sides, not rim, of a well-greased 8-inch pie pan. Prick well with fork. Bake at 400° for 12 minutes; then cool.

Coffee Filling:

1 tablespoon Nescafé
¼ cup water
16 marshmallows

1 egg yolk
1 cup heavy cream, whipped
¼ teaspoon almond extract

Combine first 3 ingredients and melt over medium heat, stirring constantly. Beat egg yolk slightly and add to coffee mixture, stirring rapidly. Cook over medium heat for 1 minute, stirring constantly. Chill until thickened, but not set. Beat whipped cream and almond extract slightly and fold into coffee mixture. Pour into cooled shell and chill several hours wrapped in Saran Wrap. Decorate with chopped nuts or drop small mounds of whipped cream flavored with crème de cacao around edge.

CHOCOLATE-COCONUT CRUST PIE
General Foods Corporation

2 squares unsweetened chocolate
2 tablespoons butter
2 tablespoons hot milk or water

⅔ cups sifted confectioners' sugar
2 cups Baker's Angel Flake Coconut, toasted or plain

Melt chocolate and butter in top of double boiler, stirring until blended. Combine milk and sugar. Add to chocolate mixture, stirring well. Add coconut and mix well. Spread on bottom and sides of greased 9-inch pie pan. Chill until firm. (Do not freeze.)

To serve with chiffon or cream pie filling: Pour filling into chilled crust and chill until firm. Remove from refrigerator and let stand 5 to 10 minutes before cutting.

To serve with ice cream: Let chilled crust stand at room temperature 5 to 10 minutes, then fill with peppermint ice cream and serve immediately.

COFFEE-COCONUT CREAM PIE
Pan American Coffee Bureau

Coffee-Coconut Shell:

1 can coconut, shredded Strong hot coffee

2 tablespoons butter or margarine

Empty can of coconut into bowl. Add enough strong, hot coffee to barely cover. Let stand 5 minutes, then drain. Pat dry between layers of absorbent paper. Rub butter or margarine on bottom and sides of 9-inch pie pan, and press coconut on pan. Bake in 350° oven for 10 minutes. Cool.

Coffee-Coconut Cream Filling:

⅓ cup all-purpose flour
½ cup sugar
⅛ teaspoon salt
1 cup coffee
1 cup evaporated milk

3 egg yolks
2 tablespoons butter or margarine
1 teaspoon vanilla
1½ cups shredded coconut

Combine flour, sugar, and salt in top of double boiler. Add coffee and evaporated milk gradually. Blend a little hot mixture into lightly beaten egg yolks, and return to double boiler. Cook 2 minutes, stirring constantly. Remove from heat. Add butter, vanilla, and 1 cup coconut. Cool. Pour into shell. Garnish with whipped cream and remaining ½ cup coconut, toasted.

PEPPERMINT SPRING PIE
National Biscuit Company

30 Shredded Wheat Juniors
⅓ cup butter or margarine
¼ cup cocoa
¼ cup sugar
1 teaspoon grated orange rind
1 tablespoon orange juice

1 3-ounce package lemon-flavored gelatin
1¾ cups hot water
1 pint vanilla ice cream
¼ teaspoon peppermint extract
Few drops red food coloring

Roll spoon size shredded wheat into fine crumbs. (Makes 1½ cups crumbs.) Melt butter; stir in cocoa and sugar. Heat mixture to boiling point, stirring constantly, until sugar is completely dissolved. Remove from heat. Stir in cereal, orange rind, and orange juice. Grease a 9-inch plate. Press the crumbs over bottom and sides of pie plate.

Dissolve gelatin in hot water. Add ice cream by spoonsful; stir until cream is melted. Stir in peppermint extract and red coloring. Chill until mixture will mound when lifted with a spoon. Spoon into cereal shell. Chill until firm. Garnish with whipped cream, if desired. Makes 6 servings.

BLACK BOTTOM PIE
Kellogg Company

Corn Flake Crust:

4 cups Kellogg's® Corn Flakes or 1 cup packaged Kellogg's® Corn Flake Crumbs	¼ cup soft butter or margarine 2 tablespoons sugar

If using corn flakes, crush into fine crumbs. Blend butter and sugar; stir in corn flake crumbs; mix well. Press evenly and firmly around sides and bottom of 9-inch pie pan. Chill.

Black Bottom Filling:

1 tablespoon unflavored gelatine ¼ cup cold water ¾ cup sugar 4 teaspoons corn starch 3 eggs, separated 2 cups milk, scalded	2 squares (2 ounces) unsweetened chocolate ½ teaspoon vanilla flavoring ½ teaspoon rum flavoring ¼ teaspoon salt ¼ teaspoon cream of tartar

Soften gelatine in cold water. Combine ½ cup sugar with corn starch. Beat egg yolks until light; stir in scalded milk slowly. Gradually stir in sugar mixture. Cook over hot water, stirring occasionally, about 20 minutes, until custard coats a metal spoon heavily. Take out 1½ cups of custard, keep remainder hot. Melt chocolate over hot, not boiling water; add to the 1½ cups custard, beating until well blended and cool. Stir in vanilla. Pour into chilled pie shell. To remaining hot custard, add softened gelatine, stirring until dissolved. Cool until mixture is ready to set. Stir in rum flavoring. Beat egg whites with salt until foamy. Add cream of tartar and beat until stiff, but not dry. Gradually beat in remaining ¼ cup sugar. Fold into custard mixture. Spread gently over chocolate filling. Chill until set. Makes 1 9-inch pie.

Topping:

1 cup heavy cream
2 tablespoons confectioners' sugar

½ square (½ ounce) un-sweetened chocolate, shaved

Whip cream; fold in confectioners' sugar. Spread over pie; sprinkle with shaved chocolate. Serve at once.

RAISIN-SOUR CREAM PIE
California Packing Corporation

2 eggs, beaten lightly
¾ cup sugar
2 tablespoons flour
½ teaspoon cinnamon
¼ teaspoon salt
1 cup dairy sour cream

½ cup milk
1 tablespoon vinegar
1½ cups Del Monte Seed-less Raisins
Pastry for 1 9-inch crust

To beaten eggs, add sugar, flour, cinnamon, and salt. Beat until smooth. Blend in the sour cream, milk, and vinegar. Add raisins and turn into a pastry-lined pie pan. Bake in 450° oven 10 minutes. Reduce the heat to 350° and bake

30 to 40 minutes longer, or until the filling is set in the center. Makes 1 9-inch pie.

AROMATIC APPLE PIE

The Angostura-Wuppermann Corp.

Unbaked pastry shell	2 eggs
4 cooking apples	½ cup thin cream
½ teaspoon cinnamon	1 tablespoon Angostura Aromatic Bitters
½ teaspoon nutmeg	
¾ cup sugar	1 tablespoon butter

Line a deep 10-inch pie plate with plain pastry. Pare apples and slice very thin, lengthwise. Arrange in crust, overlapping slices. Mix together, cinnamon, nutmeg, and sugar. Sprinkle over apples. Beat eggs well, add cream and bitters. Pour mixture carefully over apple slices. Distribute butter in bits over top of pie. Bake in 450° oven for 10 minutes. Reduce heat and bake at 350° for 50 minutes longer. Serve with confectioners' sugar dusted over top.

FRESH CRANBERRY-ORANGE PIE

Ocean Spray Cranberries, Inc.

½ cup water	¼ teaspoon allspice
Pinch salt	2 teaspoons butter
3 tablespoons quick-cooking tapioca	2 oranges, quartered and seeded
4 cups Ocean Spray Fresh Cranberries	1 9- or 10-inch baked pie shell
2½ cups sugar	Orange segments
¼ teaspoon cinnamon	

In a saucepan combine water, salt, and tapioca, and bring to a quick boil. Add cranberries and sugar, and continue cooking until berries pop. Stir in spices and butter. Put oranges through food grinder and add to fruit mixture. Cool. Spoon cooled filling into baked pie shell and chill until ready to serve. Garnish with orange segments and serve cold. Pie may be served with whipped cream or vanilla ice cream, if desired. Makes 1 deep 9-inch pie, or 1 standard 10-inch pie. Will freeze well, wrapped in Saran Wrap. (See illustration 28.)

STRAWBERRY SURPRISE PIE
Stokely-Van Camp, Inc.

Graham Cracker Crust:

1 cup graham cracker crumbs (about 18 crackers)
¼ cup sugar

⅓ cup butter or margarine, melted
1 quart vanilla ice cream

Combine graham cracker crumbs and sugar. Add melted butter and stir until well blended. Pour into lightly buttered 9-inch pie plate and press into shape. Chill about 15 minutes. Fill Graham Cracker Crust with ice cream. Store in freezer while making the meringue.

Meringue Topping:

6 egg whites, at room temperature

½ teaspoon cream of tartar
¾ cup sugar

Add cream of tartar to egg whites. Beat until frothy. Gradually beat in sugar and continue beating until mixture is stiff and glossy. Pile meringue on top of pie, being careful to completely seal the edges with meringue. Make a pretty swirl on top of pie with spatula. Then rush pie into a preheated 450° oven for 3 to 5 minutes. Take pie immediately from oven to freezer and leave there until ready to serve. When serving, dip bottom of pie plate in hot water for a few seconds. Cut pie in eights and place on individual dessert plates. Top with Strawberry Sauce.

Strawberry Sauce:

1 box (10-ounce) Stokely-Van Camp's Frozen Sliced Strawberries

1 teaspoon corn starch

Drain thawed strawberries. Add corn starch to liquid and cook over medium heat until thickened, stirring constantly. Add strawberries. Chill before serving.

MILE-HIGH LEMON CHIFFON PIE
Knox Gelatine, Inc.

1 envelope Knox Unflavored
   Gelatine
1 cup sugar
5 eggs, separated
½ cup water

½ cup lemon juice
1 teaspoon grated lemon
   rind
1 9-inch baked pie shell

Mix together gelatine and ½ cup of the sugar in top of double boiler. Beat egg yolks slightly; stir in water and lemon juice. Add to gelatine mixture. Place over boiling water and cook, stirring constantly, until gelatine is dissolved and mixture is slightly thickened, about 6 minutes. Add lemon rind. Chill until mixture mounds slightly when dropped from a spoon. Beat egg whites until stiff, but not dry. Gradually add remaining ½ cup sugar and beat until very stiff. Fold in gelatine mixture. Carefully pile into prepared shell. (Mixture should be thick enough to hold its shape.) Chill until firm. If desired, garnish with whipped cream and pieces of cherry. Makes 1 9-inch pie. (See illustration 30.)

FRENCH CONCORD TARTS
The Welch Grape Juice Company, Inc.

1 3-ounce package cream
   cheese
2 tablespoons heavy cream

1 tablespoon Welch's Fruit
   of the Vine
1 cup whipped cream,
   sweetened

Soften cream cheese, blend into heavy cream until very smooth. Spread on bottom of cooled tart shells. Fill each tart shell with Welch's Fruit of the Vine. Chill. Garnish with whipped cream just before serving.

To prepare tart shells: Prepare your favorite pastry recipe or mix. Cut out 5-inch circles to fit over backs of 3-inch muffin pans. Fold to fit, flute, prick well. Bake at 450° for 10 to 15 minutes, until crisp and golden. Cool before filling.

PARTY STRAWBERRY-AND-RHUBARB TARTS
Kretschmer Wheat Germ Corp.

3 cups sifted enriched flour
1½ teaspoons salt
⅓ cup Kretchmer Wheat Germ

1 cup shortening
7 to 8 tablespoons ice water

Sift flour and salt together. Add wheat germ and mix well. Cut in shortening until it is the size of peas. Add water slowly, tossing mixture with a fork until dough forms a ball. Roll on lightly floured board or pastry cloth. Cut dough in circles and line 3½-inch tart pans or press on the bottoms of inverted muffin pans. Prick well and bake at 425° for 12 to 15 minutes until golden. Cool.

Filling:

1 pound fresh rhubarb, cut in ½-inch pieces
½ cup sugar
2 tablespoons water
3 tablespoons sugar
1½ cups sliced strawberries

1 cup hot water
1 package strawberry-flavored gelatin
¾ cup cold water and fruit juice
Dash of salt
1 cup heavy cream, whipped

Simmer rhubarb, ½ cup sugar, and 2 tablespoons of water in covered pan for 2 minutes. Cool. Add 3 tablespoons sugar to sliced strawberries. Dissolve strawberry gelatin in hot water. Drain juice from rhubarb and strawberries and add enough cold water to make ¾ cup. Add fruit juice and water to gelatin, add salt. Cool. Whip cream until stiff and fold in ⅓ cup of cold gelatin. Place cream in bottom of tarts. Chill. Chill gelatin until slightly thickened. Fold in fruit. Place in tart shells and chill until set. Makes 15 to 16 tarts.

CAKES

SILVER CAKE
The Procter & Gamble Company

Two 8-inch layers 1½ inches deep:

2¼ cups sifted cake flour	½ cup Crisco
1⅓ cups sugar	¾ cup milk
1 teaspoon salt	4 egg whites
3½ teaspoons double-action baking powder	⅓ cup milk
	1 teaspoon vanilla

Combine flour, sugar, salt, and baking powder in mixing bowl. Add shortening and the first milk called for in recipe. Beat vigorously by hand or electric mixer, medium speed, for 2 minutes. Add egg whites, additional milk, and vanilla. Beat for 2 minutes. Pour into 2 8 x 1½-inch layer pans which have been lined with plain paper, or rubbed with shortening and floured. Bake about 30 minutes in 350° oven.

Two 9-inch layers 1½ inches deep:

2¾ cups sifted cake flour	⅔ cup Crisco
1⅔ cups sugar	1 cup milk
1 teaspoon salt	5 egg whites
4½ teaspoons double-action baking powder	⅓ cup milk
	1 teaspoon vanilla

Follow directions given above. Bake in 2 9 x 1½-inch layer pans about 35 minutes at 350°.

Variations

LEMON CAKE. In either recipe, omit vanilla in cake batter. Add 2 teaspoons grated lemon rind and ¾ teaspoon lemon flavoring.

CHOCOLATE RIBBON CAKE. In either recipe, fold into cake batter ¾ cup shaved sweet baking chocolate.

BLUEBERRY CAKE. In either recipe, fold into cake batter 1 cup fresh or drained, frozen or canned blueberries. Bake in 10-inch square pan about 45 minutes.

NESSELRODE CAKE. In either recipe, stir into cake batter 1 cup finely cut mixed candied friuts, and 1 tablespoon rum flavoring.

WHEAT GERM AUSTRIAN APPLE CAKE
Kretschmer Wheat Germ Corp.

Crust:

1 cup sifted flour	1 egg
¼ cup butter or margarine	⅛ teaspoon salt
¼ cup sugar	½ teaspoon baking powder

Mix ingredients together. Knead 2 to 3 minutes on a lightly floured board. Press evenly over bottom and up 1½ inches on sides of a 10-inch spring form pan. Chill in refrigerator 25 to 30 minutes.

Filling:

6 cups thinly sliced fresh
  apples
⅓ cup sugar
1 tablespoon flour
2 teaspoons lemon juice

½ teaspoon cinnamon
½ cup slivered almonds
½ cup raisins
2 tablespoons butter or margarine

Blend ingredients except butter or margarine together
and pour into crust. Dot with butter or margarine. Cover
pan with aluminum foil. Bake in 375° oven 40 minutes. Remove foil and continue baking 20 minutes.

Topping:

¼ cup butter or margarine
2 tablespoons flour
¾ cup Kretchmer Wheat
  Germ

¼ cup brown sugar
¼ teaspoon cinnamon

Mix ingredients together with pastry blender until mixture
resembles coarse meal. Remove apple cake from oven;
sprinkle topping over apples. Return to oven for 10 minutes, or until apples are tender and crumbs are lightly
browned. Makes 8 servings.

RUSSIAN TEA CAKE

Best Foods, Division of
Corn Products Company

2½ cups sifted cake flour
3 teaspoons baking powder
½ teaspoon salt
⅔ cup Mazola Margarine
1¼ cups sugar
1½ teaspoons grated lemon
  peel

2 eggs
¼ cup milk
½ cup strong cold tea
½ cup orange marmalade
Maraschino cherries
Lemon slices, paper thin

Sift flour, baking powder, and salt together. Cream margarine with sugar and lemon peel. Add eggs one at a time, beating well after each addition. Combine milk and tea, and add to creamed mixture alternately with flour, beginning and ending with flour. Stir smooth after each addition. Pour 2 8-inch layer cake pans which have been greased and lined with waxed paper. Bake in a 375° oven 30 to 35 minutes. Cool. Spread top of each layer with orange marmalade and put layers together. Decorate top with halves of maraschino cherries and paper-thin slices of lemon dipped in sugar.

ALL COFFEE CHIFFON CAKE
Pan American Coffee Bureau

2 eggs, separated	½ cup milk
1½ cups sugar	½ cup cold coffee
2¼ cups sifted cake flour	⅛ teaspoon baking soda
3 teaspoons baking powder	⅓ cup cooking oil
1 teaspoon salt	2 teaspoons vanilla

Beat egg whites until frothy. Gradually beat in half cup of sugar. Continue beating until very stiff and glossy. Sift remaining sugar, flour, baking powder, and salt into another bowl. Combine milk, coffee, and baking soda. Pour oil into flour mixture with ½ the coffee mixture and vanilla. Beat 1 minute using medium speed on electric mixer, or 150 strokes by hand. Scrape sides and bottom of bowl constantly. Add remaining coffee mixture and egg yolks. Beat 1 minute longer, scraping bowl constantly. Fold in egg-white mixture lightly but thoroughly. Pour into 2 deep well-greased and floured 8-inch layer cake pans. Bake in 350° oven 30 to 35 minutes. Remove from pans. Cool. Split each layer into 2 layers. Put together and frost. Chill well.

CHOCOLATE DELIGHT CAKE
The Procter & Gamble Company

Two 8-inch layers 1½-inches deep:

1½ cups sifted cake flour
1¼ cups sugar
1 teaspoon salt
1 teaspoon soda
½ teaspoon double-action
  baking powder
½ cup Crisco

2 1-ounce squares unsweetened chocolate, melted
¾ cup milk
2 eggs
⅓ cup milk
1 teaspoon vanilla

Combine flour, sugar, salt, soda, and baking powder in mixing bowl. Add shortening, melted chocolate, and the first milk called for in the recipe. Beat vigorously by hand or electric mixer, medium speed, for 2 minutes. Add eggs, additional milk, and vanilla. Beat for 2 minutes. Pour into 2 8 x 1½-inch layer pans lined with plain paper, or rubbed with shortening and floured. Bake about 30 minutes in 350° oven.

Two 9-inch layers 1½-inches deep:

2 cups sifted cake flour
1⅔ cups sugar
1 teaspoon salt
1½ teaspoons soda
½ teaspoon double-action baking powder
½ cup Crisco

3 1-ounce squares unsweet-ened chocolate, melted
⅔ cup milk
3 eggs
⅔ cup milk
1 teaspoon vanilla

Follow directions given above. Bake in 2 9 x 1½-inch layer pans about 40 minutes in 350° oven.

Variations

DOUBLE MINT CAKE. In either recipe, substitute ½ teaspoon peppermint flavoring in place of vanilla in cake batter.

CHOCOLATE ORANGE CAKE. In either recipe, substitute ½ teaspoon orange flavoring for vanilla and stir in 1 tablespoon grated orange rind.

NORWEGIAN CHOCOLATE CAKE
The Dow Chemical Company

2 cups brown sugar
½ cup butter
½ cup sour milk
2 teaspoons soda
2 cups sifted flour

½ cup boiling water
2 squares chocolate, melted
2 eggs
½ cup boiling water

Cream sugar with butter. Add sour milk and flour sifted with soda. Add boiling water and beat mixture for 2 minutes. Add remaining ingredients; beat for 2 minutes. Place batter in a lightly buttered 8 x 12 x 2-inch baking pan. Bake in 350° oven for about 40 minutes, or until cake tests done. Cool and frost as desired. Keep cake in pan, cover with Saran Wrap to keep it fresh and moist until all is eaten.

CHOCOLATE MAYONNAISE CAKE

Best Foods, Division of
Corn Products Company

2 cups sifted all-purpose
flour
1 teaspoon baking powder
½ teaspoon baking soda
½ teaspoon salt
1¼ cups sugar

⅓ cup breakfast cocoa
1 cup water
¾ cup Hellmann's or Best
Foods Real Mayonnaise
1 teaspoon vanilla

Sift flour, baking powder, soda, salt, sugar, and cocoa several times; sift into mixing bowl. Add water, mayonnaise, and vanilla. Stir until smooth. Pour into a 9-inch square cake pan which has been lightly greased and bottom lined with waxed paper. Bake in a 350° oven for 45 minutes. Makes 1 9-inch square cake.

CHERRY FUDGE CAKE

Pet Milk Company

1⅓ cups sifted all-purpose
flour
1 cup sugar
⅓ cup cocoa
1 teaspoon baking soda
¾ teaspoon salt
½ cup soft shortening

1 egg
½ cup Pet Evaporated Milk
¼ cup water
2 tablespoons maraschino
cherry syrup
½ cup cut-up maraschino
cherries

Preheat oven to 350°. Grease bottom of an 8-inch square pan. Sift flour, sugar, cocoa, baking soda, and salt into a 3-quart bowl. Add shortening, egg, and evaporated milk to dry ingredients in bowl. Beat 3 minutes with electric beater at medium speed, scraping sides of bowl often. Add water and cherry syrup, and beat hard 1 minute longer. Stir in cut-up cherries. Put into prepared pan. Bake on center rack of oven 50 to 55 minutes, or until cake pulls from sides of pan. Remove from oven. Let stand in pan 10 minutes before turning out to cool. Frost with Easy Chocolate Frosting (see page 254).

PUMPKIN CHIFFON CAKE
Best Foods, Division of
Corn Products Company

½ cup milk
6 egg yolks, beaten
2¼ cups sifted cake flour
1½ cups sugar
3 teaspoons baking powder
1 teaspoon salt
1 teaspoon cinnamon
½ teaspoon nutmeg
½ teaspoon ginger

½ cup Mazola Corn Oil
¾ cup canned pumpkin
½ teaspoon cream of tartar
6 egg whites
White Fluffy Frosting (see page 253)
Yellow, red, and green coloring
½ banana, for stem

Heat milk to boiling, pour over beaten egg yolks, and blend well. Cool. Mix and sift together cake flour, sugar, baking powder, salt, and spices. Make a well and add, in order, corn oil, pumpkin, and cooled egg-milk mixture. Beat with spoon until smooth. Add cream of tartar to egg whites. Beat until whites form very stiff peaks. Gently fold first mixture into egg whites until well blended. Fold, do not stir. Pour batter into 2 2½-quart oven-proof mixing bowls. Bake in a 300° oven 55 minutes. Then increase temperature to 325° and bake an additional 15 minutes, or until cake springs back when touched lightly with finger. Immediately invert bowls over cake rack. Let cool; then loosen side of cake with spatula. Remove from bowls.

Prepare White Fluffy Frosting; divide and set aside about ¾ cup to be colored green for the stem. Tint the larger portion a delicate pumpkin color using about 1 teaspoon yellow color and 5 to 6 drops of red.

Place one cake, top side up, on serving plate. Spread top with a small amount of frosting. Next place the matching cake, top side down, over the bottom cake. With a spatula, cover cake with a layer of pumpkin-colored frosting about ½-inch thick. Using vertical strokes, accent the pumpkin shape. Tint the small amount of frosting a deep green using about ¼ teaspoon color. To frost the stem, stick the half banana on a wooden pick or skewer. Using the pick to hold while frosting, cover the banana with the green frosting. Scoop out a small depression at the top of the cake. Insert stem. Remove banana before cutting cake.

To bake in a regular chiffon cake pan: pour batter into an ungreased 10 x 4-inch tube pan. Bake in 325° oven 55 minutes. Increase temperature to 350° and bake an additional 15 minutes, or until cake springs back when touched lightly with finger. Immediately invert pan. Let cool. Makes 14 to 16 servings. (See illustration 31.)

PINEAPPLE-HONEY UPSIDE DOWN CAKE
Dole Corporation

2 tablespoons butter or margarine	1 1-pound, 4½-ounce can Dole Crushed Pineapple, drained
½ cup honey	
Walnut halves	Batter from standard white cake recipe
Maraschino cherries	

Heat butter or margarine and honey to boiling. Pour into greased 8- to 9-inch round cake pan. Arrange nuts and cherries in honey mixture; carefully spoon drained pineapple over nuts and cherries to keep design in place. Cover with batter from standard white cake recipe, and bake in preheated 375° oven for about 40 minutes. Can be served with whipped cream or ice cream. Makes 8 to 10 servings. (See illustration 37.)

NO-BAKE RUM CHEESE CAKE
Knox Gelatine, Inc.

Cheese Cake:

2 envelopes Knox Unflavored Gelatine
1 cup sugar
¼ teaspoon salt
2 eggs, separated
1 cup milk
1 teaspoon grated lemon rind
1 tablespoon lemon juice
2 teaspoons rum flavoring
3 cups (24 ounces) creamed cottage cheese
1 cup heavy cream, whipped

Mix gelatine, ¾ cup of the sugar, and salt in top of double boiler. Beat together egg yolks and milk; add to gelatine mixture. Cook over boiling water, stirring until gelatine dissolves and mixture thickens slightly, about 10 minutes. Remove from heat; add lemon rind, lemon juice, and rum flavoring; cool. Sieve cottage cheese into large mixing bowl; or beat with electric beater until smooth. Stir in cooled gelatine mixture. Chill, stirring occasionally, until mixture mounds slightly when dropped from a spoon. While gelatine is chilling, prepare Nut-Crumb Mixture and set aside. Beat egg whites until stiff, but not dry. Gradually add remaining ¼ cup sugar and beat until very stiff. Fold into gelatine-cheese mixture. Fold in whipped cream.

Nut-Crumb Mixture:

2 tablespoons melted butter
1 tablespoon sugar
¼ cup finely chopped nuts
⅔ cup graham cracker crumbs
¼ teaspoon cinnamon
¼ teaspoon nutmeg

Mix together all ingredients. Sprinkle half of crumb mixture on bottom of an 8-inch spring form pan. Turn cheese cake mixture into pan; sprinkle with remaining crumb mixture. Chill until firm. If desired, an 8- or 9-inch square pan or a 9 x 5-inch loaf pan may be used; line with waxed paper. Makes party-size 10 to 12 servings. (For family-size, 5 to 6 servings, use half of gelatine recipe and half of Nut-Crumb Mixture in an 8-inch round pan or 9-inch pie plate.) Will freeze nicely covered in Saran Wrap.

Variations

NESSELRODE CHEESE CAKE. Reduce milk to ¾ cup; substitute 2 tablespoons light rum for rum flavoring. Fold in ⅓ cup finely chopped maraschino cherries and ⅓ cup chopped nuts.

COFFEE CHEESE CAKE. Add 2 tablespoons instant coffee to gelatine-sugar mixture in top of double boiler. Omit lemon rind and lemon juice.

CHOCOLATE CHEESE CAKE. Add 1 package semi-sweet chocolate pieces to gelatine-milk mixture in top of double boiler. Omit lemon rind and lemon juice.

JELLY ROLL
The Welch Grape Juice Company, Inc.

1 cup sifted cake flour	1 cup Welch's Grape Jelly
1 teaspoon baking powder	1 teaspoon soft butter or
¼ teaspoon salt	margarine
4 large eggs, separated	Confectioners' sugar
1 cup sugar	1 teaspoon grated lemon
1 teaspoon lemon extract or	rind (optional)
vanilla	

Sift cake flour. Mix and sift together flour, baking powder, and salt. Beat egg yolks until very light. Add ½ cup sugar and flavoring to beaten egg yolks. Beat egg whites until stiff, add remaining sugar slowly, beating until whites stand in peaks. Gently fold in yolk mixture until well blended. Turn into shallow, 7 x 11-inch pan already greased and lined with greased waxed paper. Bake in 400° oven 15 minutes. Turn onto cloth sprinkled with confectioners' sugar. Peel off waxed paper, cut away crisp cake edges. Spread surface lightly with softened butter or margarine. Now spread with grape jelly and dust with grated lemon rind. Roll gently; wrap in Saran Wrap until ready to serve.

PETITS FOURS
McCormick & Co., Inc.

½ cup shortening	3 teaspoons baking powder
1 cup super fine sugar	½ teaspoon salt
1 teaspoon McCormick or Schilling Vanilla Extract	¾ cup milk
2 cups cake flour, sifted	6 egg whites, unbeaten
	¼ cup sugar

Cream shortening thoroughly. Gradually add the 1 cup sugar, and cream until light and fluffy. Stir in vanilla. Sift flour, baking powder, and salt together 2 times; add to creamed mixture alternately with milk, adding flour first and last. Mix until smooth. Beat egg whites until they just hold up; gradually add remaining ¼ cup sugar and beat until soft peaks form. Fold into creamed batter. Pour into a paper-lined 13 x 9-inch pan and bake in a 350° oven 35 to 40 minutes. Remove from pan and cool on cake racks.

To make Petits Fours, cut cake in squares, rectangles, or triangles with knife, or in fancy shapes with cooky cutters. Line cakes in rows, about 1 inch apart, on a cake rack. Place rack on baking sheet or waxed paper. Pour glaze frosting over cakes. Decorate with cake decors or nonpareils while moist, or with butter cream frosting after glaze frosting sets.

Glaze:

1 pound confectioners' sugar, sifted	1 tablespoon McCormick or Schilling Vanilla Extract
4 tablespoons water	McCormick or Schilling Food Colors

Mix sugar, water, and vanilla extract thoroughly. (Add additional liquid if needed to get a pouring consistency.)

Tint to desired shade. Pour over small cakes on cake rack placed over waxed paper or baking sheet.

CHERRY TORTE
National Red Cherry Institute

1 can (1 pound) red sour pitted cherries (water pack)	2 teaspoons baking powder
	1 teaspoon cinnamon
1 egg	1 tablespoon melted butter
1 cup sugar	1 teaspoon almond flavoring
1 cup sifted all-purpose flour	⅓ cup chopped nuts
	2 3-ounce packages cream cheese
½ teaspoon salt	2 tablespoons milk

Drain cherries; reserve liquid. Beat egg. Gradually add sugar and beat thoroughly. Fold in well-drained cherries. Sift together flour, salt, baking powder, and cinnamon; fold into cherry mixture. Add melted butter and almond flavoring. Turn into waxed paper-lined and greased 8 x 2-inch round cake pan; sprinkle with nuts. Bake in 350° oven 45 minutes. Invert on cake rack; cool. Cut cake into wedges. Blend together cream cheese and milk; put a spoonful on top of each serving. Top with Cherry Sauce. Makes 8 servings.

Cherry Sauce:

¼ cup sugar	1 tablespoon lemon juice
1 tablespoon corn starch	⅛ teaspoon red food coloring
⅛ teaspoon salt	
Reserved cherry liquid	

Mix together sugar, corn starch, and salt in saucepan. Add enough water to cherry liquid to make 1 cup. Gradually stir into corn starch mixture. Place over medium heat, stirring constantly, until mixture comes to a boil; boil ½ minute. Remove from heat. Add lemon juice and red food coloring.

BRIDE'S CAKE
The Procter & Gamble Company

Three-tier Round Cake: Prepare 2 separate recipes of the 8-inch Silver Cake (see page 238). Place 1 recipe in an 11-inch round layer pan. Divide the batter of the second recipe between a 9-inch round layer pan and a 7-inch round layer pan. Bake in a 350° oven 30 to 35 minutes.

Four-tier Rectangular Cake: Prepare 2 separate recipes of the 9-inch Silver Cake. Bake each recipe in a 13 x 9 x 2-inch pan in a 350° oven 40 to 45 minutes. Use 1 cake for bottom layer. Cut second cake into 2 pieces, 7 x 9-inches and 6 x 9-inches, and place the 7 x 9-inch piece lengthwise on first layer. Cut 6 x 9-inch piece into 2 equal pieces, 6 x 4½-inches, and place 1 piece lengthwise on second layer. Cut remaining piece into 2 equal pieces, 3 x 4½-inches, and place 1 piece on top of third layer. The last piece is for the bride and bridegroom. Wrap in Saran Wrap and freeze. It can be saved and eaten on their first-month anniversary.

Note: To simplify your schedule, make the cake a day ahead and ice it the morning of the reception. To save time, draw a plan on paper before you decorate. Use Ornamental Icing and a cake decorating tube to make flowers or fluted edges (directions come with tube). As the crowning ornament for the top layer, use an old-fashioned bouquet or a miniature of the bride and bridegroom.

Ornamental Icing:

¾ cup Crisco
1 teaspoon salt
½ cup milk

2 teaspoons vanilla
5 cups sifted confectioners' sugar

Place all ingredients in large mixer bowl and mix at medium speed for 3 minutes and high speed for 5 minutes. Ice between layers, on side and top of each cake.

GROOM'S CAKE
The Procter & Gamble Company

Preparation of Fruits:

1½ cups halved candied
cherries
1 cup citron, small pieces
1 cup candied pineapple,
small pieces
¼ cup candied lemon peel
½ cup candied orange peel

⅔ cup brandy or grape juice
1 cup seeded raisins
2 cups seedless raisins
1 cup finely cut dates
¾ cup broken unsalted
pecan meats
¾ cup broken walnuts

Soak cherries, citron, pineapple, lemon peel, and orange peel in ⅔ cup brandy or grape juice for several hours. Wash and dry the remaining fruit, but do not soak.

Batter:

1 cup Crisco
1 cup light brown sugar
½ cup sugar
5 eggs, well beaten
1½ teaspoons vanilla
2½ cups sifted enriched
flour
1 teaspoon salt

1½ teaspoons double-action
baking powder
1½ teaspoons cinnamon
1 teaspoon cloves
¼ teaspoon ginger
½ teaspoon allspice
1 teaspoon mace

Blend shortening and sugars. Add eggs and mix thoroughly, using mixer if available. Stir in vanilla and mixed dry ingredients. Add raisins, dates, and nuts. Drain and save brandy from candied fruits. Use surplus brandy or grape juice to baste cakes after baking. Stir fruits into batter. Pour batter into 3 7½ x 3½ x 2¾-inch loaf pans which have been rubbed with shortening and lined with heavy paper. Bake in 300° oven for 2 hours. Turn out of pans and remove paper while warm. Store in tightly covered container until ready to use. Cut into thin slices for serving. Makes 3 loaves, 1¾ to 2 pounds each.

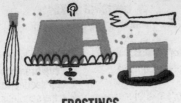

FROSTINGS

TINTED COCONUT
McCormick & Co., Inc.

Divide in half the contents of 1 can of flake coconut. Place half of the coconut in a plastic bag. Add 2 or 3 drops McCormick or Schilling Green Food Color. Toss until coconut is well tinted. If a darker shade is desired, add another drop or two of food color. Repeat with remaining coconut using McCormick or Schilling Red Food Color to get a pink tint.

WHITE FLUFFY FROSTING
Best Foods, Division of
Corn Products Company

2 egg whites
½ cup Karo Syrup, Red Label
½ cup sugar
⅛ teaspoon salt
1 teaspoon vanilla

Place egg whites, corn syrup, sugar, and salt in top of 2-quart double boiler. Beat with rotary beater until partially mixed. Place over rapidly boiling water and cook, beating constantly, until frosting stands in peaks. This will take 3 to 4 minutes depending on rate of beating and size of beater. Remove from heat and continue beating about 1 minute longer. Add vanilla and blend. Makes enough frosting to cover tops and sides of 3 8-inch layers or 1 chiffon cake.

EASY CHOCOLATE FROSTING
Pet Milk Company

¾ cup semi-sweet chocolate pieces
⅓ cup Pet Evaporated Milk

1½ cups sifted confectioners' sugar

Put chocolate pieces and evaporated milk into a heavy 1-quart saucepan. Melt chocolate over very low heat, stirring all the time. Take off heat. Add confectioners' sugar and stir until smooth. Spread on cooled cake. Makes enough to frost 8-inch cake. If frosting becomes too thick to spread easily, add a few drops of evaporated milk.

CREAM FROSTING
McCormick & Co., Inc.

½ cup butter or margarine
3½ cups sifted confectioners' sugar
¼ cup milk

⅛ teaspoon salt
½ teaspoon McCormick or Schilling Almond Extract

Cream butter until light and fluffy. Add sugar alternately with milk, beating hard after each addition. Stir in salt and almond extract. Mix well. Makes enough to frost top and sides of two 8-inch cake layers.

CREAMY DECORATOR'S FROSTING
McCormick & Co., Inc.

1 pound confectioners' sugar
4 tablespoons melted butter
2 egg whites
1 or 2 tablespoons cream

1 teaspoon McCormick or Schilling Vanilla Extract
McCormick or Schilling Food Colors

Sift confectioners' sugar and add about ⅓ of it to butter. Mix thoroughly. Beat in egg whites, one at a time, beating hard after addition of each. Gradually add rest of the sugar with cream and vanilla extract. Tint with color. If various colors are desired, divide frosting into smaller bowls and tint each bowl of frosting separately.

Note: To write names, thin frosting slightly. Keep covered with damp cloth when not in use to prevent crusting over.

PEANUT BUTTER-HONEY SPREAD

Best Foods, Division of
Corn Products Company

¼ cup (½ print) margarine
¼ cup Skippy Creamy or
  Chunk-Style Peanut Butter

¼ cup honey

Blend margarine and peanut butter with wooden spoon. Gradually add honey; continue mixing until light and fluffy. Store in refrigerator. Serve as a topping for bread, French toast, hot biscuits, waffles, or pancakes. Also ideal for a quick dessert, spooned between vanilla wafers for sandwich cookies. Makes ⅔ cup.

HONEY-COCONUT BUTTER FROSTING

General Foods Corporation

½ cup butter or margarine
2 cups sifted confectioners'
  sugar
1 tablespoon light cream

2 tablespoons honey
1⅓ cups Baker's Angel
  Flake Coconut (toasted, if
  desired)

Cream butter; then add part of sugar gradually, blending after each addition. Add remaining sugar, alternately with cream and honey, beating after each addition until smooth. Makes enough frosting for tops of 2 9-inch layers, top and sides of 8 x 8 x 2-inch cake, 2 dozen cupcakes, or 12 to 14 doughnuts.

PINEAPPLE POWDERED SUGAR FROSTING
Dole Corporation

3 tablespoons butter or margarine, softened
2½ cups sifted confectioners' sugar
1 tablespoon lemon juice

2 tablespoons syrup from can Dole Pineapple
½ cup Dole Crushed Pineapple, drained

To butter, gradually add confectioners' sugar and liquids, beating well with spoon or electric mixer after each addition. Stir in drained pineapple, beat with spoon. (It may be necessary to add a little more confectioners' sugar, depending on how thoroughly you drained the pineapple.) Spread on cool cake.

PINEAPPLE BROILED FROSTING
Dole Corporation

3 tablespoons butter or margarine
⅓ cup Dole Crushed Pineapple, drained

½ cup coconut
½ cup brown sugar
¼ cup chopped walnuts

Heat butter and pineapple, add other ingredients, and blend well. Spread lightly on hot or cold loaf or layer of plain cake, or on slices of pound cake from bakeshop or store. Place low under broiler, and broil slowly until bubbly and lightly browned. Serve slightly warm.

APRICOT FROSTING
California Packing Corporation

1⅓ cups sugar
½ cup water
2 egg whites
Few grains salt

¼ teaspoon lemon peel
½ cup puréed cooked Del
Monte Dried Apricots

Mix sugar and water; stir over low heat until sugar is dissolved. Boil until syrup spins an 8-inch thread. Beat whites with salt until stiff. Slowly pour hot syrup over whites, continuing to beat. Beat until very thick. Add peel mixed with purée, a tablespoonful at a time, beating after each addition. Makes enough for 2 cake layers.

BANANA-NUT FROSTING
McCormick & Co., Inc.

2 egg whites
1½ cups sugar
⅛ teaspoon salt
¼ teaspoon McCormick or
Schilling Cream of Tartar
½ cup water

1½ teaspoons McCormick
or Schilling Banana Extract
5 drops McCormick or Schilling Yellow Food Color
⅓ cup chopped pecans or
English walnuts

Combine egg whites, sugar, salt, cream of tartar, and water in the top of a double boiler. Cook over boiling water, beating constantly, about 7 minutes, or until frosting holds its shape. Remove from heat; add extract, food color, and nuts, and continue beating until frosting is of spreading consistency. Makes enough to frost 2 8- or 9-inch layers.

RASPBERRY FROSTING
McCormick & Co., Inc.

2½ cups sugar
⅛ teaspoon salt
⅓ cup light corn syrup
⅓ cup water
2 egg whites

½ teaspoon McCormick or Schilling Raspberry Extract
8 to 10 drops McCormick or Schilling Red Food Color

Combine sugar, salt, corn syrup, and water in a saucepan. Stir over low heat until sugar is completely dissolved. Then boil rapidly, without stirring, to 252° on a candy thermometer, or until a small amount of syrup forms a firm ball when dropped in cold water. Add syrup to stiffly beaten egg whites, a little at a time, beating after each addition. Add raspberry extract and red food color; continue beating until frosting stands in stiff peaks. Makes enough to frost 2 cake layers.

STRAWBERRY FROSTING
McCormick & Co., Inc.

1 cup sugar
⅓ cup water
1 teaspoon vinegar
⅛ teaspoon salt
2 egg whites

2 teaspoons McCormick or Schilling Strawberry Extract
About 8 drops McCormick or Schilling Red Food Color

Combine sugar, water, and vinegar; boil until syrup reaches 238°, or a small amount forms a soft ball in cold water. Add salt to egg whites and beat until stiff. Gradually add syrup, beating constantly until frosting holds shape. Stir in strawberry extract and red food color. Makes enough to frost 2 8- or 9-inch cake layers.

DATE-NUT FROSTING
General Foods Corporation

2 egg whites, unbeaten
1½ cups sugar
Dash of salt
⅓ cup water

2 teaspoons light corn syrup
1 teaspoon vanilla
½ cup chopped dates
¼ cup chopped nuts

Combine egg whites, sugar, salt, water, and corn syrup in top of double boiler. Beat about 1 minute, or until thoroughly mixed. Then place over boiling water and beat constantly with sturdy egg beater (or at high speed of electric beater) 7 minutes, or until frosting will stand in stiff peaks. (Stir frosting up from bottom and sides of pan occasionally with rubber scraper, spatula, or spoon.)

Remove from boiling water. For a very smooth and satiny frosting, pour at once into a large bowl for final beating. Then add vanilla and beat 1 minute, or until thick enough to spread. Divide frosting in half. Add chopped dates and chopped nuts to half of frosting. Spread between layers and on top of cake. Use rest of frosting on sides of cake.

RUM GLAZE
McCormick & Co., Inc.

1 cup sugar
Dash McCormick or Schilling
  Cream of Tartar

⅓ cup water
1 tablespoon McCormick or
  Schilling Rum Extract

Stir sugar, cream of tartar, and water over medium heat until sugar is completely dissolved. Cook, without stirring, until syrup reaches the hard crack stage, about 290° on a candy thermometer. Stir in rum extract, drop by drop. Excellent for glazing walnut or pecan halves.

To Glaze Nuts: Add nuts after mixing in rum extract. Stir until coated, then turn out on waxed paper. Quickly separate using two forks.

PUDDINGS

HONEY PUDDING
McCormick & Co., Inc.

3 eggs
¾ cup honey
½ teaspoon salt
½ to 1 cup raisins

3 cups milk, scalded
⅔ cup cooked rice
1 teaspoon McCormick or
   Schilling Orange Extract

Beat eggs slightly and combine with honey, salt, and raisins. Gradually mix in hot milk. Stir in rice and extract, and pour mixture into lightly greased baking dish. Set in shallow pan of hot water and bake in a 350° oven for 1 hour, or until knife inserted in center comes out clean. Serve hot or cold with cream. Makes 6 servings.

SQUAW PUDDING
Chun King Sales, Inc.

2 cups milk
1 tablespoon butter
2 eggs, beaten
½ teaspoon salt
½ cup sugar

1½ cups Nokomis Wild Rice,
   cooked
½ cup raisins
1 teaspoon vanilla
½ teaspoon cinnamon
¼ teaspoon nutmeg

Scald milk, remove from heat. Add butter and stir until butter is melted. Slowly add milk to eggs, add other ingredients except nutmeg, and mix thoroughly. Pour into greased 1½-quart casserole. Sprinkle top with nutmeg. Bake in 325° oven for 1 hour 15 minutes, or until firm. Makes 6 servings.

BAKED CRANBERRIES AND RICE
Ocean Spray Cranberries, Inc.

3 cups rice, cooked
1 1-pound can Ocean Spray Whole Cranberry Sauce

3 tablespoons butter
½ cup light brown sugar, firmly packed

Spoon 1 cup rice into 1-quart buttered baking dish. Cover with ½ cup cranberry sauce. Sprinkle sauce with ⅓ of the brown sugar and dot with 1 tablespoon butter. Repeat in 2 more layers. Bake uncovered in a 350° oven for 45 minutes. Serve warm with milk or cream. Makes 6 servings.

MAPLE-NUT RICE PUDDING
Uncle Ben's, Inc.

½ cup brown sugar
2 eggs, well beaten
½ teaspoon maple flavoring
⅛ teaspoon salt
1¼ cups milk

½ cup top milk or light cream
¼ cup chopped walnuts or pecans
1½ cups Uncle Ben's Converted Rice, cooked

Beat sugar with eggs. Blend in flavoring, salt, milk, and cream. Pour over pecans and cooked rice in buttered 1-quart baking dish. Place in pan of water and bake at 325° for approximately 1 hour, or until a knife inserted in center comes out clean. Makes 4 servings. Freezes well, covered with Saran Wrap.

COFFEE-RAISIN PILAU
Pan American Coffee Bureau

1 5-ounce package pre-
cooked rice
Regular strength coffee
½ cup golden raisins
½ cup chopped walnuts

⅛ teaspoon salt
⅛ teaspoon nutmeg
½ cup brown sugar, firmly
packed
1 cup heavy cream, whipped

Prepare precooked rice according to package directions, using coffee instead of water. Stir in remaining ingredients except cream, and mix well. Cool. Fold in whipped cream, reserving enough for garnishing. Spoon into sherbet glasses. Top with remaining whipped cream and a few chopped walnut meats. Makes 6 servings.

CONCORD BREAD PUDDING
The Welch Grape Juice Company, Inc.

6 slices day-old bread
¼ cup butter or margarine,
soft
3 whole eggs plus 2 yolks
¼ cup sugar
½ teaspoon vanilla

⅛ teaspoon nutmeg
1 quart scalded milk
½ cup Welch's Grape Jelly
2 egg whites plus 2 tablespoons sugar

Trim crusts from bread and butter 1 side. Combine 3 whole eggs plus 2 yolks, sugar, vanilla, and nutmeg. Add milk slowly, stirring until sugar is dissolved. Turn into 1-quart baking dish, and top with bread, buttered side up. Place in pan of hot water and bake in 350° oven 45 to 50 minutes, until firm. While pudding bakes, prepare meringue by beating 2 egg whites with 2 tablespoons sugar until they stand in peaks. When pudding is firm remove from oven, spread with jelly and top with meringue. Bake until meringue is golden. Serve warm. Makes 6 servings.

RUM CUSTARD
McCormick & Co., Inc.

3 eggs
¼ cup sugar
¼ teaspoon salt
2 cups milk, scalded

1 tablespoon McCormick or Schilling Rum Extract
McCormick or Schilling Nutmeg

Beat eggs slightly. Add sugar and salt, and mix well. Very slowly add the scalded milk, stirring constantly. Stir in the extract. Pour into custard cups; sprinkle with nutmeg. Place in a pan of hot water and bake in a 350° oven for 30 to 35 minutes or until a knife inserted in the center of the custard comes out clean. Makes 4 servings.

ZABAGLIONE (ITALIAN DESSERT)
Poultry and Egg National Board

5 eggs
⅓ cup sugar
¼ teaspoon salt

¾ teaspoon grated lemon rind
1 tablespoon lemon juice
½ cup sweet sherry

Beat eggs with rotary beater until thick and lemon-colored in upper part of a 1½- to 2-quart double boiler. Add sugar, salt, and lemon rind and juice, beating in thoroughly. Cook over barely simmering water (level of water in lower part should be 1½ to 2 inches below pan containing Zabaglione), beating constantly, and adding wine gradually. Scrape bottom and sides several times, and raise beater up and down while beating to assure uniform cooking. Cook until creamy and thick, 7 to 8 minutes. During the cooking the mixture expands to almost fill the pan and then settles somewhat when it is done. Serve warm or cool in sherbet glasses. Zabaglione is best served immediately. On cooling it separates in 2 layers. Makes 5 servings.

HOT CONCORD SOUFFLE
The Welch Grape Juice Company, Inc.

3 tablespoons sugar
3 tablespoons flour
1 tablespoon milk
1 cup milk, scalded
4 egg yolks, well beaten

1 cup Welch's Grapelade
1 teaspoon grated lemon rind
1 tablespoon lemon juice
6 egg whites

Mix sugar and flour together thoroughly. Blend with the 1 tablespoon milk to make a smooth paste. Add this to scalded milk and cook, stirring constantly, until mixture thickens. Remove from heat and stir in egg yolks. Add Grapelade, lemon rind, and juice. Beat 6 egg whites until they are stiff, but not dry, and fold in carefully. Pour batter into buttered and sugared, straight-sided, 2-quart soufflé dish. Bake at 350° for 35 minutes, or until soufflé is well puffed. Garnish as desired and serve at once.

CHOCOLATE SOUFFLE
Standard Brands, Inc.

1 package Royal Dark 'N' Sweet or Chocolate Pudding
1 cup milk

1 tablespoon margarine
3 eggs, separated
½ teaspoon vanilla

Blend pudding and milk in saucepan; add margarine. Bring to boil, stirring. Remove from heat. Slowly beat hot pudding into egg yolks, beaten until thick. Beat mixture until cool. Add vanilla. Fold in egg whites, beaten until stiff. Pour into 1½-quart baking dish. Set in pan of hot water. Bake in 350° oven about 1 hour 15 minutes. Serve immediately. Makes 8 servings.

COFFEE SOUFFLE
Pan American Coffee Bureau

⅓ cup all-purpose flour
3 tablespoons cocoa
¼ teaspoon salt
1 cup coffee

4 eggs, separated
½ cup sugar
Butter or margarine, soft
Sugar

Mix flour, cocoa, and salt. Stir in coffee slowly, and when well blended, cook over low heat, stirring vigorously, until mixture is very thick. Beat in 1 egg yolk at a time, and stir in sugar. Grease a quart casserole with butter or margarine, and coat with sugar. Fold well-beaten egg whites into mixture, pour into casserole, and bake about 25 minutes in 425° oven. Serve at once. Makes 6 servings.

REFRIGERATOR AND FRUIT DESSERTS

VANILLA ICE CREAM
Best Foods, Division of
Corn Products Company

¾ cup sugar
2 tablespoons Argo Corn
   Starch
½ teaspoon salt

2 eggs
1 quart milk
2 teaspoons vanilla

Mix sugar, corn starch, and salt in top of double boiler. Add eggs and mix well. Gradually stir in milk. Place over boiling water and cook, stirring constantly, until mixture is slightly thickened, about 8 to 10 minutes. Remove from heat, add vanilla; cool. Chill custard thoroughly before freezing.

With an electric freezer, follow manufacturer's directions. With hand-turned freezer, wash and scald can, cover, and dasher. Pour chilled custard mixture into can. The can should not be more than ⅔ full. Assemble freezer. Fill freezer tub with alternate layers crushed ice and rock salt, 8 parts ice to 1 part salt. Turn crank slowly at first; then increase speed, and turn until crank can no longer be turned easily. When freezing is complete, wipe cover carefully and remove dasher. Pack ice cream and adjust cover. Repack in ice and salt, in the proportion of 4 parts ice to 1 part salt. Let stand 2 hours. Makes about 1½ quarts.

Note: For a richer ice cream use 3 cups milk and 1 cup light cream or evaporated milk.

Variations

CHOCOLATE ICE CREAM. Follow recipe for Vanilla Ice Cream, adding 4 ounces unsweetened chocolate to egg and milk mixture before cooking. When mixture thickens, remove from heat and beat with rotary beater until smooth. Add vanilla and continue as above.

COFFEE ICE CREAM. Follow recipe for Vanilla Ice Cream, using 1½ cups coffee, and 2½ cups milk instead of 1 quart milk.

BANANA ICE CREAM. Follow recipe for Vanilla Ice Cream. Mix together 1½ cups mashed bananas and 1 tablespoon lemon juice; add to chilled custard mixture just before freezing.

BLACK WALNUT ICE CREAM
McCormick & Co., Inc.

2 eggs
1/8 teaspoon salt
1/2 cup sugar
1/2 teaspoon McCormick or
  Schilling Black Walnut
  Extract

1/2 cup light corn syrup
1 cup milk
1 cup light cream or evaporated milk

Beat eggs until light and lemon-colored. Add salt and gradually stir in sugar. Mix thoroughly. Stir in black walnut extract, corn syrup, milk, and cream; blend well. Pour into freezer tray. Turn control to fast freezing and freeze until there is a frozen layer 1-inch wide around tray. Remove to a chilled bowl and beat until mixture becomes light and creamy, but not melted. (Mixture may seem to separate, but this will disappear during freezing.) Freeze until firm. Makes 4 servings.

MOLDED CREAM
McCormick & Co., Inc.

2 egg yolks
1/2 cup sugar
2 cups milk
1/8 teaspoon salt
1 tablespoon gelatine
1/4 cup cold water

3 to 4 teaspoons McCormick
  or Schilling Pineapple Extract
About 6 drops McCormick or
  Schilling Yellow Food
  Color
1/2 cup whipping cream

Combine egg yolks, sugar, milk, and salt in saucepan or top of double boiler. Cook over low heat, stirring constantly, until slightly thickened. Soak gelatine in cold water until softened; add to milk mixture and stir until it dissolves. Mix in pineapple extract and food color. Pour half of this mixture into a wet mold; chill. Chill remaining mixture until it begins to set. Whip cream until stiff but not dry; fold into this remaining mixture. Pour into mold and chill until firm. Makes 4 to 6 servings.

PRUNE CREAM MOLD
The Dow Chemical Company

2 envelopes unflavored gelatine

1 cup cold prune liquid and/or water

2 12-ounce cans prune juice

1 pound prunes, cooked and chopped

2 tablespoons lemon juice

Cream cheese

Light cream

Soften gelatine in cold liquid. Heat prune juice; pour over gelatine mixture, and stir until dissolved. Cool until partially set. Fold in prunes and lemon juice. Turn into a 6½-cup ring mold; overwrap with Saran Wrap, chill until firm. Unmold and serve with cream cheese blended with light cream until consistency of whipped cream. Makes 12 servings.

Note: This dessert can be unmolded on a serving plate and the whipped cream cheese placed in the center, ready for serving an hour or so in advance. Overwrap in Saran Wrap and refrigerate. This saves last minute fuss.

EGGNOG DESSERT
Standard Brands, Inc.

1 package Royal Pineapple Gelatin

1 cup boiling water

2 eggs, separated

1 pint vanilla ice cream

1 tablespoon rum extract

Nutmeg

Dissolve pineapple gelatin in boiling water. Slowly stir hot gelatin into beaten egg yolks. Add vanilla ice cream and stir until melted. If necessary, chill until slightly thickened. Beat egg whites until stiff but not dry. Fold into slightly thickened gelatin mixture. Stir in rum extract. Pour into punch cups. Sprinkle with nutmeg. Chill until firm. Makes 6 servings.

MOLDED EGGNOG
Knox Gelatine, Inc.

2 envelopes Knox Unflavored
  Gelatine
¼ cup sugar
1 quart cold eggnog from
  local dairy

¼ teaspoon nutmeg (optional)
4 teaspoons rum flavoring
  (optional)
1 cup heavy cream, whipped

Combine gelatine and sugar in top of double boiler. Stir in 1 cup of the cold eggnog. Place over boiling water and stir until gelatine and sugar are dissolved. Remove from heat; add remaining eggnog. Add nutmeg and flavoring. Chill until mixture mounds slightly when dropped from a spoon. Fold in whipped cream. Turn into a 6-cup mold; chill until firm. Unmold. Makes 10 servings.

MARLOW
McCormick & Co., Inc.

¼ pound marshmallows
1 cup milk
1 cup whipping cream
2 to 3 teaspoons McCormick
  or Schilling Raspberry Extract

⅛ teaspoon salt
10 to 15 drops McCormick
  or Schilling Red Food
  Color

Combine marshmallows and milk; cook over hot water, stirring occasionally, until marshmallows are melted. Cool until slightly thickened. Stir in raspberry extract, salt, and food color. Mix well. Whip cream and fold into the marsh-mallow-milk mixture. Pour into freezer tray and freeze until firm. Makes 4 servings.

LIME OR LEMON SHERBET
Knox Gelatine, Inc.

1 envelope Knox Unflavored Gelatine
3 cups water
1½ cups sugar

1 6-ounce can frozen concentrated limeade or lemonade, thawed
1 egg white

Sprinkle gelatine on ½ cup of the water in saucepan to soften. Place over medium heat and stir until gelatine is dissolved. Add to remaining 2½ cups water with sugar and undiluted limeade concentrate; stir until sugar is dissolved. Pour into an 8-cup loaf pan or several refrigerator trays. Place in freezing compartment of refrigerator; freeze, stirring occasionally. Break up frozen mixture in tray; add unbeaten egg white and beat with electric mixer or rotary beater just until smooth. (Stir in a few drops green food coloring if limeade has been used.) Return to freezing compartment and freeze until firm. Makes about 1½ quarts.

CRANBERRY SHERBET
Best Foods, Division of Corn Products Company

1½ teaspoons unflavored gelatine
2 cups cranberry cocktail
1½ tablespoons nonfat dry milk solids

1 tablespoon lemon juice
1½ cups Karo Syrup, Red Label

Sprinkle gelatine over ¼ cup cranberry cocktail to soften. Stir over hot water until gelatine dissolves. Combine remaining ingredients; then add gelatine and mix well. Pour into refrigerator freezing tray. Freeze with cold control set for fast freezing until mixture is almost firm. Turn into chilled bowl; beat smooth with rotary beater or electric mixer. Return to freezing tray and freeze until firm, about 3 hours. Extremely low in calories. Makes 8 servings, ½ cup each.

FROZEN FRUIT SHERBET
Standard Brands, Inc.

1 package Royal Watermelon
   Gelatin
1 cup boiling water

1 pint lemon sherbet
1 1-pound, 14-ounce can
   fruit cocktail, drained

Dissolve watermelon gelatin in boiling water. Add lemon sherbet and stir until melted, blending in with back of spoon, if necessary. Chill until slightly thickened. Fold in fruit. Pour into a 9 x 5 x 3-inch loaf pan and freeze. To unmold, run a warm spatula around loaf pan and invert over serving platter. Slice and serve. Makes 8 servings.

PINEAPPLE FRAPPE
The Seven-Up Company

1 No. 2 can crushed pine-
   apple
1 envelope unflavored gelatine
½ cup sugar

½ cup shredded coconut
1 7-ounce bottle 7-Up
2 egg whites
¼ teaspoon salt

Drain crushed pineapple and reserve pineapple; heat drained juice to boiling. Combine gelatine and sugar in a large bowl. Stir in boiling juice and continue stirring until gelatine is dissolved. Cool. Mix in reserved pineapple and coconut; quickly stir in 7-Up. Pour into a large freezer tray or loaf pan and freeze mixture until mushy. Beat egg whites with salt until stiff. Stir mixture with fork, and gently fold in egg whites. Freeze until firm. Makes 6 servings.

KEEP-ON-HAND DESSERT
The Dow Chemical Company

1 cup butter
1 cup sugar
3 egg yolks
Juice of 1½ oranges, plus
grated rind

Juice of 1 lemon, plus grated
rind
3 egg whites
Sponge cake or lady fingers

Cream butter and sugar together. Add egg yolks and
fruit juices. Beat egg whites until stiff and fold into butter
mixture. Line a mold or loaf pan with sponge cake cut in
fingers or lady fingers and cover with mixture. Repeat for
as many layers as you wish ending with cake.

If dessert is to be frozen, first line pan with transparent
Saran Wrap. Then, the entire dessert may be removed from
pan with ease after freezing. To store in the refrigerator
overnight, simply cover dessert with Saran Wrap. Make
double recipe at one time, and keep one of the desserts
in the freezer for future use. Makes 8 servings.

COFFEE JELLY PARFAIT
Pan American Coffee Bureau

1 tablespoon unflavored gelatine
2¼ cups strong cold coffee
⅓ cup sugar

1 tablespoon brandy flavoring
1 cup heavy cream
½ cup chopped salted al-
monds

Soften gelatine in ¼ cup of the cold coffee. Heat remaining coffee to boiling point. Add softened gelatine and
sugar, and stir until gelatine dissolves. Add flavoring. Pour
into jelly roll pan, or any shallow pan, to a depth of about
½ inch. Chill until firm. Cut in ½-inch cubes. Whip cream
and sweeten to taste. Arrange alternating layers of coffee

jelly cubes, whipped cream, and almonds in tall dessert glasses. Makes 6 servings.

HANNA'S APPLESAUCE
The Angostura-Wuppermann Corp.

2½ pounds cooking apples
¾ cup sugar
2 cups water

1 tablespoon Angostura Aromatic Bitters

Wash, pare, quarter, and core cooking apples. Add water, cook until nearly soft. Add sugar and cook few minutes longer. Remove from heat. Add bitters and whip with wire whisk. Serve cool.

BAKED APPLES IMPERIAL
The Seven-Up Company

6 large baking apples
¼ cup brown sugar
3 tablespoons butter, soft
3 tablespoons slivered almonds

2 tablespoons apricot preserves
¼ teaspoon salt
1 7-ounce bottle 7-Up

Core apples and peel skin from around tops. Place in a greased shallow baking pan. Mix brown sugar, butter, almonds, jam, and salt, and spoon into centers of apples. Pour 7-Up over apples and bake at 350° for 45 to 60 minutes, basting apples from time to time. Makes 6 servings.

BAKED APPLES CANTON
Brazil Nut Association

6 large baking apples
1 cup coarsely chopped Brazil nuts
½ cup chopped pitted dates
⅓ cup chopped candied ginger

1 cup light corn syrup
1 teaspoon powdered ginger
Red food coloring
Sugar

Core apples almost through. Pare about ⅓ of the way down from stem end. Combine Brazil nuts, dates, and candied ginger. Fill centers of apples with nut-fruit mixture. Combine corn syrup and powdered ginger. Tint red with food coloring; simmer 5 minutes. Brush apples thickly with this mixture. Place in baking dish; add enough boiling water to cover bottom of baking dish; bake in 350° oven about 40 minutes, or until tender, basting frequently with the syrup. Remove from oven. Sprinkle with sugar; broil with surface of apples 4 inches below source of heat. Baste with remaining syrup and sprinkle with additional sugar, until glazed about 15 minutes. Makes 6 servings. Baked Apples Canton may be prepared in advance and frozen in Saran Wrap until needed.

BAKED GRAPEFRUIT
McCormick & Co., Inc.

Cut grapefruit in half and loosen sections with knife. Sprinkle with sugar and let stand 30 minutes. When ready to bake sprinkle with more sugar, dot with butter and drizzle 1 teaspoon McCormick Rum or Brandy Extract on top of each half. Bake 25 minutes at 450°. Serve hot as an appetizer or as a dessert.

FESTIVE ORANGE CUPS
Sunkist Growers, Inc.

8 large Sunkist Oranges, unpeeled
¼ cup maraschino cherries, sliced (reserve 1 tablespoon syrup)
¼ cup chopped nuts
½ cup chopped dates
1½ cups apricots, drained and chopped
1½ pints vanilla ice cream
½ cup heavy cream, whipped
Maraschino cherries for garnish

Cut stem end off oranges; scoop out pulp, reserving ½ cup, and chop. Combine with sliced cherries, nuts, dates, and apricots. Layer fruit mixture and softened ice cream alternately in each orange shell. Flavor whipped cream with cherry syrup and garnish filled orange cups. Top with cherries. Cover with Saran Wrap and freeze at 0°. Set in food compartment of refrigerator for 20 to 30 minutes before serving. Makes 8 servings.

To make Orange Alaskas: Garnish with meringue instead of whipped cream and brown lightly in 475° oven.

BAKED ALASKA
McCormick & Co., Inc.

½ teaspoon McCormick or Schilling Cream of Tartar
6 egg whites, have at room temperature
1 cup plus 2 tablespoons superfine sugar or ¾ cup regular granulated sugar

1 thin layer sponge cake
2 quarts hard-frozen ice cream
1 to 2 tablespoons confectioners' sugar

When ready to serve, add cream of tartar to egg whites; beat until stiff, but not dry. Gradually add sugar, continuing to beat until meringue is stiff and will hold peaks. Cover a bread board with white or brown paper. Place a thin, round layer of sponge cake on the paper. Place the ice cream on cake; make sure the cake extends ½ to 1 inch beyond the ice cream all around. (Trim cake to suit the shape of ice cream.) Completely cover the entire surface of the ice cream and cake with a thick coating of meringue. Dust with confectioners' sugar. Bake in a preheated oven at 450° just long enough to brown delicately, about 5 minutes. Slip the Baked Alaska quickly onto a chilled serving platter and serve immediately. (Individual Alaskas may be made using 3-inch circles of sponge cake and balls of ice cream. For meringue you'll need to use 1 egg white for each.)

Ice cream may be packed and hard-frozen in round or melon molds or mixing bowl. Different colors and/or flavors may be used to form layers in the molds.

Note: To serve Baked Alaska flaming, make small wells using aluminum foil, (be careful not to punch holes in foil) and lightly press them into the top of the meringue before baking. After Baked Alaska has been transferred to serving platter, fill wells with McCormick Lemon or Orange Extract. Set aflame. Serve immediately.

BANANA-COCONUT SNOWBALLS
General Foods Corporation

1 cup mashed bananas, 2 to 3 fully ripe
2 teaspoons lemon juice
¼ cup sugar
¼ teaspoon salt
⅓ cup milk
1 cup whipping cream

2 egg whites, stiffly beaten
2 egg yolks, well beaten
1 teaspoon vanilla
½ cup Baker's Angel Flake Coconut, toasted
Chopped walnuts

Mix together bananas and lemon juice. Add sugar, salt, and milk, stirring until blended. Whip cream until thickened but not stiff. Fold egg whites, yolks, cream, and vanilla into banana mixture. Turn into freezing trays of refrigerator, setting control at coldest freezing temperature. Freeze until mixture holds its shape, stirring every 30 minutes; add toasted coconut during final stirring. Freeze until firm. With scoop form into balls and roll in chopped walnuts. Cover with Saran Wrap and freeze until ready to serve. Makes 1½ quarts.

ORANGE JACK O'LANTERNS
Knox Gelatine, Inc.

6 oranges
1 envelope Knox Unflavored Gelatine
½ cup sugar
1½ cups orange juice, divided

1 tablespoon lemon juice
1 cup cooked chopped prunes
⅓ cup chopped nuts

Slice top from orange; cut around pulp with paring knife; lift out, then scrape out remaining pulp with teaspoon. Press juice through strainer. With point of paring knife, make a jack o'lantern face on each orange, being careful not to cut through inside of orange. Mix together gelatine and sugar in saucepan. Stir in 1 cup of the orange juice. Place over low heat, stirring constantly, until gelatine and sugar are thoroughly dissolved. Remove from heat; stir in remaining ½ cup orange juice and lemon juice. Chill until mixture is the consistency of unbeaten egg white. Fold in remaining ingredients. Spoon into orange shells; cover with Saran Wrap and chill until firm. If desired, serve with sweetened whipped cream. Makes 6 servings.

BLACKBERRY CHIFFON
Standard Brands, Inc.

2 packages Royal Vitamin C Gelatin, Blackberry Flavor
1½ cups boiling water
4 eggs, separated
¾ cups cold water
½ teaspoon salt
2 tablespoons lemon juice
1½ cups applesauce
½ cup sugar

Dissolve gelatin in boiling water. Beat egg yolks until light; slowly stir in hot gelatin. Add cold water, salt, lemon juice, and applesauce. Chill until slightly thickened, stirring occasionally to keep smooth. Beat egg whites until foamy; slowly beat in ½ cup sugar. Beat until stiff. Fold into thickened gelatin. Pile into 2½-quart mold. Chill. Unmold and serve with custard sauce and nuts if desired. Makes 10 to 12 servings.

CHERRY COCO-NUT
Stokely-Van Camp, Inc.

1 cup whipping cream
1 can (1 pound) Stokely-Van Camp's Red Tart Pitted Cherries, drained
¼ cup broken pecans

¼ cup flaked coconut
⅓ cup miniature marshmallows
6 medium cream puffs

Whip cream and combine with next 4 ingredients. Chill in the refrigerator until ready to serve. At serving time, cut off tops of cream puffs and fill with Cherry Choco-Nut mixture. Replace tops. Makes 6 servings. Cherry Coco-Nut will freeze well, covered with Saran Wrap.

CHERRY FLUFF
Knox Gelatine, Inc.

1 envelope Knox Unflavored Gelatine
⅔ cup sugar
⅛ teaspoon salt
1 can (1 pound) red sour pitted cherries (water pack)

2 eggs, separated
¼ teaspoon almond flavoring
¼ teaspoon red food coloring
1 cup heavy cream, whipped

Mix together gelatine, ⅓ cup of the sugar, and salt in saucepan. Drain cherries; beat together cherry liquid and egg yolks; add to gelatine mixture. Place over low heat, stirring constantly, until gelatine and sugar are dissolved, about 5 minutes. Remove from heat; add almond flavoring, red food coloring, and drained cherries. Chill until mixture mounds slightly when dropped from a spoon. Beat egg whites until stiff, but not dry. Gradually add remaining ⅓ cup sugar and beat until very stiff. Fold into cherry mixture; fold in whipped cream.

Variations

MOLDED CHERRY FLUFF. Chill in a 6-cup mold.

CHIFFON PIE. Turn mixture into a 9-inch baked pastry shell.

SOUFFLÉ. Double recipe and turn mixture into a 6 to 8 cup soufflé dish with a 2-inch high collar. To make collar, fold waxed paper into several thicknesses 3-inches wide, and long enough to go around soufflé dish with generous overlap. Attach to dish with sealing tape, leaving 1 inch of the paper around dish to make collar 2-inches high.

PUMPKIN CHIFFON PUDDING
Knox Gelatine, Inc.

2 envelopes Knox Unflavored Gelatine
½ cup brown sugar, firmly packed
½ teaspoon salt
1 teaspoon cinnamon
¼ teaspoon nutmeg
¼ teaspoon ginger
⅛ teaspoon cloves
1¼ cups evaporated milk
5 eggs, separated
1 1-pound can pumpkin
½ cup sugar

Mix together gelatine, brown sugar, salt, and spices in top of double boiler. Stir in evaporated milk and egg yolks. Place over boiling water and cook, stirring constantly, until gelatine dissolves and mixture thickens slightly, about 6 minutes. Remove from heat; stir in pumpkin. Chill until mixture is cooled. Beat egg whites until stiff, but not dry. Gradually add sugar and beat until very stiff. Fold gelatine mixture into beaten egg whites. Turn into 2-quart mold; chill until firm. Makes 10 to 12 servings.

CONCORD ROYALES
The Welch Grape Juice Company, Inc.

1 can Welch's Jellied Sauce
1 ground whole orange
1 teaspoon lemon juice
½ teaspoon almond extract
1 cup broken walnut meats
6 candied violets (optional)

½ cup drained crushed
  pineapple
1 pint commercial sour
  cream or heavy sweet
  cream, whipped
1 large or 6 individual baked
  meringue shells

Place sauce in large bowl. Break with fork. Add next 4 ingredients. Mix thoroughly. Chill. To serve, fill large or individual meringue shells with mixture. Garnish with whipped or commercial sour cream and candied violets.

CONCORD CHIFFON
The Welch Grape Juice Company, Inc.

1 tablespoon unflavored gelatine
¼ cup cold water
3 eggs, separated
½ cup Welch's Grape Juice
½ cup strained honey
Few grains salt

2 tablespoons flour
2 tablespoons water
2 tablespoons lemon juice
1 teaspoon grated lemon
  rind
2 tablespoons sugar
1 baked pie shell (optional)

Dissolve gelatine in cold water. Beat egg yolks and blend with grape juice, honey, and salt. Blend flour and water to smooth paste and stir in. Cook over hot water, stirring constantly, until mixture thickens. Add softened gelatine and blend well into mixture; add lemon juice and rind. Allow to cool, then place in refrigerator until partially set.

Beat egg whites until frothy, gradually add sugar and continue to beat until egg whites form stiff peaks. Fold into cold, thickened grape juice mixture. Pour into large or individual molds, or into crisp baked pastry shell. Chill at least 2 hours. When ready to serve garnish with ½ cup whipped cream, chilled bits of grape jelly, or candied violets.

BAVARIAN CREAM
Knox Gelatine, Inc.

1 envelope Knox Unflavored Gelatine	1¼ cups milk
½ cup sugar	½ teaspoon vanilla
⅛ teaspoon salt	1 cup heavy cream, whipped
2 eggs, separated	Sliced strawberries

Mix together gelatine, ¼ cup of the sugar, and salt in saucepan. Beat together egg yolks and milk; add to gelatine mixture. Place over low heat, stirring constantly, until gelatine is dissolved, about 6 minutes. Remove from heat; add vanilla. Chill until mixture mounds slightly when dropped from a spoon. Beat egg whites until stiff, but not dry. Gradually add remaining ¼ cup sugar and beat until very stiff. Fold into gelatine mixture. Fold in whipped cream. Turn into a 5-cup ring mold. Chill until firm. Unmold and garnish with sliced strawberries. Makes 6 to 8 servings.

CONCORD BAVARIAN
The Welch Grape Juice Company, Inc.

1 envelope unflavored gelatine	½ cup sugar
2 tablespoons cold water	1 cup plus 2 tablespoons Welch's Frozen Grape Juice Concentrate, thawed
3 egg yolks	
1 teaspoon grated lemon rind	1 cup heavy cream, whipped with ¼ cup sifted confectioners' sugar
1 tablespoon lemon juice	

Sprinkle gelatine over 2 tablespoons cold water in cup to dissolve. Beat egg yolks until thick and light. Add sugar gradually and continue beating until thoroughly creamed. Add grape juice, lemon rind, juice, and salt. Cook over hot, not boiling water, until thickened. Add gelatine and blend thoroughly. Chill in refrigerator until mixture begins to set. Fold whipped cream into partially set mixture. Pour into large or individual molds and chill several hours or overnight. At serving time crown with candied violets or any desired garnish, and serve with a hot sauce.

COFFEE BAVARIAN
Knox Gelatine, Inc.

1 envelope Knox Unflavored Gelatine	4 teaspoons instant coffee
⅓ cup sugar	1¼ cups cold water
	1 cup heavy cream, whipped

Mix gelatine, sugar, and instant coffee in saucepan. Stir in ½ cup of the water. Place over low heat, stirring constantly, until gelatine is dissolved. Remove from heat. Stir in remaining ¾ cup cold water. Chill until mixture is the consistency of unbeaten egg white. Fold in whipped cream. Turn into 3-cup mold. Chill until firm.

STRAWBERRY CREAM CHARLOTTE
Standard Brands, Inc.

1 package Royal Instant Strawberry Cream Pudding	1¼ cups milk
	1 cup heavy cream
	12 bakers' lady fingers

Make up pudding using milk and cream. Let stand 5 to 10 minutes. Fill and frost bakers' lady fingers forcing the pudding through a pastry tube to make interesting designs. If desired, garnish with strawberry slices. Serve immediately, or freeze until firm.

FRENCH CHOCOLATE CREME
Standard Brands, Inc.

1 package Royal Custard
Flavor Dessert
2¼ cups milk

½ cup semi-sweet choco-
late bits
¾ cup heavy cream,
whipped

Combine custard flavor dessert, milk, and chocolate bits.
Cook over medium heat, stirring constantly, until mixture
comes to a boil. Pour into bowl and chill. Beat with rotary
beater until smooth. Fold in whipped cream. Chill thoroughly. Serve topped with shaved chocolate.

POT DE CREME
The Nestlé Company

1 egg
⅛ teaspoon salt
2 tablespoons sugar
¾ cup milk

1 6-ounce package Nestlé's
Semi-Sweet Chocolate
Morsels
1 teaspoon vanilla

Combine egg, salt, and sugar in top of double boiler;
beat until thick. Stir in milk. Place over boiling water and
cook, stirring constantly, 5 minutes. Remove from heat.
Add semi-sweet chocolate morsels and vanilla; stir until
smooth. Pour into 6 small custard cups or pot de crème
servers. Chill several hours. Makes 6 servings.

CHOCOLATE VELVET
The Nestlé Company

2 12-ounce Jumbo packages
(4 cups) Nestlé's Semi-
Sweet Chocolate Morsels
½ cup water
1 teaspoon Nescafé

½ cup rum or cognac
3 egg yolks
3 egg whites
2 tablespoons sugar
1 cup heavy cream, whipped

Melt chocolate over hot, not boiling, water. Add ½ cup water and Nescafé, and stir until smooth. Blend in rum or cognac and egg yolks. Remove from water and cool. Beat egg whites until foamy. Add sugar gradually and continue beating until stiff, glossy peaks form. Fold whipped cream and egg whites into semi-sweet mixture. Chill at least 1 hour before serving. Makes approximately 18 servings.

MACAROON CREAM
Paul Masson Vineyards

1 envelope plain gelatine	1 tablespoon fresh lemon juice
¼ cup cold water	
1 cup milk	3 to 4 drops red food coloring
1 egg	
½ cup sugar	1 cup whipping cream
¼ teaspoon salt	¾ cup macaroon crumbs
⅓ cup Paul Masson Port	

Soften gelatine in cold water. Scald milk. Beat egg lightly with sugar and salt. Stir in hot milk and cook, stirring over very low heat until mixture coats a spoon. Add softened gelatine, and stir until it is dissolved. Remove from heat and cool slightly. Stir in wine, lemon juice, and red coloring; cook until mixture thickens. Whip cream until stiff, and fold into gelatine mixture, along with macaroon crumbs. Turn into molds and chill until firm. Unmold to serve. Makes 6 to 8 servings.

SHERRY COCONUT MOUSSE
General Foods Corporation

1 envelope (1 tablespoon) gelatine	2 cups cream, whipped
¼ cup cold water	2 tablespoons sherry
¾ cup milk, scalded	1 tablespoon butter
⅔ cup sugar	1 cup Baker's Angel Flake Coconut
¼ teaspoon salt	Dash of salt

Combine gelatine and cold water in mixing bowl; mix well. Add milk and stir until gelatine is dissolved. Dissolve sugar and salt in the hot mixture. Chill. When slightly thickened, fold in whipped cream and sherry. Turn into freezing tray of refrigerator, setting control for coldest freezing temperature.

Melt butter in skillet. Add coconut and dash of salt and sauté until coconut is delicately browned. Crush slightly.

When mousse is partially frozen, remove from tray and beat with egg beater until fluffy and smooth. Fold in sautéed coconut. Return to tray and freeze until firm, 3 to 4 hours. Makes about 1½ quarts. Store in Saran Wrap for later use.

DELLA ROBBIA DESSERT SALAD
Standard Brands, Inc.

1 package Royal Blackberry Gelatin
1 cup boiling water
1 cup cold water
1 tablespoon lemon juice
½ cup finely chopped pecans
⅓ cup commercial sour cream

Pineapple slices
Whole apricots
Pear halves
Blueberries
Bing cherries
Salad greens
Pineapple French Dressing

Dissolve gelatin in boiling water; add cold water and lemon juice. Refrigerate until slightly thickened, about consistency of unbeaten egg white. Set bowl of gelatin in bowl of ice water; beat with rotary beater or electric mixer until thick and fluffy. Quickly fold in pecans and sour cream (mixture will lose some of its volume). Turn into 1½-quart mold and refrigerate until set. Unmold in center of large plate. Surround with salad greens; arrange fruits in elaborate ring around mold. Pass dressing separately. Makes 6 to 8 servings. (See illustration 23.)

Pineapple French Dressing: Combine 1 cup salad oil with ⅓ cup lemon juice, ⅓ cup sugar, 1 teaspoon salt, ⅛ teaspoon horseradish, and ½ teaspoon dry mustard; beat with rotary beater until thick and smooth. Stir in ⅓ cup well-drained canned, crushed pineapple.

DESSERT CHEESES

The chart of Dessert Cheeses below was provided for
Food From Famous Kitchens by The Borden Company.

Kind	Country Where First Made	Color and Type	Shape
Bel Paese pronounced Bell-pa-azey′	Italy	Slate gray surface Light yellow interior Soft	Circular cake 2 inches high
Blue spelled **Bleu** on imported cheese	France	Foil-wrapped Green-mold interior Made with cow's milk Semi-soft—spicy	Cylindrical 6 inches diameter 4½ inches high
Brie pronounced Bree	France	Russet brown surface Creamy yellow interior Soft-mold ripened	Circular cake 1¼ to 1¾ inches high 6 to 16 inches diameter
Camembert pronounced Kam-em-bear	France	Gray-white mold surface Creamy yellow interior Soft-mold ripened	Circular cake 6½ inches diameter 1½ inches high

Kind	Country Where First Made	Color and Type	Shape
Edam pronounced Ee-dam	North Holland	Red coated surface Creamy yellow interior Semi-hard	Loaf or Cannon ball
Gejtost pronounced Yea-toast'	Norway	Light brown Sweetish taste Semi-hard	Cubical and Rectangular
Gorgonzola	Italy	Light tan surface Light yellow with green mold interior Semi-hard	Cylindrical 12 inches diameter 6 inches high
Gruyere pronounced Grew-yare'	Switzerland	Light yellow color Nut sweet flavor Semi-hard	Usually processed and sold in circular box in portions
Liederkranz Brand	New York U.S.A.	Russet surface Creamy yellow interior Soft with robust flavor	Rectangular 1½ x 2 x 3½ inches
Monterey or Monterey Jack	California U.S.A.	Greyish white surface White interior Semi-soft; mild	Circular wheels 9½ inches diameter Rindless blocks
Mysost (Primost)	Scandinavian countries	Light brown Sweetish taste Semi-hard whey cheese	Cubical and Cylindrical
Oka (Port du Salut)	Canada	Russet surface Creamy yellow interior Semi-soft	Circular cake
Roquefort pronounced Roke-fort	France	Green mold interior Made with sheep's milk Semi-soft; spicy flavor	Cylindrical 6 inches diameter 4 to 5 inches high

33 Coffee can be much more than a simple beverage served hot or iced. With the addition of spices, whipped cream, or chocolate, it becomes as glamorous and exotic as the countries in which these variations were first introduced. See **Beverages** (p. 289). Photo courtesy of Pan American Coffee Bureau.

34 For centuries cheese has been a principal staple of diets around the world. This sampling from the world's cheeses gives some indication of their great variety. Photo courtesy of McCall's Magazine.

35 Dinners of any size can be pleasantly concluded with nothing more elaborate than a serving of fruit, nuts, and coffee. Here, slivered Brazil nuts are served in the pod from which the whole nuts have been removed. The pod is surrounded by unshelled nuts. Photo courtesy of Brazil Nut Association.

36 Black Bottom Pie (p. 232) is a rich and luscious conclusion to a light supper or luncheon. It is equally suitable for dessert-and-coffee guests or for a break at the bridge table. Photo courtesy of Kellogg Company.

37 Pineapple-Honey Upside Down Cake (p. 246) uses crushed pineapple, cherries, and walnuts to decorate the basically simple cake. It is a welcome variation on a universally popular recipe. Photo courtesy of Dole Corporation.

38 No longer regional, the Hawaiian Luau has already been adopted by mainland hostesses as a popular American party. The food is native: fruit punch, mushrooms wrapped in bacon and alternated with pineapple on bamboo skewers. Waikiki Whip (p. 196) is in the pineapple shell. Tuna-Chicken Curry (p. 49) makes an appropriate main dish in any state. Photo courtesy of Star-Kist Foods, Inc.

39 Wines hold the memory of sun-ripened grapes, of vineyards covering the dark, rich earth. You can have confidence that these three— champagne, sherry, and rosé—will be appropriate however you choose to serve them throughout the day and evening. Photo courtesy of Paul Masson Vineyards.

40 Color today is taking its place along with taste and texture as an essential element of the culinary arts. Photo courtesy of McCormick & Co., Inc.

BEVERaGES

Coffee and tea are the basic American beverages. Recently we have become aware of exotic variations in the preparation of tea and coffee—variations that stem from the cultures of many countries.

The advent in the great American cities of the European-style coffee-house has encouraged us to experiment with their specialties—coffee served with whipped cream, spices, and liqueurs. We have come to realize that coffee, served to after-dinner guests, can be as dramatic and important as the dessert that preceded it.

The recipes in this chapter are almost certain to give you a new perspective on coffee and tea. Properly prepared, they should elicit exclamations of approval from your family and friends.

In addition to recipes for these two beverages, there are a number of soda-fountain specialties and an extra-delicious treatment of an old favorite, hot chocolate.

COFFEE

CINNAMON STICK COFFEE
The Nestlé Company

2 cups boiling water
2 2-inch sticks cinnamon or
   ¼ teaspoon ground cinnamon

4 teaspoons Nescafé
2 7-inch cinnamon sticks

Combine first 2 ingredients and simmer 5 minutes, covered. Add instant coffee and strain into 2 9-ounce coffee mugs. Serve with a 7-inch cinnamon stick in each. Makes 2 servings.

VIENNESE COFFEE
Pan American Coffee Bureau

Brew extra-strength coffee, sweeten to taste, and top with whipped cream.

HONEYPOT COFFEE
The Nestlé Company

½ cup water
1 tablespoon sesame seeds

1 tablespoon honey
3 tablespoons Nescafé

Combine water, sesame seeds, and honey, and bring to a

full boil. Cover and simmer 5 minutes. Remove from heat and add instant coffee. Strain into 2 demi-tasse cups. Makes 2 servings.

COFFEE NECTAR
Pan American Coffee Bureau

2¼ cups strong cold coffee   1 pint coffee ice cream
1 tablespoon Angostura

Place all ingredients in bowl or electric blender and beat until smooth and creamy. Pour into tall glasses. Makes 3 to 4 servings.

SPICY ICED COFFEE
Pan American Coffee Bureau

3 cups hot double-strength   2 cinnamon sticks
   coffee   4 cloves
4 allspice berries

Pour coffee over spices. Let stand 1 hour. Strain and pour over ice in tall glasses. Serve with cream and sugar. Makes 4 servings.

TEA

There are over 3,000 varieties of tea, but the instructions for brewing are the same for all:

Brew tea by the clock—not by color. Brewing time is 3 to 5 minutes, depending on the strength of tea you prefer.

Stir the tea before pouring to distribute it evenly.

Tea should be brewed in a preheated earthenware or china tea pot.

Always use fresh, cold water. Reheated water gives the tea a flat taste.

Authorities prefer milk to cream with tea in order to preserve the delicate flavor and aroma, or they use lemon to accent the flavor.

HOT TODDY
Thomas J. Lipton, Inc.

Steep a pot of strong Lipton Tea. Put 1 teaspoon sugar and 8 to 10 small cinnamon candies in bottom of tall mug. Fill mug with steaming hot tea. Stir with cinnamon stick until cinnamon flavor just pleases you.

SKI BALL
Thomas J. Lipton, Inc.

1 quart hot Lipton Tea	4 sticks cinnamon
4 lemon slices	4 tablespoons honey
8 whole cloves	

Stud each lemon slice with 2 cloves and place with a stick of cinnamon in each mug. Stir honey into hot tea and pour into mugs. Makes 4 servings.

CAMBRIC TEA
Thomas J. Lipton, Inc.

Pour cup hot Lipton Tea; fill cup with hot or cold milk and sweeten with honey or sugar.

HOT TOMATO-TEA COCKTAIL
Thomas J. Lipton, Inc.

2 cups Lipton Tea	1 teaspoon salt
2 cups tomato juice cock-tail	1 teaspoon Worcestershire Sauce

Combine all ingredients and heat to boiling. Serve in cups or mugs for first course of meal. Makes 6 servings.

LIME DELIGHT
Thomas J. Lipton, Inc.

4 cups strong Lipton Tea, cooled
Juice of 1 lime

2 tablespoons sugar
3 tablespoons maraschino cherry juice

Combine all ingredients. Pour over ice cubes in tall glass. Garnish drink with twist of lime peel and a cherry. Makes 4 to 6 servings.

TROPICAL TEA
Thomas J. Lipton, Inc.

3 cups Lipton Tea, cooled

1 6-ounce can frozen lemonade concentrate

Combine tea and lemonade concentrate. Pour over ice in tall glasses. Makes 4 servings.

ALMOND-FLAVORED TEA LEMONADE
Thomas J. Lipton, Inc.

3 cups strong Lipton Tea, cooled
1 teaspoon almond flavoring

1 6-ounce can frozen lemonade concentrate

Combine ingredients and stir until well blended. Pour into tall glasses filled with ice cubes. Makes 4 to 6 servings.

PINK TEA
Thomas J. Lipton, Inc.

1 quart Lipton Tea, cooled
2 cups cranberry juice cocktail

Juice of 1 lemon
2 tablespoons sugar

Combine ingredients. Serve over ice cubes in tall glasses.
Makes 4 to 6 servings.

HOT TEA PUNCH
Thomas J. Lipton, Inc.

2 quarts strong Lipton Tea
1 6-ounce can frozen lemonade concentrate

2 sticks cinnamon
¼ cup honey
½ cup sugar

Stir ingredients into tea and simmer 10 minutes. Serve
in mugs or tea cups. Makes 10 to 12 servings.

HOT FRUIT PUNCH
Thomas J. Lipton, Inc.

1 cup strong Lipton Tea
1 cup pineapple juice
1 cup orange juice
2 cups water

¼ cup sugar
6 pineapple spears
24 whole cloves

Combine tea, fruit juices, water, and sugar. Heat to a
boil. Place clove-studded pineapple spear in each mug.
Pour in hot punch. Makes 4 to 6 servings.

NEW ENGLAND SPECIAL
Thomas J. Lipton, Inc.

1 orange
12 whole cloves
1 cinnamon stick, in pieces
1 Lipton Family Size Tea Bag

4 cups boiling water
1 cup cranberry juice
⅓ to ½ cup sugar
1½ to 2 teaspoons rum flavoring

Stud orange with cloves, and cut into 6 or 8 sections. Drop sections into tea pot, squeezing each section slightly. Add cinnamon, tea, and boiling water. Steep for 5 minutes and strain. Stir in cranberry juice, sugar, and rum flavoring. Makes 4 to 6 servings.

TEA LEMONADE
Thomas J. Lipton, Inc.

2 quarts Lipton Tea, cooled
¾ cup simple syrup

1 6-ounce can frozen lemonade concentrate

Combine ingredients and stir until well blended. Pour over ice; garnish with lemon or orange slices. Makes 8 to 10 servings.

Simple Syrup: Simmer together ¾ cup water and ¾ cup sugar for 3 to 5 minutes.

MINTED TEA
Thomas J. Lipton, Inc.

2 sprigs fresh mint
⅓ cup orange juice, fresh or unsweetened
Juice of 2 lemons
2 cups strong Lipton Tea, hot

⅓ teaspoon powdered ginger
⅓ cup hot water
1 cup cold water

Bruise mint leaves in bowl or pitcher. Pour in fruit juices and hot tea. Stir ginger into the hot water, then blend with cold water. Add this to the fruit juice–tea mixture. Chill for an hour or more. Makes 4 to 5 servings.

HOT SPICED AFTERNOON TEA

Thomas J. Lipton, Inc.

4 quarts boiling water	1¼ cups sugar
1 teaspoon whole cloves	1 cup orange juice
1 stick cinnamon	¾ cup lemon juice
15 Lipton Flo-Thru Tea Bags or 5 tablespoons tea	

Add spices to water and bring to full rolling boil. Remove from heat and immediately add tea bags or tea. Steep for 4 minutes. Strain; add sugar and stir until dissolved. Pour in fruit juices. Keep spiced tea hot or reheat over low heat, but do not boil. Makes about 30 punch cups of tea.

BRISK TEA PUNCH

Thomas J. Lipton, Inc.

6 Lipton Family Size Tea Bags	6 quarts boiling water
3 tablespoons whole cloves	3 cups orange juice
12 2-inch sticks cinnamon	¾ cup lemon juice
	2 cups honey

Pour boiling water over tea bags and spices. Let steep 3 to 5 minutes. Strain. Add fruit juices and honey. Stir until well blended. Serve hot in mugs garnished with orange slice.

ROMAN PUNCH

Thomas J. Lipton, Inc.

1 cup sugar
2 cups boiling water
2 cups strong Lipton Tea, cooled

1 cup orange juice
⅓ cup lemon juice
1 tablespoon rum extract
1 quart ginger ale

Stir sugar into boiling water. When sugar is dissolved, add remaining ingredients and serve over ice. Makes 8 to 10 servings.

RHUBARB PUNCH

Thomas J. Lipton, Inc.

1 quart Lipton Tea
1 quart rhubarb, cut in ½-inch pieces

1 lemon, cut in sections
1½ cups sugar

Combine tea, rhubarb, lemon, and sugar. Cook until rhubarb is tender. Strain and cool. Serve punch in glasses over ice cubes. Makes 4 to 6 servings.

PLANTERS PUNCH

Thomas J. Lipton, Inc.

⅓ cup grenadine syrup
1 6-ounce can frozen lemonade concentrate

1 teaspoon almond flavoring
2 quarts strong Lipton Tea, cooled

Stir grenadine syrup, lemonade concentrate, and flavoring into the cool tea. Serve in tall glasses with ice. Garnish with pineapple wedge, lemon slice, and cherry. Makes 8 servings.

PLANTATION PUNCH
Thomas J. Lipton, Inc.

1 6-ounce can frozen orange juice

1 6-ounce can frozen grape juice

1 6-ounce can frozen lemonade concentrate

2 quarts strong Lipton Tea, cooled

1 quart ginger ale

Stir frozen fruit juices and lemonade into cool tea. Pour over a block of ice in a punch bowl. Just before serving, add ginger ale. Garnish with thin slices of orange and lemon. Makes 30 punch cup servings.

CONCORD TEA
The Welch Grape Juice Company, Inc.

4 level teaspoons of your favorite tea

3 cups freshly boiling water

¾ cup sugar

1½ cups water

½ cup orange juice

¼ cup lemon juice

2 pints Welch's Grape Juice

¼ teaspoon nutmeg

¼ teaspoon cinnamon

⅛ teaspoon allspice

Place tea and spices in square of cheesecloth and tie securely. Place in large bowl. Pour freshly boiled water over bag. Cover and allow to steep for 5 or 6 minutes. Remove bag. Add sugar, cover, and cool. When cool add grape juice, orange, and lemon juice. Pour over ice to chill. Serve with thin lemon slices stuck with whole cloves. Makes 2 quarts.

OTHER BEVERAGES

RICH HOT CHOCOLATE
The Nestlé Company

Combine in top of double boiler 6-ounce package Nestlés Semi-Sweet Chocolate Morsels, 1 cup water, and dash salt. Place over moderate heat until chocolate melts; stir until well blended. Bring to a boil, stirring constantly. Place over boiling water; add 1½ cups heavy cream and 1½ cups milk. Heat to scalding. Beat with rotary beater until foamy. Serve at once. Makes 6 servings. Serve, if desired, with topping of whipped cream, sprinkled with grated orange rind. Or place mint wafer in bottom of cup before filling with Hot Chocolate.

LA SHAKE FRANCAISE
The Nestlé Company

1 tablespoon Nescafé
1 tablespoon boiling water
½ cup vanilla ice cream
3 ounces Crème de Cacao
1 teaspoon white Crème de Menthe
6 to 7 ice cubes

Combine the instant coffee and boiling water. Blend with remaining ingredients in a blender for 2 minutes. Serve in 5-ounce glasses. Makes 4 servings.

BANANA GINGER SHAKE
United Fruit Company

1 scoop lime sherbet
½ cup cold milk
1 mashed ripe Chiquita Banana
½ cup ginger ale, well chilled

Combine sherbet, milk, and mashed banana, and beat well. Then pour in ginger ale. Makes 1 serving.

FRUIT SHAKES
United Fruit Company

1 mashed ripe Chiquita Banana   1 cup cold fruit juice

Mash a banana with a fork; combine with fruit juice in shaker, blender, or electric mixer. Mix until smooth and creamy. Makes 1 serving. For variety try combining bananas with orange, cranberry, peach, or pineapple.

BANANA MILK SHAKE
United Fruit Company

1 cup cold milk   1 ripe Chiquita Banana

Peel banana and mash with fork. Shake or beat with milk until smooth and creamy. Serve immediately. Makes 1 serving.

Variations

EGGNOG. Add an egg and a dash of salt.

COFFEE COOLER. Add a teaspoon instant coffee.

BANANA FROSTED. Add a scoop of your favorite ice cream or sherbet.

BANANA MALTED. Add 4 teaspoons flavored malted milk powder.

CHOCOLATE SHAKE. Add a tablespoon chocolate syrup.

HONEY SHAKE. Add a tablespoon of honey.

MAPLE SHAKE. Add a tablespoon of maple syrup.

STRAWBERRY SHAKE. Add a tablespoon of strawberry jam.

MOCHA SHAKE. Add a teaspoon of instant coffee and a teaspoon of chocolate syrup.

PARTY SHAKES. Just before serving, sprinkle banana milk shakes with shaved chocolate or flaked coconut.

PEACHY KEEN ICE CREAM SODAS
Standard Brands, Inc.

1 package Royal Peach Gelatin
1 cup boiling water
1 cup cold water

1 pint peach or vanilla ice cream
3 7-ounce bottles chilled 7-Up

Dissolve Royal Peach Gelatin in boiling water. Stir in cold water. Put scoop of ice cream in tall glass. Stir in ¼ cup gelatin. Fill with chilled beverage and serve with long straws. Makes 6 sodas.

SPECIAL PARTIES

EXCHANGE COOKING

Globe-trotting diplomats, students, tourists, and business men have bequeathed to the average American one of the most sophisticated and experienced taste senses in the world. Almost every American has done *some* traveling, and this chapter reflects the enthusiasm all of us have for the foods of other lands. *Food From Famous Kitchens'* parties borrow liberally from this international heritage of ours.

A good party is usually informal and colorful; the special parties that follow—each with a theme and appropriate props—are inexpensive and easy to prepare.

MEXICAN MOLLE

We'll rightly start in the Americas with our nearest Latin neighbor, Mexico. Mexican recipes reflect the high spirits of the country's countless fiestas; they are superbly suited to keynote a festive evening of your own. Turkey or Chicken Mollé, the feast dish most frequently served across the Rio Grande, is worthy of a place of honor at any gathering.

CHICKEN MOLLE
The Nestlé Company

1 5-pound fowl, cut in pieces
Water
2 carrots, cut in pieces
4 large mushrooms, sliced
1 stick celery, chopped
4 sprigs parsley
3 tablespoons salt
1 tablespoon tarragon
1 cup finely chopped onions
3 cloves garlic, minced

1 tablespoon olive oil
1 6-ounce package Nestlé's Semi-Sweet Chocolate Morsels
1 cup bread crumbs
1 cup toasted cashews or peanuts, ground
1 No. 2 can tomato purée
5 tablespoons chili powder
2 teaspoons oregano

Combine fowl, water to cover, carrots, mushrooms, celery, parsley, salt, and tarragon in a 4-quart saucepan. Bring to boil and cover. Simmer until chicken is tender, about 2½ hours. Remove chicken from broth. Take meat from bones and cut in pieces. Strain broth and return to heat. Reduce to ⅓ original volume. Skim off fat. Cook onion and garlic in olive oil until tender and golden brown. Add reduced broth, semi-sweet chocolate, crumbs, cashews, tomato purée, chili powder, and oregano. Stir until blended and chocolate is melted. Add chicken and turn into 2-quart casserole. Place in 350° oven for 45 minutes to 1 hour. Makes 6 to 8 servings.

MEXICAN FRUIT WAFERS
The Nestlé Company

2 tablespoons sifted flour	2 eggs
¼ teaspoon salt	1 cup finely chopped
¼ teaspoon cinnamon	blanched almonds
⅛ teaspoon baking powder	¼ cup chopped candied
⅛ teaspoon cloves	orange peel
⅛ teaspoon nutmeg	1 teaspoon grated lemon
1 cup sugar	rind

Preheat oven to 400°. Sift together flour, salt, cinnamon, baking powder, cloves, and nutmeg; set aside. Combine and mix the sugar and eggs until just blended. Add flour mixture, almonds, orange peel, and lemon rind. Drop by teaspoonsful 2 inches apart on brown paper-lined cooky sheet. Bake at 400° for 7 minutes. Cool 7 minutes; peel cookies off paper. Turn upside down, spread with Chocolate Brandy Glaze. Makes about 5½ dozen.

Note: If cookies stick to paper, lift paper from cooky sheet, lay damp cloth on cooky sheet. Place paper and cookies on cloth. Return to oven 3 to 4 minutes, until paper becomes softened with steam. Remove from oven and lift cookies from paper with spatula at once.

Chocolate Brandy Glaze:

1 6-ounce package Nestlé's	3 tablespoons shortening
Semi-Sweet Chocolate	¼ cup brandy
Morsels	

Melt chocolate and shortening over hot, not boiling, water; stir until smooth. Remove from heat; blend in brandy.

SWISS FONDUE

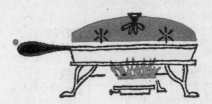

The Fondue is the national dish of Switzerland. The Swiss call it the "meal of friendship."

> 1½ pounds of Swiss cheese, grated
> 1 piece of garlic
> ½ pint of white wine
> 1 teaspoon corn starch
> 1 small glass of kirsch
> 1 pinch of bicarbonate of soda
> Pepper, nutmeg, or paprika to taste

Rub the inside of an earthenware casserole or enameled iron fondue pan with garlic. Place the pan over low heat and pour in 1 cup of wine. Stir continually and gradually add grated cheese. When bubbly, add corn starch which has been mixed into a paste with kirsch. Continue to stir and cook for about 3 minutes. Add the bicarbonate of soda and spices. To serve, place fondue pan over candle warmer or canned heat in the center of the table. Guests serve themselves from a basket of bite-size toasted bread cubes which they dip into the fondue with individual fondue forks. You will find other fondues collected in the *Appetizer* section of this book. Try them for delightful variations to this traditional fondue.

SCANDINAVIAN SMORGASBORD

In a Smorgasbord, *everything* from appetizer to dessert is served simultaneously! Generally, guests make three trips to the serving table, selecting first appetizers, then the main course, and finally dessert. Clean plates should be provided for each course. Paper plates make sense for such a meal, perhaps in three different colors.

The first course should be a mouth-watering collection of unusual, colorful tidbits. It is not necessary to offer great quantities of each dish; in fact, small quantities are preferable. Guests need only a bite or two of each.

The main course should include Swedish meat balls and a casserole of baked beans. Along with these standbys, serve a vegetable salad vinaigrette; molded salads, such as tomato aspic and a ham or chicken mousse; or a platter of sliced ham or chicken.

The desserts should comprise as wide a selection as the appetizers—cookies, fruit tarts, stuffed fruit, and a layer cake. Aged cheese and steaming coffee complete a sumptuous meal.

CURRY GALAXY

A correct curry dinner consists of a main dish and six, eight, or ten side dishes. When a guest exclaims, "The party was wonderful! She had a ten-boy curry!" he is describing the number of side dishes the hostess served. The term *ten-boy curry* stems from the ritual of the curry which dictated that a different servant be provided for each dish.

Choices are unlimited for both the curry and its accompanying condiments. Lamb, the most popular meat in the Far East, is the traditional curry. Shrimp is probably most often used in this country, but veal, chicken, and turkey are equally correct. Needless to say, you can have a festive family party by making a curry of leftover meat. In addition to the curry recipe which follows, you will find an assortment of curries throughout *Food From Famous Kitchens*. Check the index for the pages where they appear.

Suggestions for side dishes:

Chutney
Coconut
Crumbled crisp bacon
Chopped green peppers
Sliced olives
Chopped peanuts

Slivered almonds
Chopped hard-cooked eggs
Chopped onions
Raisins or currants
 (plumped with sherry)

Spinach as a salad green provides a perfect contrast to the accents of the curry. Use oil and vinegar, lightly seasoned, and top with slivered almonds. Toss and serve.

CURRIED CHICKEN WITH ALMOND RICE
General Foods Corporation

Curried Chicken:

½ cup sliced onions
1 clove garlic, sliced
¼ teaspoon ground ginger
4 tablespoons cooking oil
 or other fat
2 tablespoons curry powder
4 tablespoons all-purpose
 flour

½ teaspoon salt
¼ teaspoon pepper
3 cups chicken stock
2½ cups cooked chicken,
 cut in large pieces

Cook onion, garlic, and ginger in oil in saucepan until onion is lightly browned. Add curry powder, flour, salt, and pepper; stir until blended. Then add stock gradually, stirring constantly. Cook and stir until slightly thickened. Add chicken and simmer until thoroughly heated. Arrange hot chicken and rice on serving dish. Serve with coconut (flaked or grated) and chutney. Makes 4 servings. (See illustration 42.)

Almond Rice:

1⅓ cups precooked rice
1⅓ cups water
½ teaspoon salt
¼ cup slivered blanched almonds

2 tablespoons butter
1 cup Baker's Angel Flake Coconut
Chutney

Add rice and salt to boiling water in saucepan. Mix just to moisten all rice. Cover and remove from heat. Let stand 5 minutes. Meanwhile, sauté almonds in butter until golden brown, stirring constantly. Add almonds and butter to rice.

RHUBARB CHIFFON TARTS
General Foods Corporation

1 box Birds Eye Frozen Rhubarb
1 cup boiling water
1 package strawberry-flavored gelatin

2 egg whites
⅓ cup sugar
6 baked 3½-inch tart shells
Whipped cream

Add rhubarb to boiling water and cook until rhubarb is soft. Measure and add water, if necessary, to make 2⅓ cups. Add gelatin to hot mixture and stir until gelatin is dissolved. Chill until slightly thickened. Beat egg whites until foamy throughout. Add sugar gradually and continue beating with rotary egg beater until mixture will stand in soft peaks. Place slightly thickened gelatin in bowl of ice and water, and whip with rotary egg beater until fluffy and thick like whipped cream. Fold in meringue mixture. Turn into baked tart shells and chill until firm. Top with whipped cream. (See illustration 42.)

SOUTH SEAS LUAU

A luau is more than a special party; for Pacific islanders, at least, it is a way of life. Luaus are totally informal. Leaf fronds filled in with smaller greens are appropriate as tablecloths. Plates, forks, and spoons are used on the mainland, but sparingly.

You may scoop out melons or hard-shell vegetables for serving dishes. Coconut shells—with straws to sip from—make perfect cups, and will add considerably to the color and informality of the party.

Luaus should include three main courses, plus a mixed vegetable salad, fruit, and almond cookies. For a beverage, serve fruit punch, chilled, with frozen pineapple chunks. Or freeze fruit and punch in a ring mold; then unmold and float in a bowl filled with the punch.

Flower leis are wonderful accessories for a luau. To make them, use a 2-inch needle and number 30 thread. Six leis will require about 30 dozen carnations. (Buy tiny carnations or seconds and you will cut their cost to a reasonable figure.) String the flower heads closely together on two yards of double thread. Cut the stem just below the green calyx and cut back the calyx a quarter of an inch or more to loosen the flower petals.

Leis make an unusual party favor for a guest of honor at a shower or a bon voyage party. For example, you can alternate a rainbow of fine linen handkerchiefs with pink and red carnations or with white carnations and asters.

SWEET-SOUR PORK
McCormick & Co., Inc.

Pork:

2 pounds lean pork, un-
  cooked, cut into pieces
  ¾-inch thick and 2-inches
  long
1 cup water
6 McCormick or Schilling
  Whole Cloves

2 tablespoons soy sauce
2 tablespoons corn starch
½ cup fat for frying
Sautéed vegetables (see
  below)
Hot sweet-sour sauce (see
  below)

Combine first 3 ingredients and bring to boil, reduce heat and cook 25 minutes, or until tender. Pour off water, if there is any left. Cool. Mix soy sauce and corn starch until smooth. Pour over the cool pork; toss to coat pieces of pork. Heat fat and fry the pork until crisp and brown. Remove and drain. Combine meat with sautéed vegetables and hot sweet-sour sauce. Serve piping hot with rice as a side dish. Makes 4 to 6 servings.

Sautéed Vegetables:

¼ cup onion slices
1 green pepper, cut into
  fairly big pieces

1 carrot, cut into thin slices
2 tablespoons butter or margarine

Sauté first 3 ingredients in butter or margarine for 1 to 2 minutes. Stir once or twice. Remove from pan.

Sweet-Sour Sauce:

¼ cup butter or margarine
1 cup brown sugar
¼ cup corn starch
¼ cup soy sauce
¼ cup vinegar
1½ cups pineapple juice

½ teaspoon McCormick or
  Schilling Instant Onion
  Powder
½ teaspoon McCormick or
  Schilling Ginger

Cook ingredients over low heat until thickened, stirring constantly.

Note: Sauce may be cooked and pork cooked, but not fried, ahead of time.

PORK WITH BAMBOO SHOOTS
McCormick & Co., Inc.

2 cups bamboo shoots
2 tablespoons oil
1 pound lean pork
2 tablespoons soy sauce
½ teaspoon salt
½ teaspoon McCormick or Schilling Ginger

2 tablespoons sherry (optional)
1 tablespoon corn starch
¼ cup water
4 water chestnuts, sliced

Drain bamboo shoots; sauté in oil 2 minutes. Remove from pan and drain. Cut pork in thin, bite-size slices. Toss in mixture of soy sauce, salt, ginger, sherry, and corn starch. Reheat pan; add more oil if necessary and sauté pork until tender. Add the bamboo shoots, water, and water chestnuts. Heat thoroughly; serve hot with side dish of rice. Makes 4 servings.

CHICKEN CURRY IN PAPAYA
McCormick & Co., Inc.

⅓ cup butter or margarine

2 tablespoons McCormick or Schilling Instant Minced Onion

1 stalk celery, chopped

1 tart apple, diced

5 tablespoons all-purpose flour

1 tablespoon McCormick or Schilling Curry Powder

¼ teaspoon McCormick or Schilling Instant Garlic Powder

½ teaspoon McCormick or Schilling Dry Mustard

1 teaspoon salt

1 McCormick or Schilling Bay Leaf

3 McCormick or Schilling Whole Cloves

3 cups chicken stock

3 to 4 cups cooked chicken, cut into bite-size pieces

¼ cup milk, cream, or half and half

2 tablespoons chopped chutney

3 papayas

In a 3-quart saucepan, melt butter. Add onion, celery, and apple; cook about 10 minutes, stirring occasionally. Mix together flour, curry powder, garlic powder, mustard, and salt. Add to apple mixture along with bay leaf and cloves. Gradually stir in chicken stock and cook, stirring, until sauce thickens. Reduce heat and simmer 30 minutes. Add chicken, milk, and chutney; cook 5 minutes longer. Cut 3 papayas in half. Carefully remove all the seeds. Fill with curried chicken. Arrange in baking dish and bake in a 350° oven for 10 to 15 minutes. Serve rice as a side dish.

Note: Avocados may be used instead of papayas.

Variation

SHRIMP CURRY. Follow recipe above adding 3 cups shrimp that have been cooked, shelled, and deveined, in place of the chicken.

CHICKEN CANTONESE
McCormick & Co., Inc.

1 cup celery slices
¼ cup butter or margarine
1 cup thinly sliced raw carrots
½ cup chopped onion
¼ cup slivered almonds
¼ teaspoon salt
1 cup chopped, cooked chicken
1 tablespoon corn starch
¼ teaspoon McCormick or Schilling Ginger

⅛ teaspoon McCormick or Schilling Nutmeg
1¼ cups pineapple juice (Add water if necessary to make 1¼ cups.)
1 tablespoon soy sauce
1 teaspoon lemon juice
¾ cup pineapple chunks
1 5-ounce can water chestnuts, drained and sliced thin

Cut celery into 1 to 1½-inch slices, cutting at an angle. Heat butter in a large skillet. Add celery, carrots, onion, and almonds; brown lightly, about 2 minutes. Add salt and chicken. Combine corn starch, ginger, nutmeg, pineapple juice, soy sauce, and lemon juice, mixing until well blended. Add to chicken mixture. Cook about 3 minutes until thickened, stirring constantly. Stir in pineapple chunks and water chestnuts. Cover. Reduce heat and simmer 10 to 15 minutes. Serve over chow mein noodles or rice. Makes 4 to 6 servings.

TROPICAL BANANAS FLAMBE
McCormick & Co., Inc.

⅓ cup butter or margarine
1 cup flaked coconut
½ cup brown sugar, firmly packed
2 tablespoons corn syrup
⅛ teaspoon McCormick or Schilling Nutmeg
1/16 teaspoon McCormick or Schilling Cardamon

Dash salt
½ cup milk
½ teaspoon McCormick or Schilling Vanilla Extract
6 bananas
1 teaspoon McCormick or Schilling Imitation Brandy Extract per serving

Melt butter or margarine; add coconut and sauté until golden brown. Lift out coconut and set aside. Add sugar, syrup, nutmeg, cardamon, and salt to the remaining butter. Cook over low heat, stirring constantly, until mixture boils vigorously. Stir in milk; simmer 5 minutes. Remove from heat; add vanilla and sautéed coconut. Set aside. Cook the whole, unpeeled bananas in boiling water 5 minutes, or until soft. Peel and cut in halves lengthwise. Pour the warm sauce over bananas. Heat brandy extract slightly. Place 1 teaspoonful on each individual serving. Light with a match; serve flaming. Makes 6 servings.

SUKIYAKI

A Sukiyaki dinner is prepared at the table. Your guests will watch you cook and serve every item—onions, scallions, celery, spinach, mushrooms, bamboo shoots, water chestnuts, thinly sliced beef—all prepared and seasoned with cooking oil, soy sauce, and sugar. (Ingredients should be brought to the table carefully arranged on a serving tray in individual groupings, transferred to the skillet, cooked and served without mixing.)

Set your table with chop sticks—or forks, if you insist— and an electric skillet or chafing dish, placed in the center of the table. Serve your guests covered bowls of rice and pass a tray of Shrimp Tempura (see page 57) while the sukiyaki is cooking. Mandarin oranges and shredded coconut complete the meal.

Sukiyaki is a paradox, for it is as formal and traditional as a Japanese garden yet as relaxed and gracious a way of entertaining as any of the other special parties.

SUKIYAKI
Ac'cent International

1 pound beef (sirloin or rib), cut in paper-thin slices
1½ teaspoons Ac'cent
¼ cup salad oil
2 medium onions, thinly sliced
½ pound tender spinach
¼ pound mushrooms, sliced
12 scallions, sliced
1 can whole bamboo shoots, cut in strips
2 cups sliced celery
½ cup water chestnuts
1 10-ounce can bouillon
⅓ cup soy sauce
3 tablespoons sugar
¼ cup sherry
Hot cooked rice

Sprinkle beef with 1 teaspoon of the Ac'cent. Heat salad oil in skillet; add beef and brown quickly. Add vegetables; sprinkle with remaining ½ teaspoon Ac'cent; cook 3 minutes. Combine bouillon, soy sauce, sugar, and sherry; add to skillet. Cover and cook 10 minutes. Serve immediately with hot cooked rice. Makes 4 servings. (See illustration 41.)

TERIYAKIS
Ac'cent International

1 20-ounce can pineapple chunks
1 pound beef (sirloin or rib), cut in ¾-inch thick pieces
1 teaspoon Ac'cent
¼ cup soy sauce
1 clove garlic, minced
¾ teaspoon ginger
1 small jar (about 22) stuffed olives

Drain pineapple; reserve ½ cup of the syrup. Sprinkle

beef with Ac'cent. Combine reserved pineapple syrup, soy sauce, garlic, and ginger. Add meat cubes and pineapple chunks; marinate at least 1 hour. Alternate meat cubes, pineapple, and olives on 22 short skewers. Broil to desired doneness. Serve hot.

RECIPES FOR CROWDS

FRENCH FRIED CHICKEN
The Procter & Gamble Company

3 2½-pound frying chickens, cut in pieces	½ cup Crisco, melted
3 eggs	3 cups sifted enriched flour
2 cups milk	1 teaspoon salt
	Crisco for deep frying

Steam chicken 20 to 25 minutes. This can be done ahead of time. Refrigerate until ready to use. Beat eggs with milk and add melted shortening. Add flour and salt. Beat until smooth. Dip steamed chicken pieces into batter. Fry in deep shortening heated to 365° 7 to 10 minutes, or until golden brown. Drain on absorbent paper. Makes 12 servings.

Note: To serve 4, use 1 chicken, 1 egg, ¾ cup milk, 3 tablespoons shortening, 1 cup sifted flour, ¼ teaspoon salt. Double the measures to serve 24.

SEAFOOD NEWBURG
The Procter & Gamble Company

2 5-ounce cans shrimp	½ cup Crisco
3 6½-ounce cans tuna, flaked	¾ cup flour
1 6½-ounce can crabmeat	½ teaspoon salt
1 3-ounce can mushrooms, sliced	1 quart milk
¼ cup sherry (optional)	2 teaspoons Worcestershire Sauce
	6 eggs, hard-cooked

Combine fish, mushrooms, and sherry. Melt shortening and stir in flour and salt. Add milk and Worcestershire Sauce, stirring constantly, until thickened. Combine with fish mixture and place in 12 x 8 x 2-inch rectangular dish which has been rubbed with shortening. Bake in 350° oven about 30 minutes. Serve over hot toast or biscuits and top with hard-cooked egg quarters. Makes 12 servings. Double all measures to serve 24.

TUNA-NOODLE CASSEROLE
The Procter & Gamble Company

8 ounces noodles	⅓ cup pimiento, chopped
4 quarts boiling water	⅓ cup olives, sliced
1½ tablespoons salt	3 cups cooked peas, drained
3 tablespoons Crisco	1 teaspoon salt
3 tablespoons flour	½ teaspoon pepper
3 cups milk	1 cup corn flakes
3 cups tuna, flaked	

Cook noodles in boiling salted water until tender, about 12 minutes. Drain. Melt shortening in saucepan, stir in flour, and add milk. Cook until sauce comes to a boil and is slightly thickened. Combine tuna, pimiento, olives, peas, salt, and pepper. Place alternate layers of cooked noodles and tuna mixture in 2 9-inch square or 1 13 x 9 x 2-inch oblong baking dish which has been rubbed with shortening. Sprinkle corn flakes over top. Bake in 350° oven about 1 hour. Makes 12 servings. Double all measures to serve 24.

FRENCH TOASTED SANDWICHES
The Procter & Gamble Company

24 slices bread	1 cup milk
2 cups ham, egg, tuna, or chicken salad	1 cup bread or cracker crumbs
3 eggs	Crisco for deep frying

Spread filling between 2 slices of bread. Press bread together firmly. Dip in mixture of egg and milk. Coat on both sides thoroughly with crumbs. Press crumbs firmly on sides and around crusts of bread. Fry in deep shortening heated to 365° about 1 to 2 minutes, or until golden brown. While frying, hold under surface of shortening with spatula or spoon. Drain on absorbent paper. Makes 12 sandwiches. Double all measures to serve 24.

APPLE-CHEESE CRISP

The Procter & Gamble Company

8 to 10 medium apples	1 cup sifted enriched flour
1 teaspoon cinnamon	¼ teaspoon salt
6 tablespoons water	½ cup Crisco
2 teaspoons lemon juice	3 cups American cheese,
1½ cups sugar	freshly shredded

Pare, core, and slice apples into 2 2-quart casseroles or 2 12 x 8 x 2-inch rectangular baking dishes which have been rubbed with shortening. Sprinkle with cinnamon. Combine water and lemon juice, and add. To make topping, mix sugar, flour, and salt. Cut in shortening with knives or pastry blender until mixture resembles coarse cornmeal. Lightly stir in shredded cheese. Place topping evenly over apples and bake in 350° oven about 30 minutes, or until crust is crisp and browned and apples tender. Makes 12 servings. Double all measures to serve 24.

FLOWER FALL

A cache of plastic berry baskets and "Oasis" are all you need for a delightful decorative effect with flowers, ferns, ribbons, berries, or fruit—at any season of the year, and for any kind of party. Oasis is a water-retaining moss which

your florist stocks. It plays an important part in his wizardry
with flowers; with it you will be able to make a little magic of
your own.

Fill two baskets with Oasis and wire them together. Make
two or three others and hang them separately, or join three
together on 12-inch lengths of wire for a "fall" of flowers.

When the baskets are filled and wired, soak them in
water until the Oasis is 80% saturated, but not dripping. Insert the stems of flowers and leaves; the Oasis will keep your
flower fall fresh and lovely for many, many hours.

Suggestions for filling your baskets: dogwood, redbud, box-
wood, violets, geraniums, orange blossoms, stephanotis,
greens, chrysanthemums, bittersweet berries, holly, and
mistletoe.

PICNICS

TRAVEL LIGHT TO THE PICNIC

A picnic is any informal or impromptu presentation of food and drink that can be shared by two or more people, generally out of doors. Informality and simplicity go hand in hand. Keep picnics simple—and enjoy them more!

The following menu, tucked into a country fruit basket, accompanied by two butter-spreaders, napkins, paper plates, and a corkscrew, is ample for two on an excursion to the country or a city park.

> 2 4-ounce rolls of semi-soft cheese
> 1 crock of liver paté or meat spread
> 1 tube of fruit or berry preserves
> 1 loaf of Italian bread
> 3 bunches of grapes; red, purple, and green
> 1 bottle of rosé or dry white wine

Avoid stereotyped picnic fare; use your imagination. Convenience foods, compact packaging, safety-proof cook-

ing utensils, and flight-weight picnic accessories make today's picnic easier—and more fun—than ever before.

Saran Wrap is an indispensable adjunct to modern picnics.
With it, food can be prepared days in advance and stored in
the freezer until the day of the excursion. Sandwiches and
other picnic treats can travel to the country—or to your
own backyard—without loss of flavor, protected by the
same crystal clear Saran Wrap in which they have been
stored.

SAUCE FOR HAMBURGERS
The R. T. French Company

1 can undiluted evaporated
  milk
⅓ cup French's Prepared
  Mustard

⅓ cup catsup
1 cup grated cheese

Scald evaporated milk. With fork stir in mustard and catsup. Add cheese. Pour over cooked hamburger on bun.

FILLED HAMBURGERS
The R. T. French Company

½ pound ground beef
French's Prepared Mustard
1 thin slice onion

Spoonful of pickle relish (optional)

Press ground beef gently into 4 thin patties, about 4 inches
across. Spread or arrange remaining ingredients on 1 patty,
leaving ½ inch around edge for sealing. Top with second
patty, pressing edges together. Broil on each side. Sprinkle
lightly with salt and pepper. Serve on warm hamburger
rolls. Makes 2 servings.

Variations

CHEESEBURGERS. Cream together ¼ pound butter, ¼

pound Roquefort or blue cheese, and 3 tablespoons mustard. Spread between the hamburger patties in place of mustard, onion, and relish above.

CHEESE-RELISHBURGERS. Spread one patty generously with mustard. Place small cubes of processed cheese and a spoonful of pickle relish in the center, then top with second patty.

DIXIE SANDWICH SPREAD
United Fruit Company

1 ripe Chiquita Banana, mashed
¼ cup orange juice
¼ cup chopped raisins
¾ cup peanut butter

Blend all ingredients until thoroughly mixed. Refrigerate well for best flavor. Makes 1¼ cups spread.

EGG SALAD SANDWICH FILLING
Poultry and Egg National Board

4 hard-cooked eggs, finely chopped
2 tablespoons chopped sweet pickles or drained pickle relish
¼ cup finely diced celery or green pepper
2 tablespoons chopped parsley
2 to 3 tablespoons salad dressing or mayonnaise
Salt, pepper, and dry mustard to taste

Combine chopped eggs, pickles, celery, parsley, and salad dressing. Season to taste with salt, pepper, and dry mustard. Makes enough spread for 5 sandwiches.

TUNA CLUB SANDWICH
Star-Kist Foods, Inc.

1 6½-ounce can Star-Kist Tuna
½ cup minced celery
¼ cup mayonnaise
½ teaspoon salt
¼ teaspoon prepared mustard

Dash pepper
Sandwich bread
Lettuce
Tomato slices

For filling, combine tuna with remaining filling ingredients. Toast bread and make double decker sandwiches, using tuna filling and lettuce as one layer and tomato slices for the other. Makes 6 sandwiches.

BARBECUED TUNA BUNS
Star-Kist Foods, Inc.

3 hamburger buns, halved
1 6-ounce can Star-Kist Tuna
½ cup chili sauce
2 tablespoons mayonnaise
1 teaspoon prepared horseradish

1 tablespoon chopped pimiento
½ teaspoon lemon juice
3 drops Tabasco
Salt and pepper to taste

Spread mayonnaise on both halves of buns. Cover with chunks of tuna. Combine sauce ingredients, spoon over tuna. Place bun halves under broiler until cooked and bubbly. Makes 3 sandwiches.

PIZZA SANDWICH
George A. Hormel Co.

1 French loaf
Butter
1 can Spam
Mozarella cheese

Salt and pepper
Oregano
Chopped olives
Olive oil

Split French loaf lengthwise and butter. Arrange slices of Spam, mozarella cheese, and tomato on bottom half. Sprinkle with salt, pepper, and oregano. Scatter chopped olives on top. Drizzle olive oil over all. Top with other half of loaf. Wrap securely in aluminum foil and bake at 400° for 20 minutes. Makes 1 serving.

SPAM BOAT
George A. Hormel Co.

1 loaf Italian or French bread
1 cup bread crumbs from loaf
1 can Spam, diced or chopped
4 hard-cooked eggs, diced
1 cup diced celery
2 tablespoons chopped dill pickles

1 tablespoon minced green onions
2 tablespoons chopped stuffed olives
½ cup mayonnaise
1 teaspoon Worcestershire Sauce
Butter

Cut slice off top of loaf and hollow out, leaving a 1-inch wall. Measure bread crumbs and combine with Spam, eggs, celery, dill pickles, green onions, stuffed olives, and mayonnaise blended with Worcestershire Sauce. Spoon mixture lightly into loaf; replace top. Brush entire loaf with butter; wrap in aluminum foil. Bake over grill 30 minutes, or until heated through.

PATIO LOAVES
George A. Hormel Co.

2 cans Spam
Prepared horseradish-mus-
tard

Tiny pickled or canned
onions
Pitted ripe olives

Spread each loaf of Spam with horseradish-mustard (except the ends). Then stud the loaves with onions and olives
fastened with wooden picks. Broil on rotisserie over medium
heat until loaves are sizzling. Serve with zucchini. Makes 2
servings.

BARBECUE BUNDLES
George A. Hormel Co.

4 thick slices Spam
1 can sweet potatoes
8 stalks frozen asparagus

1 fresh apple (or banana,
halved lengthwise, then
cut in two)
Worcestershire Sauce
Brown sugar

Arrange first 4 ingredients in double thicknesses of foil,
to make 2 bundles alternating: sweet potatoes, fruit, and
Spam and edging them with asparagus. Season with Worcestershire Sauce; sprinkle brown sugar on fruit. Seal foil with
double fold. Place on grill over low heat; let cook 1 hour or
more. Makes 2 servings.

PARTY SANDWICH LOAF
George A. Hormel Co.

1 square sandwich loaf
Butter
1 can Spam
Lettuce
Mayonnaise

2 ripe tomatoes, sliced
Ripe olives, sliced
Chicken, cooked and sliced
Stiff whipped cream
Hard-cooked eggs, chopped

Cut crusts from loaf. Cut lengthwise into 4 slices. Butter. Put slices together with (1) sliced Spam, lettuce, and mayonnaise; (2) sliced tomato, sliced ripe olives, and (3) chicken, lettuce, and mayonnaise. Coat loaf with mixture of mayonnaise, stiff whipped cream, and hard-cooked eggs. Chill 3 to 5 hours. To serve cut across loaf in thick slices.

PORTABLE SUBMARINES
The R. T. French Company

4 frankfurters
4 tablespoons butter or margarine
1 tablespoon French's Prepared Mustard

1 loaf French bread
4 slices American cheese
2 tomatoes, sliced
4 slices Swiss cheese

Heat frankfurters in water just below boiling point 5 to 8 minutes. Blend together softened butter and mustard. Cut bread into 4- to 6-inch pieces; cut each of these in half, length-wise. Spread with mustard butter. On the lower half, arrange alternate slices of American cheese, tomato, and Swiss cheese. Cut cooked frankfurters in half, lengthwise. Place on top of cheese and tomato slices. Spread with additional mustard, if desired. Cover with top half of bread; skewer and wrap. Wrap in Saran Wrap and refrigerate until picnic time. At picnic area, heat on grill over charcoal, turning once. Serve immediately. Makes 4 large sandwiches.

BAKED BEAN-BACON SANDWICH
The R. T. French Company

Combine 1 cup canned baked beans, ½ cup crumbled crisp cooked bacon, and enough French's Prepared Mustard to make it of spreading consistency. Spread on rye or whole wheat bread.

APPLESAUCE-BACON SANDWICH
The R. T. French Company

Combine ¼ cup softened butter with 2 tablespoons French's Prepared Mustard. Spread on rye bread. Top with applesauce and crumbled crisp cooked bacon.

CUCUMBER-GREEN PEPPER SANDWICH
The R. T. French Company

Spread buttered white bread with mixture of equal parts of commercial sour cream and French's Prepared Mustard. Arrange thin slices of cucumber and green pepper on top. Serve open face style.

SHRIMP-MUSHROOM SANDWICH
The R. T. French Company

Combine chopped shrimp and chopped mushrooms, with a mixture of French's Prepared Mustard and cream cheese; spread on thin slices white bread.

CORNED BEEF SANDWICH
The R. T. French Company

Chop contents of 1 12-ounce can corned beef. Mix with ¼ cup chopped sweet pickle and ¼ cup French's Prepared Mustard. Mix thoroughly.

CHEESE-BACON SANDWICH
The R. T. French Company

Spread French's Prepared Mustard on 1 side toasted bread. Top with 1 slice pineapple, then with slice of process

American cheese and 1 slice bacon. Broil until bacon is brown and crispy. Serve immediately.

Sandwich filling ingredients that freeze well:

Cooked egg yolk
Peanut Butter
Cooked or canned chicken, turkey, or fish
Cooked or canned meat
Dried beef
Baked beans
Canned crushed pineapple

Roquefort or bleu cheese
Applesauce
Horseradish
Lemon or orange juice
Butter or margarine
Dairy sour cream
Milk

After filling, wrap sandwiches securely in moisture-vapor proof Saran Wrap, each in its own individual package to avoid transfer of flavors.

EASY POTATO SALAD
The Borden Company

1 package Borden's Instant Whipped Potatoes
4 hard-cooked eggs, diced
1½ cups diced celery
½ cup chopped onion
2 tablespoons chopped parsley

1 cup mayonnaise
1 tablespoon vinegar
2 teaspoons prepared mustard
1½ teaspoons salt
¼ teaspoon pepper

Prepare whipped potatoes following the package directions, but omitting the butter. Let cool; add the remaining ingredients and mix thoroughly. Chill before serving. Makes about 6 servings.

MUSHROOM POTATO SALAD WITH CABBAGE
Grocery Store Products Co.

1½ cups diced cooked potatoes
½ teaspoon salt
⅛ teaspoon pepper
¼ cup well-seasoned French dressing
1 tablespoon onion, finely diced

1 3-ounce can chopped Broiled-in-Butter Mushrooms
3 strips cooked bacon
1½ cups cabbage, thinly shredded
¼ cup mayonnaise

Place hot potatoes in mixing bowl. Sprinkle with salt, pepper, French dressing, and onion. Drain mushrooms, reserving broth for use in soup or gravy. Add drained mushrooms to potatoes. Toss lightly to mix well. Cover and chill thoroughly. When ready to serve, drain potatoes if French dressing is not all absorbed. Toss lightly until ingredients are thoroughly combined. Serve immediately, garnished with crisp salad greens and slices of tomato. Makes 4 servings.

SHRIMP-MACARONI SALAD
Grocery Store Products Co.

1 6-ounce can Broiled-in-Butter Mushrooms
⅓ cup French dressing
1/16 teaspoon powdered thyme
1 cup elbow macaroni
1 pound fresh shrimp, cooked, or 2 5-ounce cans, drained

1 tablespoon lemon juice
1 cup unpeeled cucumber, diced
½ cup mayonnaise
¼ cup chopped chives
1 bunch water cress

Drain and quarter mushrooms. Place in bowl and sprinkle with French dressing and thyme. Meanwhile, cook macaroni according to directions on package and drain thoroughly. Add to mushrooms, tossing lightly together. Chill several hours in refrigerator. Sprinkle chilled shrimp with lemon juice; add to macaroni and mushrooms with cucumber. Blend mayonnaise and chives; combine with other ingredients. Serve on bed of water cress. Makes 4 to 6 servings.

CUCUMBER-CHICKEN SALAD
Grocery Store Products Co.

2 cups diced chicken, cooked
1 6-ounce can Broiled-in-Butter Mushrooms
¼ cup French dressing
1 cup diced unpeeled cucumber
½ cup diced green pepper
¼ cup sliced stuffed olives
¼ cup mayonnaise
¼ teaspoon salt
⅛ teaspoon curry powder

Place chicken in container with a cover. Drain mushrooms. Coarsely chop ½ the mushrooms and add to the chicken. Add French dressing. Mix well and cover tightly. Chill for at least 2 hours. Pour French dressing over remaining whole mushrooms and let marinate in cold place until ready to serve. Drain chicken and chopped mushrooms, if necessary. Add the cucumber, green pepper, and olives. Blend together and add mayonnaise, salt, and curry powder. Toss lightly until thoroughly combined. Makes 4 servings.

GERMAN-STYLE GREEN BEANS AND ONION SALAD
Sunkist Growers, Inc.

1 package frozen or canned green beans
2 small onions
3 slices bacon, diced
2 tablespoons Sunkist Fresh Lemon Juice
2½ tablespoons sugar
½ teaspoon salt

Cook green beans according to package directions. (If canned, heat thoroughly.) Drain and put beans in a bowl; keep warm. Slice onions into very thin slices; separate into rings and mix with green beans. Fry bacon until crisp; save drippings. Add to skillet 2 tablespoons lemon juice, sugar, and salt. Heat mixture to boiling, stirring well. Pour mixture over beans and toss lightly. Just before serving, squeeze lemon quarters over individual servings. Makes 4 servings.

PATIO BAKED BEANS
George A. Hormel Co.

⅓ cup brown sugar
1 teaspoon instant coffee
1 tablespoon vinegar
1 teaspoon dry mustard
½ teaspoon salt

2 1-pound, 4-ounce cans baked beans
1 medium onion, thinly sliced
1 can Spam
½ cup cognac

Mix first 5 ingredients and cook over low heat for 5 minutes. Arrange beans in layers with slices of onion and most of can of Spam, cut into squares or strips. Pour the hot sugar mixture over the beans. Bake 45 minutes in moderate oven. Stir in cognac. Place strips or squares of sliced Spam on top. Bake uncovered 30 minutes longer.

GIFTS from your KITCHEN

The gifts of food we make to our friends are today's symbols of "breaking bread"—a custom as old as civilization. Originally such a gift was a gesture of truce; today it is a gift of love.

When food is prepared for giving, special attention should be given to its appearance. If the gift is a steamed pudding, use a decorative mold to enhance its appearance. Pickled relishes, sauces, jellies, and assortments of home-made bread in half-size loaves are too pretty to hide. Gift-wrap them in Saran Wrap. It is a protective showcase for your gift, transparent and tight clinging, both attractive and utilitarian. Gift ribbon is a color complement that will add the finishing touch to the most personal present you can make.

JELLIES AND JAMS

GRAPE JELLY AND BUTTER
General Foods Corporation

5½ pounds ripe Concord
   grapes
½ cup water

6¼ pounds sugar
1 bottle Certo Liquid Fruit
   Pectin

Stem the grapes and crush thoroughly. Add water; bring

to a boil and simmer, covered, 10 minutes. Place in a large sieve lined with double thickness of cheesecloth. Drain and measure 4 cups juice into a large saucepan. Use juice for making jelly; use fruit remaining in sieve for making butter. Makes about 10 medium glasses jelly and 12 butter.

To make jelly: Combine 4 cups juice and 7 cups sugar in saucepan and mix well. Place over high heat and bring to a boil, stirring constantly. At once stir in ½ bottle pectin. Then bring to a full rolling boil and boil hard 1 minute, stirring constantly. Remove from heat, skim off foam with metal spoon, and pour quickly into glasses. Cover jelly at once with ⅛-inch hot paraffin.

To make butter: Remove cheesecloth from sieve and put fruit remaining through sieve. Measure 5 cups pulp into a very large saucepan. Add 7½ cups sugar and mix well. Place over high heat, bring to a full rolling boil, and boil hard 1 minute, stirring constantly. Remove from heat and at once stir in ½ bottle pectin. Skim off foam with metal spoon. Ladle quickly into glasses. Cover butter at once with ⅛-inch hot paraffin.

ORANGE JUICE JELLY
General Foods Corporation

3¼ cups sugar
1 cup water
3 tablespoons lemon juice

¾ cup (6-ounce can) concentrated Birds Eye Orange Juice, thawed
½ bottle Certo Liquid Fruit Pectin

Measure sugar and water into a large saucepan, and mix well. Place over high heat, bring to a full rolling boil, and boil hard 1 minute, stirring constantly. Remove from heat. Stir in fruit juices. Add pectin and mix well. If necessary, skim off foam with metal spoon. Pour quickly into glasses. Cover jelly at once with ⅛-inch hot paraffin. Makes about 5 medium glasses.

FRUIT PUNCH JELLY
General Foods Corporation

1 1¾-ounce box Sure-Jell
  Powdered Fruit Pectin
2½ cups water

¾ cup (6-ounce can) con-
  centrated Birds Eye Chill-
  Ripe Punch, thawed
4 cups sugar

Measure pectin, water, and fruit punch into large saucepan, and mix well. Place over high heat. Cook until bubbles
form all around edge, stirring constantly. Add sugar and
heat until bubbles again form around edge, stirring constantly. Remove from heat. Skim off foam with metal spoon.
Pour quickly into glasses. Cover jelly at once with ⅛-inch
hot paraffin. Makes about 7 medium glasses.

BLACKBERRY JELLY
General Foods Corporation

3½ cups juice (about 2
  quarts) ripe blackberries
5 cups sugar

1 1¾-ounce box Sure-Jell
  Powdered Fruit Pectin

Thoroughly crush blackberries (not blackcaps). Place in
jelly cloth or bag and squeeze out juice. Measure into a large
saucepan.

Measure sugar and set aside. Add pectin to juice in
saucepan and mix well. Place over high heat and stir until
mixture comes to a hard boil. At once stir in sugar. Bring
to a full rolling boil, and boil hard 1 minute, stirring constantly. Remove from heat, skim off foam with metal spoon,
and pour quickly into glasses. Cover jelly at once with ⅛-
inch hot paraffin. Makes about 8 medium glasses.

Variation

APPLE JELLY. Substitute 7 cups juice (about 5 pounds) ripe
tart apples for blackberries; use 9 cups sugar. If deeper

color is desired, stir in a few drops of red coloring before skimming. Makes about 15 medium glasses.

PEACH JAM
General Foods Corporation

4 cups (about 3 pounds) ripe peaches
¼ cup lemon juice (2 lemons)

7½ cups sugar
½ bottle Certo Liquid Fruit Pectin

Peel and pit peaches. Grind or chop very fine. Measure 4 cups into a very large saucepan. Squeeze the juice from 2 medium lemons. Measure ¼ cup juice into saucepan with peaches.

Add sugar to fruit in saucepan and mix well. Place over high heat, bring to a full rolling boil, and boil hard 1 minute, stirring constantly. Remove from heat and at once stir in pectin. Skim off foam with metal spoon. Then stir and skim by turns for 5 minutes to cool slightly and to prevent fruit from floating. Ladle quickly into glasses. Cover jam at once with ⅛-inch hot paraffin. Makes about 11 medium glasses.

STRAWBERRY JAM
General Foods Corporation

3¾ cups (about 2 quarts) ripe strawberries
¼ cup lemon juice (2 lemons)

7 cups sugar
½ bottle Certo Liquid Fruit Pectin

Crush completely, 1 layer at a time, the strawberries. Measure 3¾ cups into a very large saucepan. Squeeze the juice from 2 medium lemons. Measure ¼ cup into saucepan with fruit.

Add sugar to fruit in saucepan and mix well. Place over high heat, bring to a full rolling boil and boil hard 1 minute, stirring constantly. Remove from heat and at once stir in pectin. Skim off foam with metal spoon. Then stir and skim by turns for 5 minutes to cool slightly and to prevent fruit from floating. Ladle quickly into glasses. Cover jam at once with ⅛-inch hot paraffin. Makes about 10 medium glasses.

CHERRY CONSERVE
General Foods Corporation

4 cups (about 3 pounds) ripe sweet cherries	7 cups sugar
1 tablespoon grated lemon rind	½ pound chopped seeded raisins
¼ cup lemon juice (2 lemons)	1 cup finely chopped nuts
	1 bottle Certo Liquid Fruit Pectin

Stem and pit cherries. Chop fine. Measure 4 cups into a very large saucepan. Grate the rind and squeeze the juice from 2 medium lemons. Measure 1 tablespoon rind and ¼ cup juice into saucepan with cherries.

Add sugar, raisins, and nuts to fruit in saucepan and mix well. Place over high heat, bring to a full rolling boil, and boil hard 1 minute, stirring constantly. Remove from heat and at once stir in pectin. Skim off foam with metal spoon. Then stir and skim by turns for 5 minutes to cool slightly and to prevent fruit from floating. Ladle quickly into glasses. Cover at once with ⅛-inch hot paraffin.

Note: For stronger cherry flavor, add ¼ teaspoon almond extract before ladling conserve.

COCONUT FRUIT CONSERVE
General Foods Corporation

1 medium orange	1 box powdered Sure-Jell Powdered Fruit Pectin
1 medium fully ripe pineapple	1⅓ cups Baker's Angel Flake Coconut
1½ pounds ripe apples	6 cups sugar

Remove skin in quarters from orange and discard 2 of the quarters. Lay other quarters flat; shave off and discard about ½ the white part. With sharp knife or scissors, shred remaining rind very fine, or chop or grind. Section or chop the peeled orange; discard seeds. Combine rind, pulp, and ¾ cup water; simmer, covered, for 20 minutes.

Pare and core pineapple. Chop very fine or grind. Measure 2½ cups into a very large saucepan.

Peel and core apples; chop fine. Measure 2½ cups into saucepan with pineapple. Add prepared orange.

Add powdered fruit pectin to fruit in saucepan and mix well. Place over high heat and stir until mixture comes to a hard boil. At once stir in sugar and coconut. Bring to a full rolling boil and boil hard 1 minute, stirring constantly. Remove from heat and skim off foam with metal spoon. Then stir and skim by turns for 5 minutes to cool slightly and to prevent fruit from floating. Ladle quickly into glasses. Cover at once with ⅛-inch hot paraffin. Makes about 10 medium glasses (5 pounds) of marmalade.

PLUM PRESERVES
General Foods Corporation

6 cups (about 2½ pounds) sliced ripe plums	¼ cup lemon juice (2 lemons)
1 cup water	½ bottle Certo Liquid Fruit Pectin
6 cups sugar	

Pit plums and slice thin. Measure into a very large saucepan. Add water and sugar. Place over high heat and bring to a boil, stirring carefully. Remove from heat. Let stand at room temperature 4 to 6 hours.

Measure lemon juice into saucepan with fruit. Place over high heat, bring to a full rolling boil, and boil hard 2 minutes, stirring carefully. Remove from heat and at once stir in pectin. Skim off foam with metal spoon. Then stir and skim by turns for 8 to 10 minutes to cool slightly and to prevent fruit from floating. Ladle quickly into glasses. Cover preserves at once with ⅛-inch hot paraffin. Makes about 12 medium glasses.

STEAMED PUDDINGS

Make sure molds have tightly-fitting covers. One-pound coffee cans make excellent pudding molds, provided they do not leak. The inside of the mold and the cover should be well buttered.

Never fill molds more than ⅔ full of batter. Press covers on tightly so that steam will not enter the mold and cause sogginess.

Set the mold on a rack on the bottom of a steamer containing enough actively boiling water to cover the bottom third of the mold. Molds must not touch sides of steamer.

Cover steamer and boil hard for ½ hour, then boil gently for the remainder of cooking time. If water gets low, add boiling water as necessary. It is important that the water never stops boiling. Plan the steaming so that your pudding may cook up to the last minute before it is served. However, remember that steamed puddings keep very well and may be reheated by steaming for about ½ hour before serving. If you will be pressed for time later, prepare in advance and store, wrapped in Saran Wrap until needed.

Note: A tightly covered, well-buttered double boiler may be used for steaming very small puddings.

HARVARD DATE PUDDING
Penick & Ford, Ltd.

3 tablespoons melted butter
½ cup Brer Rabbit Molasses
1⅔ cups sifted all-purpose
   flour
½ teaspoon baking soda
¼ teaspoon cloves
¼ teaspoon allspice
¼ teaspoon nutmeg
¼ teaspoon salt
½ cup milk
½ pound dates, cut in small
   pieces

Blend together butter and molasses. Sift together flour, baking soda, cloves, allspice, nutmeg, and salt; add alternately with milk to molasses mixture. Add dates; mix well. Pour into greased 1-quart pudding mold; cover tightly. Steam 2½ hours. Serve hot with a pudding sauce. Makes 6 to 8 servings.

STEAMED APRICOT PUDDING
American Skultuna Inc.

1 cup sifted flour
¾ cup sugar
1 teaspoon baking powder
½ teaspoon salt
¼ teaspoon nutmeg
¼ teaspoon ginger
½ cup seedless raisins
½ cup chopped walnuts
1 cup canned apricots,
   drained and mashed
½ cup milk
½ teaspoon vanilla (op-
   tional)

Fill base pot of Skultuna Steamer for Split-Level Cookery® with water to level of 1½ inches below top of rim. Cover and bring to full rolling boil.

Meanwhile, sift first 6 ingredients. Stir in raisins and walnuts. Blend remaining ingredients and stir into flour mixture. Turn into a greased and floured 1-pound coffee tin or 1-quart mold, filling it about ⅔ full. Cover tightly. Place mold in inset pot of steamer. Uncover base pot, place inset pot over base pot, and cover. Steam for about 1½ hours, or until center of pudding is firm to touch. Add boiling water to base pot, if needed.

To serve pudding remove from inset pot; set mold in cold water for a few seconds. Unmold pudding on heated platter. Serve with vanilla-flavored Hard Sauce. Makes 6 to 8 servings.

APRICOT-GRAHAM CRACKER STEAMED PUDDING
National Biscuit Company

20 square Nabisco Graham Crackers, finely rolled (about 1⅔ cups crumbs)
½ cup butter or margarine, melted
1½ cups sifted flour
2½ teaspoons baking powder
1 cup sugar
1 teaspoon nutmeg
1 teaspoon cinnamon
½ teaspoon salt
2 cups (1 11-ounce package) chopped dried apricots
1 cup milk
2 eggs, beaten

Combine graham cracker crumbs and melted butter or margarine. Sift together flour, baking powder, sugar, nutmeg, cinnamon, and salt. Stir into crumbs. Add chopped apricots and mix well. Stir in milk and beaten eggs, and pour into lightly oiled 2-quart mold. Cover mold tightly. Place on rack in deep kettle. Add boiling water to half way up sides of mold. Steam, covered, 2½ hours or until firm. Makes about 10 servings.

STEAMED FIG PUDDING
American Skultuna Inc.

½ pound beef suet
½ pound dried figs
1 small sour apple, cored and pared
3 cups grated bread crumbs
½ cup milk
3 eggs, well beaten
1 cup brown sugar

Force suet, figs, and apple through food chopper. Soak bread crumbs in milk; add to above mixture. Add eggs and sugar. Blend well. Steam in 1-pound coffee tin or 1-quart mold, ⅔ full, in Skultuna Steamer for Split-Level Cookery® following procedure outlined for Steamed Apricot Pudding (see page 339). Serve with Lemon Sauce. Makes 6 servings.

WHEAT GERM PLUM PUDDING
Kretschmer Wheat Germ Corp.

2½ cups sifted all-purpose flour	1 cup Kretschmer Wheat Germ
½ teaspoon salt	2 cups ground suet
1 teaspoon soda	1 cup chopped apple
2 teaspoons cinnamon	2 cups seedless raisins
½ teaspoon cloves	1 cup currants
½ teaspoon allspice	1 cup light molasses
	1 cup cold water

Sift flour with salt, soda, cinnamon, cloves, and allspice. Stir in wheat germ; set aside. In a large bowl, combine suet, apple, raisins, currants, molasses, and water. Stir in wheat germ mixture until completely mixed. Turn into greased 2-quart pudding mold. Cover tightly; place on trivet in deep kettle. Add enough boiling water to come halfway up side of mold.

Steam, covered, 3 hours. Remove from water, cool about 5 minutes; unmold. Serve warm with your favorite Hard Sauce or Lemon Sauce. Makes 10 to 12 servings.

STEAMED CRANBERRY PUDDING
American Skultuna Inc.

1½ cups raw cranberries	⅓ cup unsulphured molasses
½ cup seedless raisins	¼ cup hot water
1¼ cups sifted flour	
1½ teaspoons baking soda	

Rinse and drain berries and raisins; place in mixing bowl. Sift flour and soda together over fruit. Add molasses and water; mix until smooth. Turn into a well-greased and sugar-dusted 1-pound coffee tin or 1-quart mold, filling it ⅔ full. Steam in Skultuna Steamer for Split-Level Cookery® following procedure outlined for Steamed Apricot Pudding (see page 339). Serve with Hard Sauce or whipped cream. Makes 6 servings.

STEAMED ORANGE PUDDING
American Skultuna Inc.

¼ cup butter or margarine, soft
½ cup sugar
2 eggs
Grated rind of 1 orange
3 chopped dates
¼ cup seedless raisins
¼ cup chopped walnuts

¼ cup orange juice
3 tablespoons milk or light cream
½ cup sifted flour
½ teaspoon baking soda
Dash of salt (optional)
⅛ teaspoon ginger

Cream butter. Add sugar gradually; continue beating until creamy. Add 1 egg, beat again; add second egg, beat again. Add grated rind, chopped dates, raisins, and nuts. Stir in orange juice and blend. Add milk and the sifted 4 remaining ingredients. Blend well until smooth. Turn into well-greased 1-pound coffee tin or 1-quart mold filling it ⅔ full. Steam in Skultuna Steamer for Split-Level Cookery® following procedure outlined for Steamed Apricot Pudding (see page 339). Serve with Orange Sauce or Hard Sauce. Makes 6 servings.

GRANDMA'S BLACK PUDDING
American Skultuna Inc.

1 egg, slightly beaten
2 cups sifted flour
½ teaspoon salt

½ teaspoon baking soda
1 cup unsulphured molasses
1 cup boiling water

To egg in bowl, add the 3 sifted dry ingredients and blend; add molasses and boiling water. Blend again. Turn into a well-greased 1½-quart mold, filling it about ⅔ full. Steam in Skultuna Steamer for Split-Level Cookery®, following procedure outlined for Steamed Apricot Pudding (see page 339). Serve with Hard Sauce or whipped cream. Makes 6 servings.

OLD-FASHIONED STEAMED PUDDING
American Skultuna Inc.

1 cup sugar
1 cup sifted flour
2 teaspoons baking powder
1 teaspoon baking soda
1 teaspoon salt
1 teaspoon cinnamon
¼ teaspoon allspice or powdered cloves

1 cup finely grated raw carrot
1 cup finely grated raw potato
1 cup currants
1 cup raisins

Sift together twice the first 7 ingredients. Add remaining 4 ingredients in order given. Turn into 1-pound coffee tin or 1-quart mold filling it about ⅔ full. Steam in Skultuna Steamer for Split-Level Cookery® following procedure outlined for Steamed Apricot Pudding (see page 339). Serve with Hard Sauce, whipped cream, or your favorite pudding sauce. Makes 6 servings.

COOKIES

MADE-AT-HOME COOKIE MIX
The Procter & Gamble Company

6 cups sifted enriched flour
1 tablespoon salt

1 pound (about 2⅓ cups) Crisco

Mix flour and salt in a large mixing bowl or on a large square of waxed or wrapping paper. Cut shortening into flour with two knives or a pastry blender until pieces are about the size of peas. Store in a covered container such as an empty 3-pound Crisco can. (No refrigeration needed.) Makes 7 to 8 cups.

Variation

RICH BROWNIES. Stir together 1½ cups Cookie Mix, 1½ cups sugar, ½ teaspoon double-action baking powder. Add 3 eggs, 3 1-ounce squares unsweetened melted chocolate and 1 teaspoon vanilla, and stir vigorously. Add ½ cup chopped nuts, and blend well. Pour into 9-inch square pan which has been rubbed with shortening. Bake in 375° oven for 25 to 30 minutes, or until inserted toothpick comes out clean. Sprinkle with confectioners' sugar. Cool. Makes 3 dozen 1½-inch brownies.

REFRIGERATOR COOKIES
Best Foods, Division of
Corn Products Company

3 cups sifted flour
¼ teaspoon salt
1 teaspoon baking powder
1 cup butter or margarine
½ cup Karo Syrup, Blue Label

⅔ cup sugar, brown or granulated
1 egg, beaten
1 teaspoon vanilla
1 cup chopped shredded coconut or nuts

Mix and sift together flour, salt, and baking powder. Beat butter until soft and creamy. Add corn syrup and sugar, and beat until thoroughly blended. Add egg; blend well. Add vanilla and coconut or nuts. Add sifted dry ingredients; mix thoroughly. Chill dough about 1 hour. Shape into 2 rolls about 2 inches in diameter. Wrap in Saran Wrap and chill in refrigerator at least 4 hours or overnight. With a very sharp knife, cut in ⅛-inch slices. Place on ungreased cooky sheet. Bake in 350° oven 10 to 12 minutes. Makes about 6 dozen.

Variations

CHOCOLATE COOKIES. Omit baking powder and sift ¼ teaspoon soda with flour. Add 2 squares melted unsweetened chocolate or ⅓ cup cocoa to batter before adding sifted dry ingredients. Stir until well blended.

PEANUT BUTTER COOKIES. Omit coconut and nuts. Add 1 cup peanut butter to batter before adding sifted dry ingredients. Stir until well blended.

ORANGE COCONUT COOKIES. Substitute light corn syrup for dark corn syrup. Use granulated sugar. Add 2 tablespoons grated orange rind and ¼ teaspoon nutmeg with the coconut.

SUGAR COOKIES. Substitute light corn syrup for dark corn syrup; use granulated sugar; omit coconut and nuts. Sprinkle tops with sugar after placing cookies on cooky sheet.

ALMOND COOKIES
Best Foods, Division of
Corn Products Company

2½ cups sifted flour	2 teaspoons almond extract
1 teaspoon baking powder	1 teaspoon vanilla
¼ teaspoon salt	1 egg white
¾ cup sugar	1 egg, slightly beaten
⅔ cup Mazola Corn Oil	1 tablespoon water
1 egg yolk	⅓ cup blanched almonds, slightly toasted
1 tablespoon orange juice	

Sift together flour, baking powder, and salt. Combine sugar and corn oil in large mixing bowl; beat in egg yolk. Beat in orange juice, almond extract, and vanilla. Stir in ½ of sifted dry ingredients. Beat egg whites until stiff but not dry; fold into batter. Add remaining dry ingredients, kneading slightly with fingers to make a smooth dough. Shape and bake at once. Shape dough in 1-inch balls and place on ungreased cooky sheet. Press with bottom of flat glass.

Combine beaten egg and water and brush each cooky lightly. Press almond in center of each cooky. Bake in 350° oven about 12 minutes. Makes about 3 dozen.

CHOCOLATE CEREAL BARS
National Biscuit Company

1 6-ounce package semi-sweet chocolate pieces
1 cup miniature marshmallows
¼ cup chopped nuts
8 Shredded Wheat Juniors

Line 9 x 4-inch loaf pan with waxed paper. Melt chocolate over hot water. Add marshmallows and nuts. Break spoon size shredded wheat in half and add to chocolate mixture. Mix well. Pack mixture into prepared pan. Chill until firm. Remove from pan. Peel off paper and cut into small bars. Makes 18 cookies.

FILLED OATMEAL GIFT COOKIES
The Quaker Oats Co.

Dough:

1½ cups sifted enriched flour
½ teaspoon soda
½ teaspoon salt
¼ cup milk
1 egg
1 cup sugar
¾ cup shortening, soft
1 teaspoon vanilla
1½ cups Quaker or Mother's Oats (quick or old-fashioned, uncooked)
Confectioners' sugar frosting

Sift together flour, soda, and salt; add milk, egg, sugar, shortening, and vanilla. Beat until smooth, about 2 minutes. Lightly stir in rolled oats. Turn out half the dough on lightly floured board. Knead gently 2 or 3 times. Roll very thin. Repeat with other half of dough. Cut dough with floured cooky cutters. Place a small spoonful of Date Filling in center of half the cookies; cover with remaining cookies, pressing edges together. Place on greased cooky sheets. Bake in 375° oven 8 to 10 minutes. Remove immediately from cooky sheets. Cool. Frost with confectioners' sugar frosting and decorate as desired. Makes 3 dozen.

Date Filling:

1 cup dates	1 cup sugar
1 cup water	Juice of 1 lemon

Combine dates, water, sugar, and lemon juice in saucepan; cook until thick, stirring frequently.

ORIGINAL TOLL HOUSE COOKIES
The Nestlé Company

1 cup plus 2 tablespoons sifted flour	½ teaspoon vanilla
½ teaspoon baking soda	¼ teaspoon water
½ teaspoon salt	1 egg
½ cup butter or shortening, soft	1 6-ounce package Nestlé's Semi-Sweet Chocolate Morsels
6 tablespoons sugar	½ cup coarsely chopped walnuts
6 tablespoons brown sugar	

Preheat oven to 375°. Sift together flour, baking soda, and salt. Blend butter or shortening, sugar, vanilla, and water; beat in 1 egg. Add to flour mixture and mix well. Stir in semi-sweet chocolate and walnuts. Drop by half teaspoonsful on greased cooky sheet. Bake at 375° 10 to 12 minutes. Makes 50 cookies.

TEA TIME PASTRIES
Best Foods, Division of
Corn Products Company

1 cup Argo Corn Starch	½ cup butter or margarine
1 cup sifted flour	½ cup sugar
½ teaspoon salt	2 to 3 tablespoons water

Mix and sift corn starch, flour, and salt. Cream butter until soft, add sugar gradually and continue creaming until light and fluffy. Add sifted dry ingredients to creamed mixture; blend well. Add enough water to bind together. Dough will be stiff but soft. Roll dough on lightly floured board and cut with fancy cooky cutter; or force dough through cooky press. Bake on ungreased cooky sheet in 350° oven for 12 to 15 minutes, or until cookies are set and only very delicately browned. May be decorated with candy sprinkles before baking. Makes about 4 dozen.

HOLIDAY COOKIES
Red Star Yeast & Products Co.

2 packages Red Star Special Active Dry Yeast	1 teaspoon salt
½ cup warm water (110°-115°)	3 cups sifted all-purpose flour
⅓ cup sugar	2 eggs at room temperature
	⅓ cup soft shortening

Add the yeast to the warm water in a cup. Let stand a few minutes, then stir. Measure sugar and salt into mixing bowl, and add the yeast mixture. Mix in ½ of the flour and beat until smooth. Stir in the eggs and shortening. Mix in, a little at a time, all the rest of the flour with spoon or hand until well blended. Scrape down dough from sides of bowl. Cover and let rise in warm place about 30 minutes. The dough should double.

Drop dough by heaping teaspoonsful into Fruit Mixture,

3 or 4 at a time. Take each piece in the hands and work in some of the fruits and nuts, then stretch into pencil-like strips. Shape into snails, twists, knots, or figure 8's. Continue with the rest of the dough. (Dough may also be shaped in tiny balls and baked in small muffin tins.)

Place on lightly greased baking sheets and let stand 10 minutes. Bake 10 to 15 minutes, or until golden brown, in preheated 375° oven. Remove to rack to cool. Makes 2 to 2½ dozen.

Fruit Mixture:

¼ cup finely chopped nuts
½ cup sugar

½ cup finely chopped fruit cake fruits

Mix together in shallow pan.

COCONUT MACAROONS
General Foods Corporation

1⅓ cups Baker's Angel Flake Coconut
½ cup sugar

1 egg, well beaten
1 teaspoon almond extract

Combine coconut and sugar, and mix well. Add egg and flavoring, and blend; let stand 5 minutes. Then drop from teaspoon on greased baking sheet. Bake in 350° oven 15 minutes, or until golden brown. Remove from baking sheet at once. Makes about 1 dozen large macaroons.

COFFEE COCONUT MERINGUES
General Foods Corporation

2 egg whites
¼ teaspoon salt
1 tablespoon instant coffee
½ cup sugar

1 cup Baker's Angel Flake Coconut
¼ teaspoon vanilla extract

Beat egg whites with salt until foamy. Mix instant coffee and sugar together and add to egg whites, 2 tablespoons at a time, beating after each addition until sugar is blended. Then continue beating until mixture will stand in peaks. Fold in coconut and vanilla. Drop from teaspoon onto well-greased baking sheet. Bake in 250° oven 30 minutes, or until done. Makes 2½ dozen meringues.

ANISE COOKIES
McCormick & Co., Inc.

1 teaspoon salt
4 eggs
2 cups sugar

1 teaspoon McCormick or Schilling Anise Extract
4 cups sifted all-purpose flour

Add salt to eggs, and beat until thick and lemon-colored. Gradually add sugar and continue beating until dissolved. Stir in anise extract; add flour, mixing well (makes a moderately stiff dough). Chill dough for several hours. Roll into a rectangular sheet, ½-inch thick, on a floured board; cut into 1½-inch squares. Place on greased baking sheet. Chill, uncovered, for about an hour. Bake in a 350° oven 15 to 20 minutes. Cool and store in a covered container. Makes about 5 dozen.

Note: If desired you may make impression using a Springerle rolling pin, then cut into cookies.

CANDIES AND CONFECTIONS

MOLASSES POPCORN BALLS
Penick & Ford, Ltd.

3 quarts popped corn
1½ cups Brer Rabbit Molasses
½ cup sugar
¼ cup water

2 teaspoons cider vinegar
½ teaspoon salt
2 teaspoons vanilla extract
5 tablespoons vegetable shortening

Pick over popped corn, discarding all hard kernels. Combine molasses, sugar, water, vinegar, and salt; cook slowly, stirring constantly, to 270°, or when a small quantity dropped into cold water forms hard ball. Remove from heat; add vanilla extract and shortening, stirring only enough to mix. Pour over popped corn, stirring constantly. Grease hands; shape lightly and quickly into balls. Cool. Wrap in Saran Wrap. Makes 28 to 30.

GLAZED NUTS
Penick & Ford, Ltd.

⅓ cup Brer Rabbit Molasses
⅓ cup light corn syrup

2 cups sugar
1 cup water
Nut meats

Combine molasses, corn syrup, sugar, and water; cook slowly, stirring constantly, until sugar is dissolved. Cook, without stirring, to 300°, or when small quantity dropped into cold water forms very brittle ball. Quickly dip nut meats into syrup; drain on Saran Wrap.

41 Sukiyaki (p. 315) is becoming increasingly popular with American hostesses. Prepared at the table, it is fun for the cook and entertainment for the guests. **Photo courtesy of Ac'cent International.**

42 Curried Chicken with Almond Rice (p. 307) can make a special party even out of leftovers. Serve with asparagus, Rhubarb Chiffon Tarts (p. 308), and coffee. **Photo courtesy of General Foods Corporation.**

43 A gift from your kitchen—a picnic basket filled with candied apples and popcorn balls. Pound cake and pumpernickel marbled with rye are similarly appropriate presents. Saran Wrap serves as a protective covering and moisture guard for these warmly personal gifts. **Photo courtesy of The Dow Chemical Company.**

44 A plate of cookies, kept crisp and flavorful in a wrapper of Saran Wrap. **Photo courtesy of The Dow Chemical Company.**

45 Saran Wrap is a gift wrap, ideal for protecting the jellies and candies you are delivering to friends. Its transparency also makes it the perfect showcase for your gifts of food. **Photo courtesy of The Dow Chemical Company.**

46 A picnic tray with its salads wrapped in Saran Wrap for flavor protection and continued freshness. The Persian melon shell contains grapes, melon balls, and pineapple. Frozen mixed vegetables, first cooked, then marinated in French dressing, fill tomatoes and peppers for individual servings. Alternate tomatoes are filled with herbed cottage cheese. Meat and cheese sandwiches are individually wrapped in Saran Wrap. **Photo courtesy of The Dow Chemical Company.**

47 A bowl of salad greens retains its original freshness when prepared in advance and wrapped in Saran Wrap. **Photo courtesy of The Dow Chemical Company.**

48 Sculpture moves into the kitchen with the introduction of Kitchen Clay (p. 366), a modeling material formed of elements readily available to every housewife. It's a new, exciting medium in which to work—for professional or amateur from 4 to 40. **Photo courtesy of Best Foods, Division of Corn Products Company.**

41

44

BUTTERSCOTCH PRALINES
The Nestlé Company

2 cups sugar
1 cup light brown sugar,
  firmly packed
¾ cup water
¼ cup light corn syrup
1 teaspoon vinegar

½ teaspoon salt
1 6-ounce package Nestlé's
  Butterscotch Morsels
1 cup coarsely chopped
  walnuts

Combine first 6 ingredients in 2-quart saucepan and bring to full boil over high heat, stirring constantly. Boil over highest heat 3 minutes. Do not stir. Remove from heat; add butterscotch and walnuts, and stir quickly until butterscotch is melted. Drop by tablespoonful on ungreased heavy brown paper. If mixture becomes too thick, stir in small amount of water. Let stand at room temperature until set. Makes about 4 dozen.

BUTTERSCOTCH THINS
The Nestlé Company

1 6-ounce package Nestlé's
  Butterscotch Morsels
½ cup butter or margarine
⅔ cup light brown sugar,
  firmly packed

1 egg
1⅓ cups sifted flour
¾ teaspoon baking soda
⅓ cup chopped nuts
¾ teaspoon vanilla

Preheat oven to 375°. Melt first 2 ingredients over hot, not boiling, water. Remove from heat, add brown sugar and egg, and beat until light colored. Sift together flour and baking soda, and stir into butterscotch mixture. Add chopped nuts and vanilla. Chill until firm enough to handle. Shape on Saran Wrap in 1 12-inch roll. Roll up and chill thoroughly. Cut in very thin slices. Place on ungreased cooky sheet and bake at 375° for 5 to 6 minutes. Let cool approximately 1 minute; then remove from pan. Makes about 8 dozen.

PEANUT BUTTER-MARSHMALLOW BARS
The Quaker Oats Co.

5 cups Quaker Puffed Rice
¼ cup butter or margarine
⅓ cup peanut butter

½ pound (about 32) fresh
marshmallows

Heat puffed rice in shallow pan in 350° oven 10 minutes; pour puffed rice into a large greased bowl. Melt butter, peanut butter, and marshmallows in double boiler, stirring occasionally. Pour over puffed rice stirring until puffed rice is evenly coated. Pack into a greased 7 x 11-inch pan; cool and cut into bars. Makes 2 dozen bars.

COCONUT-STUFFED PRUNES
General Foods Corporation

1 cup Baker's Angel Flake
Coconut
1 cup walnuts
¼ cup honey

2 teaspoons lemon juice
3 dozen drained, cooked,
pitted prunes

Grind coconut and walnuts in food chopper; mix well. Add honey and lemon juice, mixing thoroughly. Fill prune centers with mixture. Makes 3 dozen stuffed prunes.

COCONUT FRUIT BALLS
General Foods Corporation

1½ cups mixed dried fruits
½ cup figs
¼ cup dark seedless raisins
¼ cup chopped walnuts

2 tablespoons honey
½ teaspoon almond extract
1⅓ cups Baker's Angel
Flake Coconut, toasted

Put mixed fruits, figs, and raisins through food chopper. Combine fruit mixture with nuts, honey, and almond extract.

Mix together well. Shape into ¾-inch balls. Roll in toasted coconut. Allow to ripen in refrigerator 2 to 3 days. Makes about 3 dozen fruit balls.

COCONUT-WALNUT BARS

Best Foods, Division of
Corn Products Company

½ cup brown sugar, firmly packed
½ cup Mazola Margarine
1 cup sifted flour
2 eggs, well beaten
½ cup brown sugar, firmly packed
½ cup Karo Syrup, Blue or Red Label
1 teaspoon vanilla
2 tablespoons flour
1 teaspoon baking powder
½ teaspoon salt
1 cup shredded coconut
1 cup coarsely chopped walnuts

Blend sugar and margarine. Stir in flour. Pat out mixture onto bottom of an ungreased 9 x 9 x 2-inch pan. Bake in 350° oven 10 minutes. Meanwhile, blend eggs and brown sugar. Stir in syrup and vanilla. Add flour, baking powder, and salt, mixing well. Stir in coconut and nuts and spread over bottom layer. Return to oven and bake 25 minutes longer, or until top is golden brown. Cool in pan; cut into finger length bars. Makes 24 bars.

COCOA PEANUT SQUARES

Kellogg Company

¼ cup corn syrup
½ cup brown sugar, firmly packed
½ cup peanut butter
3 cups Kellogg's® Cocoa Krispies

Combine corn syrup and sugar in medium-size saucepan. Cook over moderate heat, stirring frequently, until mixture bubbles. Remove from heat. Stir in peanut butter. Add cereal, stirring until well-coated with peanut butter mixture. Press into buttered 9 x 9-inch pan. Cut into squares when cool. Makes 36 1½-inch squares.

PEANUT BUTTER CLUSTERS
Kellogg Company

1 cup (6 ounces) butter-
  scotch pieces
½ cup peanut butter

3 cups Kellogg's® Corn
  Flakes

Melt butterscotch pieces over hot, not boiling water; stir in peanut butter. Remove from heat. Add cereal, mixing until well-coated. Drop by teaspoonsful onto buttered baking sheets. Set in cool place to harden. Makes 35 confections, 1½-inches in diameter.

CIRCUS TREATS
The Chun King Corp.

⅓ cup butter or shortening
1½ cups brown sugar,
  firmly packed
½ teaspoon salt
1 cup sifted all-purpose
  flour

2 eggs, beaten
1 teaspoon vanilla
1 cup Chun King Chow Mein
  Noodles, crushed
1 cup salted peanuts,
  chopped

Cream butter, ½ cup sugar, and salt thoroughly. Mix in flour. Press mixture in greased 9 x 13-inch pan. Bake in

350° oven for 15 minutes. Add remaining sugar to eggs and beat until fluffy. Add vanilla, noodles, and peanuts, and mix. Spread over already baked layer, return to oven and bake 25 minutes more. Cool. Cut in squares. Makes 30 squares.

CHOCOLATE TING A LINGS
The Chun King Corp.

12 ounces (2 cups) semi-
sweet chocolate pieces
1 cup salted peanuts

1 5½-ounce can Chun King
Chow Mein Noodles

Melt chocolate pieces over hot water. Pour over the peanuts and noodles. Mix thoroughly and drop from teaspoon on Saran Wrap. Chill. Makes 36 clusters.

QUICK NO-COOK FONDANT
Best Foods, Division of
Corn Products Company

⅓ cup Mazola Margarine,
soft
⅓ cup Karo Syrup, Red
Label

½ teaspoon salt
1 teaspoon vanilla
4½ cups (1 pound) sifted
confectioners' sugar

Blend margarine, syrup, salt, and vanilla in large mixing bowl. Add sifted confectioners' sugar all at once. Mix all together with a spoon; then with hands knead in dry ingredients. Turn onto board and continue kneading until mixture is well blended and smooth. Makes 1⅓ pounds. Store in Saran Wrap in cool place. Divide into portions and tint and flavor as desired. May be shaped into balls and rolled in multi-colored candy, coconut, or nuts. Or fondant may be rolled, cut in fancy shapes, and decorated.

CANDY BALLS
The Quaker Oats Co.

6 cups Quaker Puffed Rice
¾ cup light corn syrup
¼ cup light molasses
½ teaspoon salt

1 teaspoon vinegar
2 tablespoons butter or margarine
1 teaspoon vanilla

Heat puffed rice in shallow pan in 350° oven 10 minutes; pour into large greased bowl. Combine syrup, molasses, salt, and vinegar in saucepan; cook, stirring frequently, until a few drops in cold water form a hard ball. Remove from heat; add butter and vanilla, stirring only enough to mix. Mixing quickly, gradually pour cooked syrup over the puffed rice. With greased hands immediately form mixture into balls. Wrap cooled candy balls in Saran Wrap; tie tops together with colored ribbon. Makes 10 to 12 balls.

Note: If mixture hardens before shaping is complete, place it in a moderate oven to soften for a few minutes.

HOLIDAY BOURBON BALLS
The Nestlé Company

1 6-ounce package Nestlé's Semi-Sweet Chocolate Morsels
½ cup sugar
3 tablespoons light corn syrup

½ cup Bourbon
2½ cups vanilla wafers, finely crushed (about 5 dozen)
1 cup finely chopped walnuts

Melt chocolate over hot, not boiling water. Remove and stir in sugar and corn syrup. Blend in bourbon. Combine vanilla wafers and walnuts; add to semi-sweet mixture. Form in 1-inch balls and roll in sugar. Let ripen in container covered with Saran Wrap at least several days. Makes approximately 4½ dozen balls.

CHOCO-NUT PIZZA SPECIAL
The Nestlé Company

Cookie Crust:

⅔ cup sugar
½ cup soft butter
½ teaspoon vanilla

¼ teaspoon salt
1 cup sifted flour

Combine first 4 ingredients and beat until light. Gradually stir in flour. Press evenly over bottom of ungreased 12-inch pizza pan. Bake in 350° oven approximately 16 to 18 minutes. Cool 5 minutes, then cover with Walnut Meringue Topping.

Walnut Meringue Topping:

1 cup sugar
2 eggs
1 teaspoon vanilla

¾ teaspoon salt
3 cups finely chopped walnuts

Combine first 4 ingredients and beat till light. Add walnuts and stir to blend well. Spread over cooled Cookie Crust and bake at 350° for 20 minutes. Cool and frost with Glossy Chocolate Frosting.

Glossy Chocolate Frosting:

½ cup evaporated milk
Dash salt
1 teaspoon vanilla

1 6-ounce package Nestlé's Semi-Sweet Chocolate Morsels

Combine evaporated milk and salt and bring just to boil over moderate heat. Add vanilla and chocolate and stir until smooth. Cool until thick enough to spread, approximately 5 minutes. Spread over Walnut Meringue Topping. Cool and cut in wedges. Makes about 16 to 24 wedges.

MAPLE PECAN FUDGE
McCormick & Co., Inc.

3 cups sugar
2 tablespoons brown sugar
½ cup water
1 cup milk
2 tablespoons butter

¼ teaspoon McCormick or Schilling Vanilla Extract
¼ teaspoon McCormick or Schilling Maple Extract
1 cup chopped pecans

Combine sugar, brown sugar, water, and milk in a saucepan; cook, stirring constantly until sugar dissolves. Continue cooking, without stirring, until syrup reaches 236° or a small amount forms a soft ball in cold water. Remove from heat; add butter and let cool, without stirring, until lukewarm (110°). Then beat until mixture thickens and loses its gloss. Quickly mix in nuts. Spread at once in an 8-inch square pan; cut in squares.

GOLDEN CRUNCHIES
Kretschmer Wheat Germ Corp.

¼ cup butter or margarine
¾ cup sugar
2 eggs
1½ teaspoons vanilla
½ cup dry milk powder

½ teaspoon baking powder
¼ teaspoon salt
1 cup Kretchmer Sugar 'N' Honey Wheat Germ
1 cup chopped walnuts

Cream butter or margarine with sugar. Add 2 eggs and beat well. Add vanilla. Combine dry milk powder, baking powder, salt, and wheat germ. Add dry ingredients to butter-sugar-egg mixture and blend thoroughly. Fold in nuts. Bake in greased 8-inch square pan at 350° 35 to 40 minutes. Cut into squares.

GIFT BREADS AND MUFFINS

GINGERBREAD

Best Foods, Division of
Corn Products Company

2 cups sifted flour
½ teaspoon salt
¾ teaspoon ginger
½ teaspoon cinnamon
½ teaspoon nutmeg
1 teaspoon baking powder
½ teaspoon soda

⅔ cup molasses
½ cup Karo Syrup, Blue Label
½ cup Mazola Margarine, melted
1 egg, well beaten
½ cup warm water

Mix and sift first 7 ingredients into a bowl. Make a well; add in order molasses, syrup, margarine, and well-beaten eggs. Beat until smooth. Add water and beat until thoroughly blended. Turn into a greased 9-inch square pan. Bake in 350° oven 35 to 40 minutes. Makes 9 servings.

MOLASSES GINGERBREAD

Penick & Ford, Ltd.

½ cup shortening
1¼ cups Brer Rabbit Molasses
1 egg
2½ cups sifted all-purpose flour

1½ teaspoons baking soda
1 teaspoon cinnamon
1½ teaspoons ginger
½ teaspoon salt
¾ cup hot water

Melt shortening in 3- or 4-quart saucepan over very low heat. Remove from heat; let cool. Add molasses and egg; beat well. Sift together flour, baking soda, cinnamon, ginger, and salt; add alternately with hot water to first mixture. Line 8 x 8 x 2-inch pan with greased waxed paper; pour in batter. Bake in 350° oven 40 to 45 minutes, or until done. Cool 5 minutes. Remove from pan.

ALMOND MERINGUE GINGERBREAD
Penick & Ford, Ltd.

¼ cup shortening
¼ cup sugar
2 egg yolks
½ cup Brer Rabbit Molasses
1½ cups sifted all-purpose flour

½ teaspoon ginger
½ teaspoon cinnamon
⅛ teaspoon salt
¾ teaspoon baking soda
½ cup boiling water

Cream together shortening and sugar. Add egg yolks; beat well. Add molasses. Sift together flour, ginger, cinnamon, salt, and baking soda. Add to creamed mixture; mix well. Quickly stir in water; beat smooth. Line greased 8 x 8 x 2-inch pan with greased waxed paper; pour in batter. Top with Almond Meringue Topping. Bake in 350° oven 35 to 40 minutes.

Almond Meringue Topping:

2 egg whites
6 tablespoons sugar
½ teaspoon vanilla extract

½ cup blanched almond nut meats, cut in long shreds

Beat egg whites stiff, but not dry. Gradually add sugar, beating constantly. Add vanilla extract; spread on top of cake batter. Sprinkle with nut meats. If necessary, increase heat last 10 minutes of baking time to toast almonds.

MOLASSES WHOLE WHEAT NUT BREAD
Penick & Ford, Ltd.

2 tablespoons brown sugar
2 cups whole wheat flour
1 cup sifted all-purpose flour
¾ teaspoon baking soda
2½ teaspoons baking powder

1¼ teaspoons salt
¾ cup milk
¾ cup water
¾ cup Brer Rabbit Molasses
1 cup chopped walnut meats

Mix together sugar, whole wheat flour, baking soda, baking powder, and salt. Combine milk and molasses; add to dry ingredients. Mix smooth. Add nut meats. Pour into greased 9¼ x 5¼ x 2½-inch loaf pan. Let stand 20 minutes. Bake in 350° oven 1½ hours. Cool 5 minutes. Remove from pan. Cool. Bread will slice in uniformly thin slices if stored overnight.

BOSTON BROWN BREAD
Penick & Ford, Ltd.

1 cup yellow corn meal
1 cup whole wheat flour
1 cup sifted all-purpose flour
1½ teaspoons salt
½ cup sugar
1 teaspoon baking soda

⅔ cup Brer Rabbit Molasses
1½ cups buttermilk or sour milk
3 tablespoons melted shortening

Mix corn meal, whole wheat flour, flour, salt, and sugar. Stir baking soda into molasses; add to flour mixture with milk. Mix well. Add shortening. Pour into greased 2-quart pudding mold, having mold not more than ¾ full; cover tightly. Steam 3¼ hours. Makes 6 to 8 servings.

APPLESAUCE SPICE CAKE
Penick & Ford, Ltd.

½ cup shortening
½ cup sugar
2 eggs
½ cup Brer Rabbit Molasses
2 cups sifted all-purpose flour
1 teaspoon baking soda

½ teaspoon salt
1 teaspoon cinnamon
½ teaspoon nutmeg
¼ teaspoon cloves
1 cup strained thick applesauce
⅔ cup seedless raisins

Cream together shortening and sugar. Add eggs, one at a time, beating after each. Add molasses. Sift together flour, baking soda, salt, cinnamon, nutmeg, and cloves; add alternately with applesauce to first mixture. Add raisins; mix well. Pour into greased 8 x 8 x 2-inch pan. Bake in 350° oven 55 minutes. Cool 5 minutes. Remove cake from pan; cool on wire rack. Serve plain or top with frosting.

HOLIDAY BREAD
Best Foods, Division of
Corn Products Company

2 eggs
¾ cup Skippy Creamy or Chunk-Style Peanut Butter
2 tablespoons margarine
1 cup milk

1¾ cups sifted flour
2 teaspoons baking powder
1 teaspoon salt
⅔ cup sugar
½ cup candied fruit

Beat eggs until foamy. Add peanut butter and margarine, and blend until smooth and creamy. Gradually add milk stirring constantly. Sift flour, baking powder, salt, and sugar together. Add to creamed mixture with fruit, and stir until well mixed. Pour batter into 8½ x 4½ -inch loaf pan which has been greased and lined with greased wax paper. Bake in a 350° oven 1 hour and 10 minutes. Remove from pan and cool.

To Frost: Blend 1 cup confectioners' sugar and 1 tablespoon milk. Spread on top of loaf and allow it to drip down the sides. Decorate with candied fruit.

HOLIDAY FRUITCAKE
The Borden Company

1 cup Borden's Instant None Such Mince Meat
1 cup coarsely chopped walnut meats
1 cup (8 ounces) mixed coarsely chopped candied fruit
1⅓ cups (15-ounce can) Eagle Brand Sweetened Condensed Milk
1 egg, beaten
¾ cup flour
½ teaspoon baking soda

Mix mince meat, nuts, candied fruit, condensed milk, and egg. Stir in flour and baking soda. Pour into a greased 9 x 4 x 3-inch loaf pan, lined with greased waxed paper. Bake at 350° for 1½ hours, or until center springs back. If glass baking dish is used, reduce heat to 325°.

CHEESE MUFFINS
Penick and Ford, Ltd.

2 cups sifted all-purpose flour
3 teaspoons baking powder
¼ teaspoon baking soda
½ teaspoon salt
1 egg
½ cup milk
½ cup Brer Rabbit Molasses
¼ cup melted shortening
⅔ cup grated American Cheddar cheese

Sift together flour, baking powder, baking soda, and salt. Beat egg; add milk. Add to dry ingredients. Add molasses and shortening, stirring just enough to moisten. Add cheese. Fill greased muffin pans ⅔ full. Bake in 350° oven, 20 to 22 minutes. Makes 12 muffins.

KITCHEN CLAY

Kitchen Clay modeling is a delightful arts-and-crafts activity with the homely virtues of safety (since *everything* goes into a baby's mouth), cleanliness, and immediate availability on your kitchen shelf. Kitchen Clay is ideal for modeling decorative fruits, nuts, and vegetables, as well as other interesting shapes and designs.

Argo Corn Starch, table salt, and water are the elements of this amazing new medium. Kitchen utensils and toothpicks make perfect sculpting tools, and a cheese grater will finish or "grain" the surface as you desire.

Mix 2 cups of salt and ⅔ cup of water in a saucepan over low heat, stirring constantly, about 2 to 4 minutes. Remove saucepan from heat; mix 1 cup Argo Corn Starch and ½ cup cold water and add immediately to the mixture. Stir quickly to combine all ingredients. The mixture should thicken to about the consistency of stiff dough. If it does not, return to low heat for another minute, stirring until proper consistency is obtained.

Turn out on wooden board or kitchen table and knead to form a smooth mass of clay. Use immediately or keep on hand in the refrigerator. The clay will store indefinitely if wrapped in Saran Wrap.

Shape the clay and dry the modeled objects at room temperature from two to six days, depending on the size and thickness of the model. Paint with water colors, all-purpose dye, or food coloring, and finish with several coats of clear shellac. The natural texture of this kitchen-based craft lends itself wonderfully to a natural, realistically imperfect look. Color washes into each object in such a way that your non-edible edibles look sun-ripened.

These make lovely gifts. Have your baby make beads on his high-chair tray and string them for the Christmas tree. Toddlers and the kindergarten set can flatten their clay with a rolling pin and cut it into pretty shapes with cooky cutters. String them on wire for an unusual holiday mobile—one to which everyone in the family can contribute. (See illustration 48.)

INDEX